HOMEBUILTS
A HANDBOOK FOR THE
FIRST-TIME BUILDER

FRANK J. O'BRIEN

TAB TAB BOOKS Inc.
Blue Ridge Summit, PA 17214

To Marge—a VFR haven in the IFR world of airplane
building.

FIRST EDITION

FIRST PRINTING

Copyright © 1985 by TAB BOOKS Inc.

Printed in the United States of America

Library of Congress Cataloging in Publication Data

O'Brien, Frank J.
Homebuilts—a handbook for the first-time builder.

Includes index.
1. Airplanes, Home-built. I. Title.
TL671.2.035   1985   629.133′343   85-4642
ISBN 0-8306-2375-2 (pbk.)

Contents

Acknowledgments   v

Introduction   vi

1   Before You Begin   1

2   Preliminary Considerations   7

3   Getting Ready   14

4   Fuselage Frame Construction   22

5   Plywood Skins for the Frame   26

6   Spar Construction   29

7   Tailfeathers   34

8   Wood Sealers   38

9   Wing Fittings   40

10   Joining the Spars and Fuselage   44

11   Truss Assemblies   47

12   Seat Back and Floor   57

13   Rudder Pedal Assemblies   60

14   Control Systems   63

15   Canopy and Windshield   68

16   Outer Spar Installation   76

17   Landing Gear and Retract System   80

18   Cockpit Interior   106

19   Electrical System   114

20   Fuel System   121

21   Engine Mount   130

22   Miscellaneous   135

23   Foaming and Fiberglassing   143

24   Test-Flying   150

25   Conclusion   160

Appendix   162

Selected Bibliography   168

Index   169

Acknowledgments

Writing a book, like building an airplane, is rarely a solo event. There are innumerable bits and pieces of information on the techniques and procedures of homebuilding that must be garnered from others who are more experienced in these areas. Without their help and encouragement, neither this book nor my airplane would have gotten far.

First and foremost among these was Paul Roberts, whose expert technical advice and patient understanding were key factors in the development of so many of the ideas and procedures discussed in the text.

The willing cooperation shown by members of EAA Chapter 176, in providing comments and suggestions on quite a few of the topics talked about here, is sincerely appreciated. Particularly noteworthy was the assistance given by Joe Wieger, Keith Caulton, and Frank Liberti, whose expertise in homebuilding provided the answers to many knotty problems.

I am also indebted to another Corsair builder, Joel Biggs, who was kind enough to share his experiences in building this airplane. One of the more pleasurable facets of working on both the book and the airplane projects has been the people involved in putting together their own airplanes, and their readiness to lend a hand whenever needed.

Many thanks to a bunch of real tigers.

Introduction

Throughout this book you will find quite a few suggestions, recommendations, and opinions about homebuilding in general and construction techniques for the Corsair in particular. These are based strictly on my personal experience in going through the throes of building my first airplane. They are reinforced by the advice and help of a lot of people who are very knowledgeable in the homebuilding business. These tips may not be the only solutions to particular problems, nor possibly the best. But they are offered here mainly because they work, and/or have proven helpful on the Corsair project. Another reason for their inclusion is that they are geared for someone building his first airplane, keeping in mind the possibility that shop equipment and resources might be a trifle limited.

Hopefully, these ideas will spare the new builder the lengthy trial and error process by which they were developed.

There are also many references to the costs and time involved in the various phases of the project. These cannot be taken as absolutes for a variety of reasons. What is expensive to one builder may be a drop in the bucket to another, and the prices for the materials needed to build an airplane increase with alarming regularity. Also, the amounts charged for work that is farmed out can vary from the sublime to the ridiculous. Here again, the basis for these relative comparisons is my perception of things while putting together the Corsair.

While it is an exacting hobby, homebuilding does permit the individual a certain amount of latitude in the way its problems are solved. It is in this context that the opinions presented in this book are offered.

Chapter 1

Before You Begin

Building an airplane is probably the most challenging and complex project you'll ever undertake. Even the simplest of aircraft is fairly complicated when considering the number and variety of systems that must function properly and in unison. A glance at the inner workings of any homebuilt bird—or looking over the plans for the same—will certainly emphasize the point that this is not for the casual weekend whittler. For someone who has not been involved in projects of this scope before, the enormity of the task appears quite staggering—and in many respects it is.

But how does one who has been bitten by the airplane building bug come to grips with so difficult a problem? This is where this book comes in. Its purpose is to smooth off some of the rough edges of homebuilding, and hopefully make the project more enjoyable than frustrating. Although the task is demanding, it is not impossible for anyone who is somewhat handy with tools—and is willing to learn.

The scope of this book will be expansive in some areas and restricted in others. All of the discussions herein will approach each topic from the standpoint of the first-time homebuilder. Although some of the procedures and techniques may appear to belabor the obvious, they might be real stumbling blocks for someone who hasn't been there

before, if they are left unexplained. Also, some of the more basic techniques are those recommended by the "old heads" in the homebuilding business. In this light, it is hoped that the methods and ideas covered in this book will, at the very least, save the fledgling builder some valuable time. A good many of the problems encountered on your initial trip through the homebuilding maze are very knotty ones indeed. As such, they require an inordinate amount of "sittin' and thinkin'" time in order to work things out.

In many cases this ends up with your reinventing the wheel when this time could have been spent more profitably in other areas. There are relatively few "new" problems in homebuilding, only new people trying to address problems that have been solved elsewhere. Therefore, the basic idea behind this book is to prevent new people from undertaking vast projects with half-vast preparations. The techniques and procedures discussed will try to illustrate the best way to get there from here, based on the experiences of other homebuilders.

It is highly recommended that if you are tackling the Corsair project you first read through all the chapters dealing with construction techniques up to the point where the bird is ready to be foamed. This should be done *before* actually starting work—not only to get a general overview

1

of the project, but in a more important vein, to become aware of a sequence of events that should be followed to make life easier while building this airplane. There are quite a few times during the construction process when provisions should be made for the installation of a part that won't actually be put on the bird until some time later—but if the holes are drilled or the cutouts made when things are not so cramped and/or inaccessible, the entire process will go a lot quicker and with a lot less sweat. Listing all these "special notes" at the beginning of the book would only confuse the issue, since they cannot be taken out of context and discussed as a separate entity without a frame of reference. Therefore, all of these items are addressed in conjunction with the major system or installation with which they are associated. In this way, you can visualize the relationship between these parts and those immediately around them. Identifying these potential problem areas before they actually crop up will allow you to avoid the difficulty altogether by taking pre-planned actions early in the game.

Along this same line, there are undoubtedly many "extras" that you would like to include on your airplane, but are unsure at the outset whether finances, space, or weight and balance will permit their installation. As you get downstream in the project, and the "extras" have taken on the air of "musts," it would be a good idea to make provisions in the framework for their attachment as you go along. Then, if things work out to the point where they are now "givens," installing them will be much less of a problem. Should events work out to the contrary, only a small investment in time and effort will have been made.

The building techniques talked about herein will be exclusively concerned with one method currently in vogue among homebuilders. This is the composite construction approach, where a basic wooden frame is utilized for the intrinsic strength of the design. This wooden frame is then overlaid with styrofoam to achieve the shape desired: this, in turn, is covered with fiberglass for added strength and protection. A majority of the construction on this type of project deals with wood, and the main thrust of this book will be focused on that area.

However, since there are a considerable number of metal pieces used on an aircraft built by this method, their fabrication and installation will be dealt with where warranted. Welding and other metalworking techniques (such as those performed with machine tools) will not be covered, since they are well beyond the scope of this book.

The project that will be used as a background for the discussions that follow is a half-scale F4U Corsair designed by War Aircraft Replicas. The techniques used for building this bird can be applied to others utilizing the same method of construction. The gull wing of the Corsair does introduce some problems that would not appear in a straight-wing design. However, these are explained fully, and their solutions include many features and procedures that can be applied to any homebuilt.

There is one other point that should be made at this time concerning the purpose of this book. It is not intended to be a minutely detailed, step-by-step construction manual for all parts of the WAR Corsair. It is assumed that anyone undertaking a project of this magnitude is of average intelligence, can read and interpret a set of plans, and knows how to use some basic hand tools. The more-or-less routine phases of construction will be touched on very lightly, if at all. The majority of these are either self-explanatory, or can be figured out quickly after looking over the plans. There is no area in a project of this sort, no matter how rudimentary, that does not require some thought, and preliminary study before proceeding. However, some of these areas generate more problems, or more *difficult* problems, than others. This is where the main theme of this book will be concentrated. Hopefully, some of the blind alleys that crop up so repeatedly when trying to solve some of the tough puzzlers will be avoided. By keeping the number of wrong turns to a minimum, and presenting at least one possible solution to each, an enormous amount of time will be saved—to say nothing of frustration.

Anyone getting into homebuilding should realize—or will soon discover—that putting an airplane together is not a cost-free proposition. Naturally, there is a given amount of raw materials, hardware, and manufactured parts that must be obtained. And, unless the aspiring builder has a fairly complete shop, the purchase of some tools will be unavoidable. You could probably count on one hand the number of homebuilders—especially first-timers—who are lucky enough to be in a situation where money is no object. Therefore, throughout all the procedures and techniques discussed below, the approach will be that of keeping costs to a minimum. This should be in no way construed as a suggestion to save money at the expense of safety.

There should be *no* compromise on the design specs listed for your bird, or for any other safety-of-flight item. In these areas, the best course of action is to bite the bullet and ante up whatever it takes to get what is called for. Some of the price tags are frightening, and your only solace is to remember that when the project is finished, you'll be strapping it to your frail pink body and slipping the surly bonds of Earth.

Thus, in the critical areas, nothing but the best will do. The first time you page through an aircraft parts catalog, you are almost guaranteed a case of the homebuilder's version of "sticker shock." However, this is an area where some savings can be realized by a little research and/or some judicious shopping. Substitutions, along with alternate procurement sources, can bring down the tab for a considerable number of otherwise high-cost items. Also, construction schedules and ancillary equipment such as work tables and lighting can have a significant impact on the cost of a project.

Selection of a Project

Possibly one of the most vexing problems facing anyone who decides to try homebuilding is the selection of a project on which to begin. The aesthetics of the decision will undoubtedly have a major influence on the ultimate choice. Old fighter pilots or those who get a kick out of the "big iron" will probably opt for one of the many fighter replicas currently available. Antique buffs will most likely decide on a biplane design with fabric covering. Those leaning toward sportplanes will have a wide variety of designs to choose from. A realistic approach to the selection of a first project might dictate looking for one that is relatively simple. This would increase the chances of its being completed, rather than being shelved after awhile because of frustration.

However, all homebuilders are thought to be a little crazy by their earthbound contemporaries, and maybe this is a good reason why aesthetics and realism should both be a part of the decision process. A great deal of time and money are going to be invested in this project, and if you end up with something less than what you *really* wanted, this investment might not yield the expected dividends. Within reasonable limits, a more complex project would no doubt take additional time and effort, but the end product would be well worth it—you will have the airplane of your dreams. Can you imagine an old fighter jock building an Air Camper, or the antiquer being happy with a Dragonfly? Therefore, don't neglect your "druthers" when looking over the market for your first project.

There are, however, some things that should be kept in mind during the search. These are factors that have to be applied while deciding on the *type* of plane to build, as well as when making the final selection of the particular plans and/or kit. The first of these is the size of the bird you are planning to build. Will it fit the work table your shop or garage can accommodate? If you anticipate starting this project in the basement, be sure to carefully check

that completed subassemblies such as the fuselage frame can be maneuvered up the stairs and/or out the door. Once built up, these structures become a little unwieldy and could present some serious problems during the move from the cellar to the garage. You will definitely *not* make any points with the distaff side of the house when you bring up the subject of cutting new doors and windows. It may even be worth your time to tack a few pieces of scrap lumber together to approximate the size of the completed wing or fuselage so that you can try it for size. Be sure to look downstream in your project to consider what size it will be when the wings are attached. Here, selecting an airplane for which the outer wing panels are removable will certainly solve many problems. If the wings are all in one piece, the work area where the bird will be after they are installed will need some detailed planning. Can the completed framework be moved through the door? Can it be moved around inside the shop to facilitate the installation of other components?

The external size of the project at various stages of completion is only one side of the coin in this area. Another very important aspect of the size problem deals with the available room in the cockpit. Most homebuilts are small by nature, and this results in fairly cramped quarters once you climb in. For a large person, this could present difficulties when attempting a rapid egress from the aircraft during an emergency. It may also make the operation of certain controls a real chore that can only be accomplished with a lot of squirming around. The Corsair we will talk about later is a prime example of a tight fit. When seated in the cockpit, the main spar is just under the pilot's knees, and getting in or out requires a little practice. Your feet have to be gotten over the spar without catching on the overhead fuel tank, while at the same time keeping your knees low enough to clear the instrument panel. The top of the spar must have cushions to make it bearable on the back of the knees, but these also contribute to narrowing the space through which you must draw your feet. The close sides of the cockpit also make for a cumbersome operation of the canopy and hand-cranking the gear up and down.

While thinking about these problems it might also be wise to consider what happens in wintertime. A heavy jacket and boots may make some of these tasks well-nigh impossible. This size problem may force some builders into a larger aircraft to be comfortable, which in turn will require more building and storage space. However, since small cockpits are almost a given with homebuilts, you should not expect significant size differences between the various designs unless you select something close to a full-size aircraft. While cockpit size is not a major stumbling block unless you are dealing with the extremes, it should nevertheless be given some thought before a final choice is made.

Costs

Overall cost is obviously another factor that must be taken into account when deciding on what to build. You are taking up one of the world's most expensive hobbies, and should steel yourself for some *nasty* shocks along the way in this area. The cost of plans varies widely, and, in the main, are proportional to the size and complexity of the project. In many cases, kits are available that contain the basic construction materials cut to the proper cross-section, but not to length. It may be wise to order the plans first, and calculate from the enclosed list of materials what it would run to order the wood separately. However, on a project like the Corsair, the wood kit includes pre-formed laminated spars. These are well worth the small added expense since they will save considerable time and heartburn.

Naturally, kits that contain other extra components will be more expensive, so be sure to determine if these can or should be made at home, or are available from other sources at a lower price. A couple of projects, such as the Christen Eagle or the Venture P-51D, are just about the ultimate in kits, with almost everything included—and nearly half the work completed. Of course, the price tag on these birds reflects all these additional goodies.

With these and a few other notable exceptions, the plans and kits for most homebuilts can be obtained fairly reasonably. But these initial costs are just the tip of the iceberg, and once construction gets to the point where metal parts and other components have to be added, things start to mount up. The variables affecting the overall costs of homebuilding are infinite, and a great many of them depend on the whims of the builder. As an example, the Corsair project described herein will probably run between $8,000 and $10,000 before all the dust settles.

While reviewing the many offerings on the market today, it is safe to assume that homebuilts requiring larger or special engines, or such complexities as retractable landing gear or full instrumentation, will end up costing a lot more than the smaller, simpler projects. The thing to beware of here is that the initial outlay for the plans and the kit for either of these selections may be pretty much the same. It is not until you are well into the project that the costs begin to escalate for the one that is more complicated.

The subject on the complexity of a project deserves a little more elaboration, since it is one of the major factors that should influence the selection of a project. Building any airplane is not a "piece of cake" undertaking; however, some are considerably more difficult than others. The caveat here is: Don't get in beyond your depth, or, if you do, be prepared to swim a lot longer. Retractable landing gear adds immeasurably to the problems of construction, and almost guarantees lengthening the project by *at least* a year. The alignment and structural problems associated with retractable gear tend to drive the average homebuilder up the wall in short order.

A primary consideration to keep in mind for a first project is not to select something that involves difficulties that are beyond your abilities, or that you are unwilling to tackle. However, if you have your heart set on a bird that looks like it will have more than its share of problem areas, it would certainly be advisable to know an A & P mechanic who can help you over some of the rough spots.

Similarly, biplanes and triplanes have construction problems unique to these designs, which are over and above those found in monoplanes. The problems associated with the rigging procedures for the wings can be quite formidable for the newcomer to homebuilding. The alignment of the flying surfaces with respect to each other, and in compliance with the aerodynamic features called for in the plans, can be a very exasperating and time-consuming task. If a bird of this type is still your choice, be sure to get in touch with someone who is knowledgeable of the rigging procedures, and who can give you some sound advice on what you'll be facing.

The same can be said of flaps, trim systems, or additional electrical equipment. Projects that include items such as these, either in the original design or as add-ons by the builder, will certainly increase the number of problems that must be faced. This is not meant to imply that extra features will make for an impossible project. Although they do create difficulties, they are not insolvable, and if they are an integral part of the airplane you want to build, then press on! Such things are only mentioned here to forewarn you of the added time, effort, and costs they will involve.

Building the plane of your dreams should not be avoided simply because it happens to have a few complicated areas of construction, unless you feel they are completely beyond your capabilities. However, it would be a rare homebuilt project that could *only* be completed by an experienced A & P mechanic. All the answers and advice you need for any project can usually be found after a little careful searching. Also, many construction problems can be solved by a liberal application of the long green—and, in the end, this may be the easiest and least frustrating way to go. Farming out some of the more complex components to someone skilled in that particular area definitely enables the first-time homebuilder to consider a more difficult project. However, keep in mind that such people do not work free.

One final note on the selection of an A & P mechanic to help you with your project: If at all possible, try to get someone who is familiar with lightplanes in general, and homebuilts in particular. Even though a person holds an A & P ticket, his specialty may be jet transports, and thus he would not be attuned to the problems of the average homebuilder. If you have any questions on something he suggests, it may be advisable to run it by your EAA chapter designee for confirmation. (More will be said about this individual's role in your project later on.)

Plans

Adequacy of plans is another thing to think about when deciding on what airplane to build. It would really water your eyes to be all psyched up about a particular design, only to find out that it takes a master mechanic to interpret the instructions. The ease of use and clarity of plans offered on the market varies widely, and some would make everything a real chore for anyone on his first project.

Most of the people who sell plans also offer an information packet (for a few dollars) that spells out in greater detail the major specifics of the project. This may be a wise investment before plunking down the cost of the complete plans package.

It would be even wiser to write to the designer for the answers to certain questions that are not covered in the ad or the information pack. Examples of these would be: Are all the plans completed or are some still to be drawn, for delivery at a future date? Are the drawings full-size, or must they be scaled up on the workbench? Is a follow-up service available so that builders will be automatically advised of changes and updates in the plans? The absence of one or two drawings from the set is not too crucial at the outset, and will not keep you from getting started on your project. These sheets will normally deal with something that will be added to the airplane at a much later date, such as the electrical system or the interior cockpit layout. Full-size drawings are relatively rare, with only a few firms offering this definite advantage. However, if they are available, and with all other things being equal, they are certainly the way to go.

Enlarging a set of plans to the actual size of the airplane is cumbersome, very time-consuming, and pregnant with the possibility for errors.

A wrinkle used by some plans makers for modifications and updates is a newsletter. However, these must be subscribed to, and may or may not be worth the added expense. They consist mostly of letters written by other builders discussing progress and problems found on their airplanes, and quite often contain hints on how others solved the same difficulties you are facing. But it would seem that anyone selling plans for an aircraft should supply all changes and modifications to the basic design as part of the purchase price. Charging for timely updates via a newsletter indicates an outfit that is more profit- than product-oriented.

A final note of the cost of a set of plans: The prices on this item vary widely, and are usually in proportion to the clarity and the detail of the drawings. The first-time homebuilder should look for the best in both these areas, because quality here will make the job a lot easier. Even though the price of the plans seems high, in the long run it is fairly insignificant in comparison to the overall cost of the project. Therefore, if a certain bird has caught your eye, don't be deterred by an expensive set of plans. Over the length of the project, you'll undoubtedly spend a lot more than that just on the beer used to fuel hangar-flying sessions and "think time" about the project.

Also to be considered is the availability of a construction manual, and *its* thoroughness. The plans don't tell everything, and some narrative instructions on the procedures to be followed are essential, particularly on your first time around. Also, good plans do not guarantee a well-written construction manual. (The Corsair project is a perfect case in point. The plans are excellent—full-size, clear, well-drawn, and detailed. However, the construction manual is far from satisfactory, consisting of only a few typewritten pages dealing with the entire building process up to the application of the foam. The crowning blow is the sparse treatment given to the major problem area in this project—the landing gear and retract system. *One* sentence made up of eight words was all that was deemed necessary to describe a procedure that took over *two years* of relatively steady work and a lot of help and advice from friends. The manual was apparently written for those having a PhD in homebuilding, and thus is almost useless for the first-timer.)

Pictures, sketches and drawings are just about a must in any manual, since they can certainly save a lot of head-scratching. The pictures should be detailed illustrations of how a component is installed, or the way a construction procedure was accomplished. They should not be merely a collection of long-range shots of the project at various stages of completion. If the manual for your dream machine is less than desirable, all is not lost. If the plans are good, and you can find an A & P mechanic to suggest the right way of attacking the various construction problems, then everything is *go*!

A logical question comes up about the search for "the" project: "Where do you find out what's on the market?" The trade magazines carry ads for only a small percentage of all the plans and kits that are available. In order to save a lot of time and effort, your best bet is to order a copy of *Sport Aircraft You Can Build* from the Experimental Aircraft Association. This publication contains an extensive list of homebuilts that are currently obtainable, and gives their dimensions, specifications, type of construction, and approximate costs. Pictures of just about every airplane are also included. Having all this data on a variety of homebuilts at your fingertips for easy comparison really simplifies the decision process.

An important factor in making the final selection of an airplane to build is to choose one that is a proven design. "Proven" in this sense means that the airplane has been built from the plans supplied, by more than just a couple of builders, and has been flown successfully. Ads for the various designs usually picture the prototype—which was undoubtedly put together by some old hands in the homebuilding game who had access to all kinds of equip-

ment and building space. A way to check on this is to look over articles in the trade magazines that deal with major airshows and fly-ins. Is the bird you have chosen mentioned, or can it be spotted in the pictures? Ask the members of the local EAA chapter what they have heard or read about the airplane.

This is not meant to imply that each new design offered on the market is not an airworthy or reliable machine. The point is that it is not recommended that the first-time homebuilder be a pioneer on a brand new airplane. There are problems aplenty in any homebuilding project, but its success is more assured if you can turn to someone who has been there before to find the right answers.

But, as mentioned earlier, if you have your heart set on a particular design that is fairly new, do not let this one factor override all other considerations. Just about any problem that may come up during the project can be solved by an A & P mechanic experienced in homebuilding. However, you should expect that this type of project will take longer, and will most likely cost you more money than one that has been around for a while.

Once your choice is made, the urge to get under way is almost uncontrollable. However, before sending away for the plans and materials, it is a good idea to pause momentarily and evaluate the project as an entity. Some of the things to look at before you leap are discussed in the next chapter.

Chapter 2

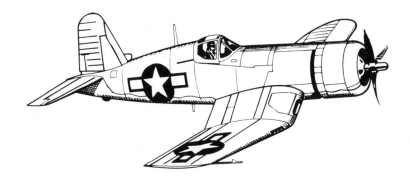

Preliminary Considerations

There are times when homebuilding, like war, is very difficult! Therefore, if you are thinking about getting into the ball game, give some thought to the overall problems of building an airplane before taking the plunge. A little preplanning here will certainly pay dividends later on.

As alluded to earlier, cost is one of the major considerations in this undertaking; it is one that cannot be avoided, and should not be underestimated. Although the total cost of the project may be a little difficult to swallow initially, remember that it will be spread out over a number of years. This is one of the great features of homebuilding—when the money gets short, the project can be temporarily shelved. It sure is a less painful way of going than meeting the monthly payments on the purchase of a completed airplane. Also, once the plans and wood have been obtained, occasional restricted finances do not mean that work on the project comes to a complete halt. There is just about always *something* that has to be cut out or trimmed for installation later on to keep you busy.

There is an old adage about homebuilding that states: "A project should never be held up because parts have not been delivered." Whoever coined this phrase was obviously well-heeled, but his idea does have merit. Whenever you find yourself a few bucks ahead, look downstream

in the project and see what items will be needed next, and get an order in for them. It's a terrible thing to see the UPS truck in your neighborhood and know that it didn't stop at your house.

Although you can order just about anything you'll need from the aircraft parts supply houses, keep in mind that for many items, there are alternate sources. Such high-priced components as instruments, radios, or brake systems may be available from someone who deals in wrecked aircraft. *Trade-A-Plane* and the classifieds in the EAA's monthly magazine, *Sport Aviation,* are also good places to find things of this nature. It is also a good idea to check with local fixed base operators who may be able to offer some good prices on certain stock items. Do not overlook auto stores and catalogs, where quite a few things can be obtained at a considerable savings over similar parts from an aircraft catalog.

Unfortunately, there are certain times during a project when relatively large expenditures are unavoidable. The engine, prop, and navcom are examples of single items that will put a real dent in your checkbook. Components that must be ordered in pairs—such as brake and disc assemblies, or landing gear struts and retract mechanisms—can do likewise. Just like everything else, the prices on aircraft parts and materials go up every year.

Therefore, the name of the game here is to order the big items as soon as you can swing it, because they won't get any cheaper as time goes on. For the *real* backbreakers (like the engine and possibly the navcom), your best bet is to scan the ads in the trade publications religiously until you find what you're looking for at a price that's in the ball park.

If you are handy with a soldering iron, and have had a little experience in building electronic devices from kits, some savings can be realized by making the navcom from scratch. At first glance, wiring up such a complicated piece of gear may seem like a Herculean task, but by following the instructions carefully and using the proper construction techniques, the job is not too difficult, and can actually be fun. There are no special tools required for this undertaking, with the exception of a soldering pencil and a continuity checker of some sort. Both of these items are readily available at any electronics store at a very moderate cost. (The name and address of the firm offering navcom kits is listed in the Appendix.)

Another high-cost item that seems to be gaining in popularity in light aircraft these days is Loran. If you plan to do any cross-country work in your bird, this is certainly the best way to go, since the accuracy and versatility of these units is truly amazing. The price tags will also raise your eyebrows, so some thought should be given to investigating the possibility of using Loran sets designed for marine use. But, before viewing these as the answer to your prayers, be sure to discuss the installation with someone knowledgeable in avionics. These sets were not intended for aircraft use, and may have some undesirable tendencies or anomalies when used in a bird.

Time and Space

Time is another consideration that you should give some thought to before committing yourself. It is assumed here that this project will be accomplished in your spare time. (Unfortunately, nearly all homebuilders must work at another job to keep bread on the table.) An even more important requirement for this drudgery is that it keeps parts in the pipeline from the aircraft supply houses.

You will soon find that time is at once your worst enemy and your best friend. There are days when it is your intention to move mountains and accomplish a great deal of progress on the bird, yet some knotty little problem invariably crops up that must be solved before going on to the next step. Jobs that appear relatively simple can gobble up huge chunks of time when it actually comes to fitting the parts together for final installation.

There is one very basic rule that should be adhered to closely in this situation: *Never* rush the last bit of trimming that will make a part fit perfectly before it is put on the airplane for good. Hurrying in this area almost invariably produces shoddy work, which will come back to haunt you later on. Parts that end up being installed "almost right" will be a constant source of problems as subsequent items are attached or mounted nearby. You really get a feel for the interdependence of the various systems in an airplane when you first start bolting major components together, and can see how the cumulative effect of small errors can impede your progress.

On the other hand, if everything turns into a can of worms, you can always step back and think about it for a while. There are no deadlines in homebuilding other than those that you set for yourself—and you will soon realize that you've got to be very flexible with these, or you'll be a basket case in no time at all. There is no sense in kidding yourself about a part-time project. Expect from the outset that it will take at least three or four years to complete, even if you work at it fairly steadily. "Fairly steadily" here means putting in a couple of hours three or four nights a week, plus a good percentage of the weekend. Unless you're a night owl, this doesn't leave much time for some of the more mundane but necessary tasks in life, such as cutting the grass, changing the oil, or fixing the faucet that can't be put off any longer.

Another thing that can be counted on with the same certainty as death and taxes is delays over which you have little or no control. Parts and materials do not always arrive in a timely fashion, and components that have been farmed out are not always done when promised. In cases like these, the resourceful builder moves on to another area of construction and gets some of the preliminary work out of the way rather than letting the whole project sit idle. There never seems to be an end to the small peripheral jobs that must be tackled eventually, yet can be done out of sequence. Later on, when these parts are ready to be installed, it sure is nice to be able to go over to the shelf and get the completed unit, rather than starting from scratch to build it. It's a good idea to have a list of these subprojects in your hip pocket so that even short delays—such as waiting for glue to dry—can be turned into productive time.

You can anticipate waiting at least three weeks for delivery from most supply houses, and this is another reason—along with costs—that local sources of parts and materials should be investigated. Occasionally a point is reached where some item is needed right away, and the thought of waiting two or three weeks is just too much to bear. This is the time to contact the Dillsburg Aeroplane Works in central Pennsylvania. Delivery time from this outfit is just a little slower than instantaneous, and on hardware and small items, the ink on your check will hardly be dry before the parts are in your mailbox. Generally speaking, the prices at Dillsburg are only very slightly higher than other sources, and in just about every case the service is well worth it. They are also great people to deal with on the phone for inquiries or corrections to orders. They do have one request, however—one that should pose no problems to most homebuilders—and that is to make all orders a minimum of $10.00.

Adequate space seems to be another chronic problem faced by homebuilders, and definitely should be addressed before the plans and materials are ordered. Once your project is under way, the space committed to it is down the tubes for quite a while. Very early in the game you will find that this is not a project that can be cleaned up and put away after each work session. After things start to take shape, the airplane becomes a permanent fixture in your cellar and/or garage. As such, it becomes something that must be worked around whenever you're doing any other job about the house. If the work area is not too spacious, this can develop into a constant source of worry: Will one of the kids run into it with a bicycle? Might it get bumped while you're wrestling with the garbage cans? Will someone use the framework as a convenient drying rack for wet bathing suits and towels?

Adequate room for the actual structure is not the only space problem. As things go along, you start collecting boxes of parts to be installed later, and other odds and ends that will be needed at some time during the project. Add to this the small power tools you'll probably want to get, and the not insignificant space required for storing materials, and you find that your shop is quickly filling up. In this vein, tools and materials kept in the cellar will quickly generate a lot of stair-climbing once the project is moved to the garage. This is due to the irrefutable maxim of homebuilding, more properly known as O'Brien's First Corollary to Murphy's Law, which deals with situations where there are two possible work areas on the premises. This states: "No matter how many tools are taken to a work area, the one that is absolutely essential for completing the job, and which is needed at the most crucial time, will always be found in the other work area." Therefore, make it easy on yourself and, if possible, arrange your project area so that tools and materials can be stored securely between work sessions.

Since constructing an airplane is a lengthy undertaking, involving a large outlay of time and money, the prudent homebuilder will consider his family before launching. The better half should be made aware of the impact this project will have on the household budget, and the approximate spacing of the major expenditures. There's no sense in setting yourself up for a fall by announcing that you're ready to get the engine or landing gear about the same time she is eyeing wall-to-wall carpeting for the home.

Normally, you need young kids around a project about as much as Custer needed more Indians. However, with the proper briefing about the relative frailty of "that thing on the table," kids can be useful at times when an extra hand is required to hold the other end of something.

As the time and money you spend on the project start to mount up, you may begin to get the fisheye from your wife every time the word "airplane" is mentioned. A last-ditch countermeasure you might use in this situation is to casually mention that you plan to paint her name on the nose—a little nautical perhaps, but in a crisis like this, desperate measures are called for.

More About Plans

A few more words about plans for homebuilt aircraft are appropriate here. Although they illustrate the construction procedure for the basic airplane—which should be followed fairly closely—they merely provide guidelines in other areas. Such things as engine mountings, landing gear and retract systems, and cockpit interiors allow a fair amount of latitude for the whims of the builder—within certain limits, of course. But remember: All modifications are made at your own risk! The plans may call for an oleo landing gear strut, yet one utilizing a coil spring works just as well, and is simpler and cheaper to build. Perhaps gussets should be welded on the landing gear support brackets to provide for better side load protection. A different gearing may be advisable for the retract system to make it work easier, or an electric drive motor may be added. Even small modifications like these should be checked carefully beforehand to make sure that the changes will not interfere with the operation of other systems.

This point cannot be overemphasized, because what may look great and work well when first installed may be a major source of trouble when follow-on components are added later in the project. This is also true when modifying one of two items that are already installed, and are in close proximity to each other. If one of these has moving parts, temporarily install both pieces and check for adequate clearance throughout the full range of movement.

About the only way to keep from painting yourself into a corner when installing a modification in a relatively clear area, and/or early in the project, is to carefully check the plans to see if any other items will interfere with it. Make sure you check all the sheets in the plans pack that show the area in question, since for purposes of clarity, some things may be shown on one view but not another.

If it appears that the clearances might be tight after checking the plans, the best course of action is to build a mockup of the parts concerned. Naturally, this is time-consuming, but it is the only safe way to go, rather than starting to drill holes in things only to find out later that they won't fit.

Should problems develop after a modified part is installed, it is not advisable to alter the design of the unchanged system to accommodate the modification. For example, if a part that has been changed interferes with the operation of the flight control system, don't vary the dimensions of the latter so that the modified component will work properly. This will produce different moment arms, which could easily cause significant problems when it comes to rigging the control surfaces for proper deflection. Either do away with the alteration or redesign it so that it will work within the existing parameters. If you are up a tree to the point where a small change in the basic system is absolutely essential, don't proceed without having an A & P mechanic review your idea carefully.

Wholesale alterations to the basic design should *never, never* be made, especially by the first-time homebuilder, without having the whole game plan checked over by an A & P mechanic. Just about every mod that you want to make will affect the CG of the bird, and some may even be detrimental to the airplane's flight characteristics.

Therefore, if you feel that you can't live without a particular feature on the airplane—especially if it is to be placed in the tail area—make it as light as possible. Putting weighty items in the extreme aft area of the bird will, in all probability, only result in having to add counterbalances in the nose that are many times the weight of the added components. The way to proceed in this area is to consider both the weight and the moment arm effect of any addition to the asic design.

One thing to remember about modifications is that they will most likely add to the complexity of the project, and this in turn will increase the time you must spend solving additional problems. As mentioned earlier, just about every difficulty in homebuilding has a solution, but it's your decision as to how much time and money you are willing to invest in order to find it. The plans—and some of the techniques discussed in this book—only show one way of attacking a given problem. In most cases there are many other ways of achieving the same end, some of which may be better adapted to *your* particular situation, and thus should not be ignored. (Probably the main advantage of the mods and techniques talked about here is that of time. They have been tried and have proven workable, which may preclude your ending up in a few blind alleys.)

There are certain parts of the project where everything is left to the builder's discretion. Examples of these would be the design and installation of the fuel and electrical systems. Here, there are too many variables that must be decided upon by the builder for a standard set of plans to be published. These systems are normally shown by schematics that indicate how the various components should be installed in relation to each other.

The choice of construction materials is another area where the builder has a few options. Substitutions can be made for the type of wood and metal parts called for in the plans, but this should be done *only* with care, and *only* after consulting with an A & P mechanic. Although most plans are based on the use of sitka spruce because of its strength-to-weight ratio, there are other woods that can be utilized. Caution must be exercised here, though, because the substitute may have to be cut with a larger cross section to achieve the required strength. This could generate a lot more problems than the substitution is worth if the new sizes interfere with the installation of other components. (The plans for the Corsair call for 2 1/2 inch 7075 aluminum extrusions to be used for the control surface hinges. The major supply houses do not carry extrusions of that hardness in the size required; therefore steel was substituted. The use of steel made it more practical to braze bushings on each hinge, which made for smoother operation at less cost than the original design.) Manuals listing substitution criteria for some of the materials commonly used in homebuilding are found in Appendix B.

There is one overriding consideration that should be kept in mind when you are thinking about substitutions or modifications, particularly the latter. Whatever changes you are planning, remember to *keep it simple*. Involved additions or alterations to a set of plans are guaranteed to create more than their share of problems.

Getting into the Swim

Once the die is cast and you've sent off for the plans, there is some initial groundwork that should be done while you're waiting for them to arrive. The first and foremost of these is to contact your local chapter of the EAA and join up. The fees are not that steep and the magazine is quite good, but most of all you'll be rubbing elbows with guys who have been in the homebuilding game for a long time. The members of your chapter are an invaluable source of information on *how* to do it, *where* to find it, and *why* it needs to be done. Just about all these folks have been there before, and thus have seen and solved most of the problems you are confronted with. There is nothing a homebuilder likes to talk about more than his project, and a little listening time will pay handsome dividends in the form of tips on construction techniques and procedures.

Equally important is their knowledge of where to locate some of the oddball parts for airplanes. In any given area there are usually a few homebuilders who buy up supplies in bulk lots, or have a collection of not-so-common parts for selling or swapping. Often there are excellent prices available from these sources, and they are well worth checking out.

Along with hard-to-find parts, chapter members are usually helpful in locating some of the exotic tools needed for homebuilding. These are the unusual things that may be required only once or twice during the entire project, but are the only tools that will do the job. Because of their uniqueness they are usually not found in the normal home workshop; however, it's a good bet that someone in the chapter has one—or knows where to get it. Cylinder wrenches, swaging tools, and cutters for instrument panel holes are examples of these items.

Another good reason for being active in a local EAA group is the ready availability of the Chapter Designee. This is a member of the chapter who is an experienced homebuilder, and who may even be an A & P mechanic, and who stays particularly up-to-date on the rules and regs governing homebuilding. These guys are worth their weight in gold if a problem crops up and you require a quick answer, or if you need some reassurance that the way you are doing something is correct. And most of these guys will make house calls!

Another very important facet of the preliminary groundwork is to visit some projects under construction. Even if it is not the same kind of airplane you are planning to build, such a visit is time well spent. It gives you an idea of the space and tool requirements you'll soon be facing, as well as a chance to look over the different parts of the bird at various stages of construction. Here again is another great opportunity to gather some ideas on the actual building techniques you'll be using, along with a foretaste of some of the problems.

During these visits, be sure to pick the brains of the builder as much as possible, particularly on those areas of construction that are similar to the bird you'll be putting together. Concentrate your questions on points dealing with the basic framework and systems, rather than focusing on fiberglassing and painting. Your *immediate* problems are not in these latter areas, and by the time you get to them, you'll have had the opportunity for adequate research and questions on these topics.

If you're lucky enough to find someone in your locality who is building the same airplane as you, establish a rapport that will permit a series of visits and questions as you approach each major phase of the project. If this is the case, it's a good idea to go over the plans carefully before starting each section and make up a list of specific questions to ask about any area that is not perfectly clear. A note of caution here: Before accepting this guy's advice as gospel, ask around the chapter about his qualifications as a homebuilder. Although he may appear to have all the answers, his thinking and methods may not be in line with normally accepted procedures. This could possibly lead to a lot of heartburn for you when your project is a lot further along and corrections will be more costly and time-consuming.

A lot has been said up to this point about how much an A & P mechanic can help with your project. Now is the time to start learning from his expertise. Talk to one before you receive your plans to get an idea of the generalized problems you can anticipate. A topic of particular importance during this dicussion is the FAA requirements that must be met while building your aircraft. There are certain points during a project where construction must stop and an FAA inspection be accomplished before proceeding. There is also the necessity of making gluing samples and welding samples along the way.

After getting your plans, it's a good idea to see your A & P again and get some more specific advice on the different areas of the project. Also, as you near any of the inspection points, it's advisable to have the Chapter designee look over your work before you call the FAA for an inspection. He may be able to save you some embarrassment by indicating any discrepancies or omissions that must be corrected before the inspector arrives.

You may run into problems when calling the FAA office to set up an inspection. Because of personnel shortages, many offices do not have the manpower to perform any initial inspections, such as the one on the spars and fuselage of the Corsair, or the precover inspection. Their position on these two inspections is outlined in "Amateur Builders Information and Guidelines, Revised March 1984." This revision states: "This FAA no longer conducts precover inspections. Pre-closure and in-progress inspections will have to be signed off by you [the builder] and you may and should reference that a qualified individual inspected your work prior to closure." The "qualified individual" referred to here is an A & P mechanic or the EAA Chapter Designee. Your logbook must contain a statement that the required inspection procedure has been complied with. A suggested entry for the logbook is as follows: "I certify that I have completed the construction of (name of the assembly), and have inspected it for precover requirements. The work was reviewed by Chapter Designee/A & P mechanic (name if desired), and is satisfactory and ready for finishing or covering as applicable."

The revision referred to above also states that when the major portion of the aircraft is foam/fiberglass construction, the builder must sign off that the correct procedures have been followed and there is no evidence of bubbles or delaminations during construction. The FAA still requires that they make the final inspection before the first flight; therefore, if you are dealing with a regional office that has been caught in the personnel crunch, expect some delays in getting your bird looked at. Any waiting time experienced can be put to good use by checking all the required paperwork to make sure it is in the proper order.

Except for this final inspection, any reference made to the FAA in this book is with the assumption that they are available. If this is not the case, an A & P mechanic will have to be contacted. Throughout this book there are many, many suggested revisions to the basic design of the WAR Corsair as presented in the plans. If these—or any others—are used in your airplane, they *must* be documented as you go along. When the FAA man arrives for the preflight inspection of your bird, he will expect to see all such minor changes noted on the drawings, initialed, and dated. This is also a good opportunity to comply with the FAA requirement to supplement your builder's log with photographs of your work throughout the project.

Another important part of this preliminary groundwork deals with assessing your own capabilities to handle the project. This is especially true when looking at other aircraft under construction, and when talking the whole thing over with an A & P mechanic. If there ever was a time to be honest with yourself, *this is it.* Should you decide, after thinking it through, that you are in beyond your depth, now is the time to bail out. Waiting until you are partway through the construction, will result in the expenditure of considerable time, effort, and money, nearly all of which can't be recouped.

However, if only certain parts of the project seem to be impossible, remember to consider the possibility of farming out some of the more difficult components. Don't be discouraged after looking through the plans for the first time. They are a bit overwhelming initially, but after a little study and advice from other homebuilders, the murky waters of planemaking become a lot clearer. All of the problems don't have to be solved at once, and by going at the project one step at a time, it is surprising to see how soon things start to fall into place.

References and Manuals

Something else that should be done concurrently with all of the above is to start collecting some of the information and references that you'll be needing later on. The EAA publishes a large number of manuals dealing with every type of sportplane construction, and the titles cover both generalized and specific areas of homebuilding. These manuals are relatively inexpensive, and provide a concise source of some very basic information that is invaluable to homebuilders.

Again, not all these manuals have to be purchased at the same time. Those devoted to foaming and fiberglassing and engine overhaul should be delayed until you are getting ready to start on those phases of the project.

There probably isn't any area of homebuilding that hasn't been covered in detail in *Sport Aviation.* Therefore, if you are interested in reading up on any specific subject, the back issues of this publication are a virtual gold mine of information. There are always a few members of the chapter who have saved every copy of *Sport Aviation* since they first joined the organization. However, these collections are jealously guarded treasures because of most people's negligence in returning borrowed magazines. In nearly all cases you will be expected to sign in blood before anyone will lend out back issues from their personal libraries.

Along with the manuals mentioned above, it is also a good plan to obtain a few catalogs from the aircraft parts supply houses. There are things that can and should be ordered right at the beginning of your project, so you might as well be ready to roll on that score. These supply houses are innumerable, so for openers it would be advisable to get a catalog from Aircraft Spruce and Specialty Company, Dillsburg Aeroplane Works, Wag Aero, and Wicks Aircraft Supply.

The first offers the most complete line of items, and also includes a lot of additional information on the various grades of wood and metal. While the Dillsburg catalog contains fewer items, it should be on hand for ordering the more common parts that are needed in a hurry. The last two supply houses also have more restricted lines than Aircraft Spruce and Specialty Company, with Wag Aero leaning more toward the restoration and refurbishing of commercially built lightplanes.

Within reason, prices from as many sources as possible should be compared before making any purchase for your bird, and these should include local non-aviation firms, who may specialize in just what you need.

Once you are committed to a project and are waiting for the plans and/or wood to arrive, there are many things that should be done to ease your transition into the world of homebuilding. Chapter 3 will outline the tasks that must be accomplished—and some of the decisions that should be made—before work actually starts on the airplane.

Chapter 3

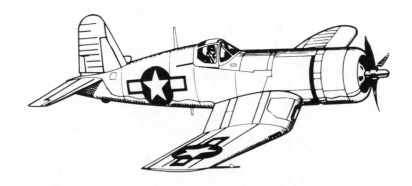

Getting Ready

The first item on the agenda for setting things up to start work on your bird is selecting the space. As a minimum, you'll need an area 8 feet by 20 feet, or about the size of a one-car garage. The latter is a perfect solution if you don't mind putting the family bus out in the weather for a few years. The above dimensions are arrived at by the room needed to set up an 8 × 16 foot table, with about two feet of working space on each side and end.

Try to select an area with adequate clearance above the table. You need a little room here when gluing the plywood skins to the fuselage frame, and after installing the fin spar. Another reason for a little extra space above the table is for the installation of proper lighting. If possible, use a pair of fluorescent fixtures, each about four feet long with its own switch. Trying to get by with a couple of bare bulbs hanging over the table is not the best way to go. The illumination never seems to be sufficient, and definitely contributes to eyestrain during long work sessions.

The availability of electrical power near the work table is another consideration. An existing junction box may be tapped in order to provide a line for the overhead lights. However, at least one socket should be located near the table so that small power tools can be used without long extension cords, which seem to be forever getting in the way. Sockets are also needed to plug in the trouble light. This portable light source is highly recommended, since despite the overhead fixtures, there always seems to be a spot that needs some extra illumination.

If available sockets are at a premium in your work area and extension cords must be used, there are a few points worth remembering. Be sure to use wire that is a little sturdier and more heavily insulated than lamp cord. These lines are subject to a large amount of abuse, and should be capable of handling the load of a drill or sander for long periods without overheating. If power must be brought to your work table or workbench by means of an extension cord, considerable time and aggravation can be saved if it is connected to some form of multiple plug receptacle. There are times during a project when a drill, saw, and sander have to be used repeatedly and in rapid succession. Having to switch plugs to a single power source all the time gets a little trying. When choosing this receptacle, be sure it can accept a three-prong plug, if any of your tools are so equipped. Once the bird is moved to the garage, a roll-around light stand, as shown in Fig. 3-1, comes in very handy.

Just about anyone living in a moderate or colder

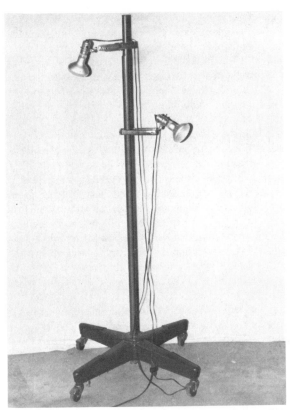

Fig. 3-1. A portable light stand made from the base of a swivel chair, a TV antenna pole, some wood clamps with ball and socket joints attached, and light fixtures.

climate will eventually have to face the problem of heat in the work area. This is not only important for personal comfort, but also for gluing procedures, since many epoxies specify minimum curing temperatures. If your project is slated to be started in the cellar and finished in the garage, the latter portion may impose some restrictions on your building schedule unless heat is provided. On a cold day it takes a fair-sized unit to keep an uninsulated and drafty garage up to an acceptable temperature for glue and/or people.

Therefore, once construction gets to the point where it must be moved to a garage that is impractical to heat, you are faced with certain limitations in wintertime. No gluing can be done on the framework until spring, when the minimum curing temperature can be maintained for the required length of time. There are, however, some five-minute epoxies available that are unaffected by temperature, and these can be used for any *small* gluing job that may crop up.

Cold weather does not mean that work on the bird comes to a screeching halt, since this is a good time to make some giant strides on the metalwork. If possible, try to plan your work during the warmer months to install all the wooden blocking necessary to mount the metal components. Then, when things get colder, everything will be all set to bolt the metal parts in place as they are made. This is also a good time to put together and glue up small wooden units that can be made in the cellar and be ready to install in the spring.

The final thing to get nailed down as far as space is concerned is a place to store your materials. Here again, a considerable amount of room is necessary. One of the boxes in the wood kit for the Corsair is about 15 feet long, and the plywood is delivered as 4 × 4 foot sheets in a slightly larger crate.

Wood should be kept in a dry place that is relatively accessible to the project. If the long pieces of wood and the subsequent scraps are stored in the shipping box, everything can be put right under the work table. Along with wood, there will be other materials that must be kept on hand, such as long lengths of steel tubing, strips of corner blocking, and aluminum tubing for brake and fuel lines. Since these items are usually sent in cardboard shipping tubes, the easiest solution is to suspend these containers from the rafters. Having a definite place to keep all these loose items sure helps when you need a certain kind of wood, in just the right size, and need it right away.

As the project wears on and you start to accumulate a variety of hardware and other small parts, cabinets or shelving become just about a necessity if things are to be kept orderly. Something that helps considerably here is a couple of dozen baby food jars to store all the numerous sizes of hardware you're bound to collect. Some of the expensive and relatively fragile items, such as radios and instruments, should be put out of the way in a cabinet because of the things that can be dropped and/or spilled in any shop area.

Tools for the Job

It's probably an unwritten law of homebuilding that no beginner ever starts a project with all the tools he will need. Naturally, everyone would like to have a complete wood and metal shop available, along with all the hand tools in the Sears catalog. While this would be ideal, an airplane can be built with quite a bit less. The tool list compiled below does not represent the maximum or minimum required, either in numbers or varieties. For the most part, these are the relatively common tools found in any do-it-yourselfer's workshop—and with a few exceptions, are those that were found to be handy in building the Corsair. The terms "Required" and "Nice to have" are definitely relative, since it is no doubt possible to do the job with a lot less. However, this is the hard way to go, and you'll certainly find that the more hand tools you have, the easier things will be.

Another thing to keep in mind when reviewing the list below is that the Corsair is a wooden airplane. Homebuilts that are all-metal or have fabric covering require different or additional tools peculiar to these construction methods.

Required

- ☐ 1/4-inch drill and bits.
- ☐ Belt sander.
- ☐ Saber saw with blades for wood and metal.
- ☐ Clamps—"C", spring, and furniture.
- ☐ Files and wood rasps.
- ☐ Saws—miter and hack.
- ☐ Squares—large (18″ × 24″) and small.
- ☐ Scissors.
- ☐ Hammers-claw and tack.
- ☐ Open-end and socket wrenches—particularly 7/16″ and 3/8″.
- ☐ Vise-medium or small size.
- ☐ Levels—large and small.
- ☐ Screwdrivers—common and Phillips.
- ☐ Pliers—regular, lineman's, and needlenose.
- ☐ Vise Grips.
- ☐ Wire strippers.
- ☐ Soldering iron.
- ☐ High-speed hand drill.
- ☐ Miter box.
- ☐ Long straightedge.
- ☐ Set of X-acto knives.
- ☐ Plumb bob and line.

Nice to Have

- ☐ Portalign drill attachment.
- ☐ Drill press.
- ☐ Taps.
- ☐ Plastic cutting wheel.
- ☐ Pop riveter.
- ☐ Flycutter.
- ☐ Bench-mounted grinder.

A few words of elaboration should be added about some of the items mentioned here. If you own a Craftsman belt sander, Sears has an attachment that will make this tool one of the handiest in your shop, next to the 1/4 inch drill. This is the Belt Sander Stand, which supports the machine in a vertical position and allows you to sand true 90 degree edges. Since these belts can be used for both wood and mildly hard metals, it is really a versatile tool.

Clamps are something that probably no one ever has enough of, and nothing that can hold two pieces of material together should be overlooked. When starting out, it's a good idea to have at least a dozen C-clamps available in a variety of sizes, and, if possible, some of the deep-throated design. Along with these, you will also need a few of the adjustable furniture clamps mounted on a section of pipe. These find many uses during a project, particularly when working on the spars. During this phase of the work, it will be necessary to borrow a few more of these clamps so that about six or eight are on hand when the spars are assembled.

A variety of files and wood rasps will definitely make life a lot easier during some of the trying moments of the project. At the very least, you should have the following shapes on hand for each: flat, round, and half-round. There is one type of wood rasp on the market that is flat on one side and half-round on the other, with each side having two degrees of coarseness. While working on a wooden airplane, you'll find that this one tool is worth its weight in gold. It is also recommended that a set of small model builder's files, in a variety of shapes, be picked up. These too will prove invaluable in many instances.

Unless you've had to buy one at some other time, a small, hand-held, high-speed rotary drill may seem like an extravagance. However, after working on something over your head with a wood rasp for any length of time, the merits of this tool become patently obvious. Using this tool with a round or drum-shaped burr will save an inordinate amount of time, effort, and barked knuckles. The saying goes that it only costs a little more to go first class, and in this case it is really worth it.

Other Necessities

Along with tools, the homebuilder's workshop ought to have the following items in order to facilitate the construction process:

A prime necessity is a good workbench that is separate from the table on which the airplane will be built. There are a great number of times during a project when another work surface is needed while the framework rests undisturbed on the table as the glue dries. Also, on the size table that will be described below, there really isn't a lot of extra room once the fuselage and center spars are joined.

As touched on above, it will be well worth your time to scrounge up a few cabinets and small tables. These are needed to store the million-and-one things you'll need at some time during the project, and are good places to set up the sander, table drill press, and grinder. Something that might be considered here if you don't want these items permanently installed is a mounting board for each. This is a piece of 3/4 inch plywood, about two feet by three feet, to which the unit is secured. This allows these very handy tools to be moved up to the garage for a work session when they will be used heavily, while at the same time providing an adequate base and support. This type of arrangement also makes for easy storage between projects.

Another useful addition to help fight clutter in the shop is a tool board. This doesn't take much time to set up, and it sure helps to keep things organized as far as hand tools are concerned.

There will be times during the project—especially when you start working on the metal parts—that long periods will be spent at the workbench trimming something to just the right size. A big help here, if you can come across one, is a tall stool like those used by draftsmen. Of even greater importance is a pair of small stools or stepchairs to be used around the worktable. Often, a certain phase of construction will require that you climb up on the table to get a measurement, climb back down to cut and shape the piece, climb up again for a trial fit, and so on. After doing this number about a hundred times a day you'll really appreciate just how handy a small stool can be.

A couple of other things you'll find useful are a mechanic's drop light, or trouble light, with a long extension cord, and a shop vacuum. This latter item will make a lot of points with the better half, and also keep things livable in the shop. Building a wooden airplane generates a prodigious amount of sawdust, and the first time you track some up from the cellar you'll get an earful on the virtues of vacuuming.

Getting the worktable built will probably take a weekend or so after the materials are delivered, so plan for this in advance. If you intend to do the preliminary work on the airplane in your cellar, you'll have to make a table that can be moved with the bird. In this case, your best bet is two 4 × 8-foot sheets of plywood or particle board, arranged end-to-end and supported by sawhorses.

An awful lot of work will be done on the framework after it starts to roost on the work table. Therefore, make it easy on yourself and set the height of the table at a convenient level to avoid a lot of bending or reaching. Something to keep in mind here—particularly with the Corsair—is to make the table high enough to allow the gear to fully extend once it is installed.

Because of the length of the table, at least three sawhorses will be required to support it adequately. If the one in the middle is positioned lengthwise to spread its support over a larger area, some form of bracing along the sides of the table at the butt joint will probably be necessary.

Three-quarter-inch plywood or particle board should be used for the table. The latter is cheaper than plywood, but each 4 × 8 sheet is extremely heavy, and is a very cumbersome load for a minimum of two people. When both sheets are joined, it becomes a real task to manhandle the completed table up onto the sawhorses. Even when three supports are used, you will probably find that the table will sag a little between the sawhorses whenever any weight is placed on it. Therefore, some form of under-table bracing will be required. This problem can be minimized or alleviated by screwing long 2 × 3-inch planks, on edge, to the bottom of the table. When securing these pieces, be sure to countersink the wood screws in order to keep a smooth work surface.

Something to keep in mind as you construct the work table is that the sturdiness of this item can't be overemphasized. You will be spending a considerable amount of time on the table, nearly all of which will be standing on the outside edges, or on the very ends. In this light, make sure that the perimeter of the table is adequately supported—particularly the end where the nose of the aircraft will be, since this area gets most of the heavy use.

It is also recommended that diagonal braces be used between the legs on the same side of the sawhorse. This will minimize side-to-side sway of the table, which really becomes important when you try to jockey the bird on and off the table with the gear attached. It would really spoil your whole day to have the entire weight of the framework resting on one edge of the table, and then have the legs on that side give way while you're getting a better grip.

If the plans you purchase are full-sized, you'll soon realize that you've got quite a few rolls of paper to deal with. Often, many different sheets of the plans are printed on one continuous piece of paper. These should be cut into convenient—and, if possible, related—sections, re-rolled, and labeled on the outside of the roll.

These plans will be referred to countless times during the project, and thus should be kept out of harm's way while still being readily accessible. An easy solution to this is a U-shaped structure made from scrap paneling or thin plywood and some leftover 2 × 3s and nailed to the rafters.

Record-keeping is another area that should be addressed before construction gets under way. One of the handiest sets of information to keep is a list of all the questions you encounter during the building process—questions that you must ask of other homebuilders, the Chapter Designee, or an A & P mechanic. When you get the answers, be sure to jot them down so that they can be referred to later on, when you are actually ready to make and install the part that caused the problems.

Another list that is well worth your time to keep up-to-date is a catalog of all the bolts and other pieces of hardware that are ordered, along with a notation as to where they will be installed. Very often such hardware sits around for extended periods before the part is ready to be bolted on, and a record of what is on hand for each component saves the time and expense of reordering. It's also a good idea to put scraps of paper in the plastic bags hardware is shipped in to identify where each piece will be used. Although not absolutely necessary, other records that could be kept are the cost and from whom each part is ordered, and a log of the time spent on each work session and what was accomplished.

Glues and their Characteristics

Hopefully, before your plans and wood kit arrive, you'll have received a couple of the supply house catalogs. Now is the time to get some general things ordered, items that will be needed early in the game. One of the most important of these is the glue you are planning on using, and here again, some research is needed.

Probably one of the best sources of information on the many types of glue available on the market is a publication by the EAA entitled *Building the Custom Aircraft with Wood, Volume 2*. The articles in this manual discuss the good and bad properties of a number of the more common adhesives used in homebuilding. For your convenience, a summary of the characteristics of the major types is listed below.

	Resorcinol	Epoxy	Plastic Resin
Strength	Good	Best	Better
Gap Filling	Fair	Good	Fair
Working Life	Good	Excell.	Better
Shelf Life	Indef.	Indef.	Indef.

	Resorcinol	Epoxy	Plastic Resin
Contact Pressure	Yes	No	Yes
Wood Penetration	Fair	Best	Good
Staining Quality	Bad	Good	Best

The above chart is by no means all-inclusive, since it only reflects the results of tests on a few of the more commonly used glues. However, these tests were fairly exhaustive, and thus lend a high degree of validity to the findings. The epoxies tested were Aerolite and Hughes FPL 16A, and the plastic resin was made by Weldwood. The Corsair project described in this book utilized Aerolite throughout, and everything they say about this adhesive is true—it's really great.

It is evident from the chart that epoxies are pretty much the way to go, since they possess more of the qualities important to the first-time homebuilder than the other types. But there are a few things that should be mentioned on the minus side with respect to all of these adhesives. The most important is toxicity. The fumes from resorcinol and plastic resins are injurious, and thus large or continuous applications of these glues should *only* be done in a well ventilated area.

The bad feature about epoxies is that they are prone to causing rashes and other problems with the skin. Aerolite, for example, will peel the hide off your hands just like a bad case of sunburn. In severe cases epoxies have been known to induce a coronary because of the inflammation of the tissues in the lungs and around the heart. The name of the game here is to read *all* the precautions on the can, and *believe what they say*. These are definitely harmful substances, but their effects can be circumvented by utilizing the proper protection while they are being used.

People who are susceptible to allergic reactions should be especially careful in this area. If such things as breathing masks, hand creams, or rubber gloves are recommended, *don't* try to be a hero by disregarding these warnings. The kitchen variety of rubber gloves found in all supermarkets is just what the doctor ordered. They are cheap, fairly durable, and thin enough to allow a sense of touch to be retained while they are being worn.

Another drawback with epoxies is their costs, which is usually above the other types. However, over the long run, this added expense is well worth it when considering all the good points about these glues.

A note of caution should be added here that applies to all kinds of glue that come in two parts and must be mixed. Follow the directions as to proportions *exactly*, and be *very* careful in measuring out the amounts of each. A few slip-ups here could result in a glue with entirely different properties than those on the label.

After looking at the plans for any homebuilt made of wood, you will find that, in many respects, it goes together like a model airplane. Where pins were used to hold the balsa strips in place for the model, blocking pieces will be used for the real thing. These blocks are cut from 3/4-inch square white pine, and are about 2-1/2 to 3 inches long. A piece of pine about eight feet long should provide enough of these blocks to get you started. After the pieces are cut, they should be drilled with two holes for the nails that will hold them in place on the work table. These holes will prevent any splitting when they are nailed down for the first time.

While you're at the lumberyard getting the white pine strips, pick up some 1/4-inch plywood or lauan for the fuselage jig. The latter is a bit cheaper and is strong enough to do the job satisfactorily.

Some other things that will definitely be needed and can be purchased at this time are glue brushes. The type to look for are called "acid brushes," and are used to brush on acid flux for soldering and welding jobs. They are quite inexpensive, and you'll probably need at least a half-dozen or so.

A final item that can be obtained beforehand is tracing paper. This, however, is not essential, and is only needed if you do not wish to cut up the plans in order to get patterns for the various parts that must be cut from plywood, metal, and stock lumber. Using patterns made from tracing paper is recommended since it preserves the plans as a master; this is particularly important when they must be used for other measurements.

On the big day when the plans and wood kit arrive, the first order of business is to make a complete inventory of both. There should be a list that identifies every sheet in the plans package, and all should be accounted for. On aircraft that are relatively new on the market, there may be some parts of the plans that are not drawn as yet, but these should be for some system or component considerably downstream in the project. The wood in the kit will normally be listed as the total number of feet for each of the sizes required. If the plans call for special pieces cut to two different sizes, such as the Corsair longerons, make sure that they are included, and the lengths of each size are correct.

A note of caution here: The amount of wood supplied in a kit is calculated very closely to the amount called for in the plans. Also, each board is designed to supply the wood for very specific pieces, and the total length of these does not leave much scrap. Therefore, before making the final decision on what patterns to assign to each board, make sure you are getting the maximum possible utilization of the available length. Not getting the most out of each board may cause you to end up with insufficient wood for one of the larger patterns. This, in turn, will necessitate your ordering more wood at prices that will *really* water your eyes.

Metal Components

As you look over your plans for the first time, it's a good idea to give considerable thought to the metal parts of the airplane. Due to the long lead time usually needed to procure these items from whatever source, some fairly important decisions should be made at this point. The big question is: Do you plan to make *some, all,* or *none* of the metal parts required?

As you mull over this problem, there are a few things to keep in mind as you consider each option. Those who plan to do it all themselves would have to have access to a lathe, a metal-cutting bandsaw, a drill press, and a grinder. Along with the skills necessary to operate these machines, a fairly high proficiency in welding is required. Your adroitness in this latter area will be checked by the FAA inspector, who will want to see samples of joints you have weleded. These samples will be cut apart to check for the depth of the weld at each junction. Naturally, there are a lot of other special tools that are needed in conjunction with the machine tools mentioned above, such as precision measuring instruments, reamers, special clamps and jigs, etc. The two biggest advantages of doing-it-yourself are savings in time and costs. The parts will be ready when you want them, and your only outlay will be for materials.

At the other extreme is ordering all the metal parts from supply houses or custom manufacturers. There are usually a few of the latter available that specialize in making parts for specific airplanes on the market. The names of these are normally available from the company producing the plans for your homebuilt, or from the various trade publications. The main drawback to this course of action is the *staggering* cost of these custom-built components. This is a quick way of getting all the metal parts from one source, but their price lists usually read like the national debt. Another problem normally encountered here is the very long wait for the parts to be delivered. And, even when you get them, you may find that they do not fit together perfectly, especially if the various parts were not all ordered at the same time. Probably the biggest headache occurs when there is something wrong with the parts. They have to be packaged up and shipped back to the manufacturer, where you hope your description of the problem is sufficiently detailed to allow them to correct the difficulty—*more* time and money down the drain!

Without a doubt, the preferred way to go in this area is it take advantage of the best of both worlds. This is done by trying to find an A & P mechanic in the local area who has the necessary machine tools and will build the parts for you. In all probability he will not charge as much as the custom houses, and even if he does, it is still by far the better deal. If the part doesn't fit exactly, or there are modifications or refits to be done later on, he is relatively available to fix the problem. Most of these people do not make parts for homebuilders on a full-time basis; therefore, you still must plan on a long lead time for these components.

Another advantage is that A & P mechanics are licensed by the FAA to do aircraft welding. However, it is best to ascertain if the mechanic is current and proficient in the type of welding you need. He may have been working strictly on jet engines since obtaining his rating.

Even though you do not have the tools and the skills to work metal, there are a lot of preliminary things you can accomplish on certain parts before they are given to the A & P mechanic. On those made from sheet stock or steel tubing, you can do the initial cutting, fitting, and trimming to get the pieces ready for welding and/or final assembly. This type of work is relatively simple, yet fairly time-consuming. Therefore, you are better off price-wise doing the easier tasks yourself, rather than paying an A & P mechanic to do rote work. Doing it this way will also expedite getting the part completed and ready to install.

While we're on the subject of metal parts, it's a good time to discuss some common denominators of all metal components. Once the unit is finished, it should be cleaned and primed even if it is not to be installed for some time. You don't want to let rust and corrosion get a toehold since this could be a source of trouble later on, when removing and replacing the part could be a real can of worms. Wire-brush the entire component thoroughly, being particularly careful to remove the scale around welded areas.

After the part is cleaned, it should be wiped down with a solvent to remove all traces of grease and oil. Use a stiff brush or an old toothbrush to get at the more stubborn or inaccessible spots. Lacquer thinner is great for this job. However, if you're temporarily out of this solvent and the parts aren't too big, stick them in the dishwasher for the wash and rinse cycles. It's probably a good idea to remove them before the drying cycle, since this may allow a little rust to begin forming. After the parts have been cleaned by solvent or in the dishwasher, they should not be handled, since a fingerprint will prevent good paint adhesion.

As soon as possible after cleaning, each unit should be hung up and given a coat of primer. The most economical and handiest thing to use here is a spray can of the red or gray auto primer found in all auto parts stores. If the component will end up on the inside of the bird and will not be painted again when the entire airplane is done, a second coat of primer would be advisable.

Although it may seem a little obvious, there is one facet of priming that deserves extra attention here. When assembling or installing parts that have been primed, expect some problems fitting them together and getting bolts through the mounting holes if there is paint in these areas. This is particularly true when dealing with close-fitting surfaces such as the torque tube and its bushings, or the gear retract shaft. Since it is a good possibility that metal parts will be cleaned and primed well in advance of their final installation, make sure that all surfaces—even those in bolt and shaft holes—are primed. Then, when it comes time to put them on the bird, clean out the tight-fitting holes with a cotton swab dipped in lacquer thinner. Shafts may have to be wiped entirely clean of paint in order for them to be inserted without having to resort to hammering. After all the adjustments have been made, and the part has been installed permanently, clean and touch up any exposed surfaces with primer.

As the project goes on, quite a few metal parts will have to be removed and reinstalled frequently. This will invariably cause dings and scratches to appear in the painted surfaces. An area that is particularly prone to such problems is the top of the trusses. These are all-too-convenient footrests, once they are installed, while you are doing work in the cockpit area.

With these factors as just about givens throughout the project, a little preventive maintenance is in order on a periodic basis. Every once in a while, when time is hanging heavy on your hands, go over all the metalwork on the bird and sand, clean, and reprime as required.

Aircraft Hardware

Aircraft hardware is another area dealing with metals that should be touched on at this time. Only nuts, bolts, and washers designated AN and NAS should be used on aircraft because of their strength and resistance to corrosion. *Do not* use nuts and bolts from the hardware store, since these will be unacceptable to FAA inspectors. *All* bolts on an airplane must be secured by nuts incorporating either a plastic or a metal device to keep them from working loose. The metal locknuts are used in areas where high temperatures are expected. The only exception to the use of locknuts is when castellated nuts are employed, and these are secured with a cotter pin.

All AN bolts are coded by thickness and length, and the latter must be determined fairly carefully. Trial assemble the parts to be bolted together, and measure the overall distance from one end of the bolt hole to the other. This is the "grip length" needed for that assembly, and is the factor that determines the length of the bolt to be used. If the standard sizes in the catalog do not list the exact length you need, order the next larger size. When the bolt is installed, all threads should be visible, and washers are used to compensate for excess shank length. However, the maximum acceptable number of washers is two. Washers should always be used under the nut to prevent scoring the metal part when it is tightened.

If either end of the bolt is resting on a wood surface, a larger washer is needed at the end to distribute the load over a larger area. An AN-970 washer is the most common type used here.

A glance through your parts catalog will indicate that aircraft bolts are not exactly free. Also, the locking feature of a locknut can be worn out by repeated removal and installation. Therefore, it's advisable to get two or three dozen standard nuts in both the 3/16-inch and 1/4-inch sizes. This will allow you to assemble and disassemble these components as many times as needed without ruining either the bolts or nuts.

If you have your druthers, there is a good rule of thumb to follow when installing any bolt on an aircraft. The head of the bolt should be pointing either *up* or *forward*. This practice may provide some margin of safety in the unlikely event of a nut working loose and falling off. As with most rules of thumb, there are some exceptions dictated by necessity or common sense. There are some places where it is impossible to install a bolt without its head being down or tailward. Also, if a bolt is in a critical spot—especially one that is subject to vibration—and you want the nut visible for periodic inspections, then install it that way.

The various other types of hardware that are used less frequently will be discussed in connection with the applicable portion of the project.

Now that everything you need to get under way has arrived, and you've got a pretty good idea of your overall game plan, it's time to start cutting some wood. The next chapter will deal with building the box frame of the fuselage, and although it's not an absolute requirement to start here, it's as good a place as any.

Chapter 4

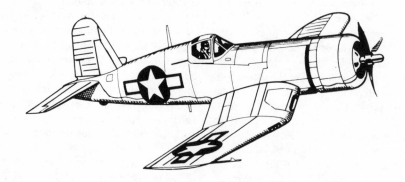

Fuselage Frame Construction

The fuselage frame is relatively easy to build, yet despite its simplicity, care should be exercised in fitting all the pieces because this structure forms the basic strength of the airplane. As you start to cut and slash your way through your pile of sitka spruce, remember that this is precious stuff. Save every scrap, no matter how small, because there always seems to be a need for pieces of every size and shape as you go along through the project. You will find this to be particularly true with respect to the birch plywood used for the fuselage skins and ribs. This 1/16-inch sheet stock is needed in all phases of construction to make mounting pads for the control surface hinges and various other metal components.

This saving of scrap and mistakes also extends to the metal parts for your bird. These too come in handy when you need an oddball size of a certain type of metal that is too small to warrant placing an order.

Before laying out the plans on the work table, the latter should be leveled in both directions over its entire length. Cellar or garage floors are rarely, if ever, level; therefore, the legs of the sawhorses should be blocked up to achieve a flat work surface. Normally, the proper use of a level doesn't sound like a very big deal, but in airplane building, the trueness and squareness of each part in relation to the others assumes critical proportions.

Therefore, in order to achieve consistency in measurements of levelness made throughout the project,

a certain technique is called for. Whenever a level is used to check the bird or the table in any given direction, the same end of the level should always point in the same direction. As an example, when checking for levelness in a spanwise direction, the same end of the level should always point toward the same wingtip.

After the table has been squared away, drive a small nail in each end, halfway between the sides. Unroll the plans for the fuselage frame on the table and smooth them out, using weights to hold things in place temporarily. Run a string between the nails on the ends of the table, make it taut, and tie in place. Then line up the plans under the string so that the latter falls along the centerline of the frame, as drawn on the plans. Smooth out the paper again, recheck the alignment, and secure it to the table top with short strips of masking tape.

Before any of the wood pieces are blocked in place, prepare a stack of wax paper squares, about 4-6 inches on an edge. These will be placed over the plans at every glue joint to keep the paper from sticking to the wood, and to help protect the drawings from the glue components. If you use Aerolite, be particularly careful about keeping the hardener from running off the wax paper and contacting the drawing. This chemical tends to react with blueprint lines, making them very diffuse or even causing them to disappear entirely.

When blocking the longerons into place, the only

precaution to be observed is the placement and orientation of the thinner section aft of the cockpit area. The wood strip supplied with the kit will be slightly longer than necessary. Therefore, it must be placed on the plans so that the thin section starts at the proper spot. Any excess on the ends is cut off after the side frame is completed.

The orientation of this thin section depends on which side of the fuselage you are building. The cutout side of each longeron faces the interior of the airplane. Thus, when you are building the left side of the fuselage, this cutout side must be down, facing the plans. This in turn will require that a number of 1/4-inch blocks be prepared to elevate the crossmembers in this section above the table and flush with the outside of the longerons.

When making the crossmembers, mark the various angles right from the plans, and cut them a little oversize using a miter box whenever possible. Both surfaces should be in complete contact across the joint, with no spaces. Regardless of its gap-filling properties, don't rely on the glue to take up the slack for a poorly made joint.

Gluing Procedures

A couple of tips on gluing that might be worth remembering: Have all the blocking to hold the pieces nailed in place before any glue is applied. This will preclude the piece from being moved around and the glue squeezed out of the joint while the blocks are being nailed. If you are using Aerolite, there are a few things to be aware of that are a little different from the procedures used for adhesives that go on in a single application. With Aerolite, the epoxy is put on one surface of the joint, and the hardener is applied to the other. This is one of the great advantages of Aerolite, because the glue does not start to set up until the pieces are joined. This gives you a large amount of flexibility, time-wise, during the gluing and assembly operations. However, if you are working on a joint where more than two pieces are involved, it pays to plan ahead as to which surface gets the hardener and which gets the epoxy. This also helps avoid a situation where epoxy has to be applied to a surface that already has hardener on it. Some of the hardener will most likely be carried back to the epoxy jar on the brush, and your entire glue batch will start to set up. If you should inadvertently get hardener on the glue brush, be sure to wash out the brush *thoroughly* with water before putting it back in the epoxy.

When gluing in the fuselage frame crossmembers, or any other joint involving the butt end of a piece of wood, another precaution about Aerolite is in order. If the water-thin hardener is applied to the end of a piece of wood, there is a marked tendency for it to be absorbed into the grain of the wood. This could set up a situation where the hardener is drawn away from the surface of the joint in an amount sufficient to prevent a complete reaction with the epoxy. The resulting joint would certainly not be as strong as required. Therefore, whenever possible, apply the epoxy to the end of the piece, and the hardener to the other surface. If this is not possible, be sure to keep applying hardener to the end of the wood until all signs of absorption have stopped and the surface is saturated.

The birch plywood used throughout the Corsair also deserves a little attention when it comes to gluing. You will notice that this plywood has a hard, somewhat shiny surface as it comes from the supplier. Regardless of the type of glue you are using, better adhesion will be obtained if the surface of the plywood to be glued is given a light sanding to remove the shine.

As the project goes along you will probably find it more economical to mix up quite a few small batches of glue rather than a couple of large ones. Before each batch is used up, be sure to make a sample joint that the FAA inspector can break apart to check on your mixing and application procedures. These glue samples should be identified by batch number, and your work log should reflect what portions of the assembly this batch was used on. The sample should be a simple lap joint with an inch or so of glued surface, and made from scraps of either plywood or strip stock.

After the fuselage frame sides have been completed and the glue has dried, carefully inspect each joint for crevices or gaps that the adhesive has not filled entirely. If any of these are apparent, follow-on gluing (FOG) should be used. If Aerolite is your glue, each gap should be thoroughly brushed with hardener and then filled with epoxy. A handy gadget to apply the epoxy in narrow crevices is an L-shaped piece of music wire, with the short side of the L being about a half inch long. When FOGing joints, it's a good idea to pour out a little epoxy on a piece of cardboard and dip the wire in this, rather than risk spoiling the whole batch. When this glue has dried, carefully remove the frame from the plans without taking out the blocking pieces. Turn the frame over and FOG the underside of each joint as required. The other side of the fuselage frame is done in the same manner, with the exception of the differences needed with respect to the thin section of the longerons.

A hint here that may make life easier for you when the fuselage frame sides are joined together: When each side is finished, it's a good idea to sand off the rough spots made by the glue on the interior side of the frame. This little extra work will pay dividends when you are installing the crossmembers and everything is under tension—including you.

While the second fuselage side is drying, the top and bottom crossmembers should be measured, cut, trimmed, and labeled. When measuring for these pieces, check along the edge closest to the center of the airplane. This will prevent undercutting, since the further you get from the center of the bird—particularly tailward—the more of a bevel will have to be sanded into each piece. Once the bevels are made, those pieces should also be marked as to which side is forward. This will come in handy during installation, since things go fairly quickly here and are a little hectic at best.

Other items that have to be made now are the clamps to hold the fuselage sides when the top and bottom crossmembers are installed. On the Corsair (or similar projects), the wooden strips with the end pieces, as described in the instruction booklet, are completely adequate. But be sure to label each clamp, and mark on the frame approximately where it goes. This will facilitate their rapid placement when everything is happening at once.

Another area where the instruction manual serves its purpose is the part concerning the building of the fuselage jig. Construct these items according to the directions, align over the centerline as described, and secure in place. It would also be advisable to build some sort of a device to be erected in front of the frame while it's in the jig. This is to prevent the entire assembly from moving forward, thereby keeping the entire frame in its proper position within the jig. Before arranging the frame sides in the jig, make about eight to ten thin wedges from scrap material. These will be used to move the assembled frame slightly within the jig and hold it in the proper alignment until the glue dries. Probably their most important function is to help bring the frame into squareness after the top and bottom crossmembers are glued into place.

Completing the Fuselage Frame

When all the crosspieces, clamps, and wedges have been prepared, place the side frames in the jig and loosely secure them in an upright position against the sides of the jig. Be sure that the front of each frame is flush against the forward stop, then insert a couple of the top and bottom crossmembers in the cockpit area. Do not use any glue here, since this is just a trial run to see if any problems will develop when the frames are squeezed to their final positions at the front and back ends. Attach

the frame clamps where indicated as additional crossmembers are fit into position. This operation is a little tricky since only friction and pressure are holding these pieces in place, and inadvertently jostling one may cause others to fall out.

This drill actually amounts to a practice session for the actual gluing of the crossmembers. What you are looking for here is significant alignment problems and pieces that are somehow too long or too short. The fuselage should taper evenly from the cockpit area, with no bumps or depressions in the longerons that would indicate a measurement that is off (Fig. 4-1).

Another thing that is of prime importance here is squareness, and what must be done to achieve it. Check the squareness of the frame at various spots along the sides to see where any adjustments will have to be made. The way to shift the frame into proper alignment is to drive one of the thin wedges between the frame and the jig until the 90 degree angle between the sides and the top or bottom is obtained. This may necessitate using another wedge diagonally from the first to decrease the total movement required in any one spot. Make a mark where each of these wedges is needed for quick reference later.

After everything is lined up satisfactorily, remove all the cross pieces and start gluing them in, again beginning with the center section. If you thought things were tedious during the trial run, you ain't seen nothing' yet! Now that there's glue on each end of the crossmembers, they become fairly slippery and thus a lot harder to keep

Fig. 4-1. Looking through the fuselage frame from the nose to check for the symmetrical alignment of the four sides.

in place—particularly where the taper of the longerons is more pronounced.

If it has been just one of those days, and a few of these pieces seem bound and determined to slip to the point where they will not stay put as the fuselage clamps are placed into position, use a C-clamp immediately in front of the cross piece. Given the anxiety of the moment, it would probably be a wise move to have a couple of these prepositioned and opened to just the right width.

Time is somewhat of a problem here because once the joint is made and the glue starts to set up, it should be disturbed as little as possible. Glue in these pieces rapidly, and install the frame clamps and wedges. Immediately recheck the entire frame for squareness and adjust the wedges as needed.

Check constantly for slippage of the crossmembers, which may have occurred when the clamps and wedges were tapped into place. Also recheck that the frame is tight against the forward stop.

There is one thing you should be aware of during the dry run and the actual gluing operation that will nearly cause cardiac arrest in the first-time builder. As the front and back sections of the frame are squeezed together when the cross pieces are installed, there is a possibility of joint separation at the end of the vertical pieces in the frame sides. This usually happens with a sudden snapping noise, which has the same effect as an icicle driven through your heart. An imperfect glue joint is the cause—probably from too much hardener being absorbed into the end of the wood. The break is clean and along the glue line, and merely has to be cleaned up and reglued at a later time. Don't stop the gluing and alignment procedure to fix a joint separation, since the former is much more crucial at this point. However, with the whole frame under stress from the clamps, and the large number of things that have to be done quickly, it really is a sinking feeling when one lets go.

Gussets, Doublers, and Webs

While the fuselage frame is still in the jig, the various gussets and doublers can be installed. The gussets should be cut out and trimmed fairly carefully to ensure a good tight fit. Gaps between the gluing surface of the gusset and the fuselage frame members should be minimized as much as possible. This is done by holding the piece in position and placing the drop light very close behind it at the proposed glue line. Then, with your eye level with the glue line, check for light coming through the joint. Any unevenness between the two pieces will be readily apparent, and trimming can be done accordingly.

Clamping these triangular blocks in place for gluing presents somewhat of a problem. Without a lot of extra blocks of the correct angles, C-clamps cannot be used. Since Aerolite doesn't require clamping pressure, a handy device to hold the gusset in place while drying is made from a nail and a rubber band. Attach one end of the rubber band to the nail with a girth hitch, stretch the other end around the parts to be joined, and loop it back over the nail. A few of these afford a quick and easy method of providing enough pressure to hold the parts together for a good joint.

If you are using a glue that requires clamping pressure, then angled clamping blocks must be employed. Some of these gusseted junctions also require plywood doublers over the outside of the assembly. Be sure to sand smooth any excess glue that was squeezed out of the gusset-frame joint prior to gluing the doubler in place.

Before the frame is removed from the jig, the plans should be checked to see if any plywood webs have to be added to the interior. The Corsair has a few of these in the tail section, and it is considerably easier to add these pieces now, as opposed to after the frame has been skinned. However, don't forget that the frame is inverted in the jig, and care must be exercised to ensure that each web is installed with the proper up-down orientation. Some of these webs are fairly large and it takes a good bit of twisting and turning to get them into place. Also, their edges may have to be trimmed a little to allow the webs to be worked into position. But since the purpose of these webs is to add strength, all trimming should be kept to a minimum.

A lot of times these webs seem to defy every effort to get them located properly, and major surgery appears to be the only answer. However, before resorting to this, keep trying to twist, bend, or angle them into place. For some unexplained reason, there is usually one—and only one—procedure for slipping a given piece into position. Once this is found, make some mental notes on how you went about it, and practice it once or twice. After the glue has been applied to each surface, you don't want any hangups in getting them joined correctly.

When all the glue has dried, the frame can be carefully removed from the jig. Each joint should then be inspected and FOGed where necessary. The frame is still somewhat fragile at this point, especially to diagonal loads, so cautious handling of the structure is advised.

The next step in the process is to eliminate this weakness and increase the overall strength of the frame by the addition of plywood skins. The following chapter details the construction and installation of these sections.

Chapter 5

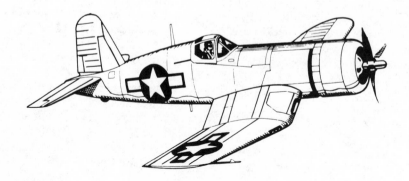

Plywood Skins for the Frame

One of the things that contributes to the strengthening of the frame by the plywood skins is the fact that each is installed as a single, complete piece. The various sections are glued together beforehand, and the skin for each side of the frame is applied as a unit. Fabricating these parts before they are put on the frame allows for better glue joints between the individual pieces than would be possible if these same sections were glued together after they were mounted on the frame. This is because once they are in place, adequate clamping pressure cannot be maintained across the entire joint to ensure a good bond between the edges of the skins.

One of the best methods of making a joint such as this, where the thickness of the material should be kept as uniform as possible, is by scarfing the edges of the pieces to be joined.

Scarfing

Scarfing is the beveling of the edge of the material at a very slight angle (about 5 degrees), which results in a slanted gluing surface extending back from the edge about 1 to 1 1/2 inches. The scarfed areas of the two sections to be joined are then overlapped. This permits a very strong glue joint to be made, with little or no increase in the thickness of the fuselage skin.

There are many ways to do the actual scarfing of the plywood pieces concerned. The simplest is to do it by hand, using a flat wood rasp. The plywood is clamped down with the side to be scarfed along the edge of the shop bench. Work along the entire edge, holding the rasp at a very slight angle from the horizontal. The evenness and the depth of the scarf can easily be determined by the alternate light and dark layers of the plywood. These color lines should be straight and fairly parallel along the scarfed area (Figs. 5-1, 5-2).

Scarfing may also be done with a table saw by having the blade tilted 5 degrees from the vertical. This, however, requires a jig that is clamped to the work surface of the saw to support and guide the plywood as it moves across the blade. It is constructed of scrap wood, and the saw projects up through the base piece of the jig about an inch to an inch and a half. Two vertical pieces are nailed and/or clamped to the base to form a guide slot parallel to the saw blade, and just far enough apart to allow the plywood to slide through smoothly. Once the jig is constructed and installed on the table saw, the scarfing operation is a piece of cake. The construction and mounting procedures for this type of jig are described in detail in the Corsair builder's manual.

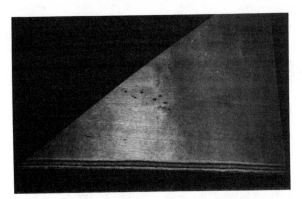

Fig. 5-1. Example of a good scarf on the bottom of a scrap piece of plywood. The color lines of the various layers of wood are evenly spaced and parallel.

Another method of scarfing is using a drum-shaped sander in a 1/4-inch drill. The technique here would be the same as that described above for using a wood rasp as far as the evenness and depth of the cut is concerned.

Assembly and Preparation of Skins

Before gluing the sections together to make a complete skin for any side of the frame, they should be lined up over the plans for the side in question. The reason for this is that there is not much excess material along the sides of the skin panels. It may be necessary to realign the sections slightly in order to completely cover that side of the frame, and now is the time to determine what adjustments are necessary. If this check is not made, you may find that the assembled skin will not completely overlay the frame to the edges of both longerons along their entire length. Once they are aligned properly, mark each piece for easy reference later.

Before any gluing takes place, be sure to spread a sheet of wax paper across the plans where the scarfed joint of the skin will be located. Line up the first piece of plywood skin according to your marks and, using a staple gun, secure it directly to the table top through the plans. After the glue has been applied, cover the joint with wax paper, and use one of the fuselage frame clamps you made earlier to hold everything in place. Adequate clamping pressure can be obtained across the entire glued surface with a few staples through the frame clamps, the plywood, and into the table.

When the complete assembly has dried, the joints should be sanded smooth, particularly where they will come in contact with the fuselage frame.

Attaching the full-length skins to the frame does pre-

sent a few problems that must be worked out before any gluing is attempted. Joining two items of this size is cumbersome at best, and since time is of the essence, you don't need any hangups during the gluing procedure. As mentioned above, the proper alignment of the skin over the frame is critical. Also, the inside of the skin should be lightly sanded where it touches each structural member of the frame.

Therefore, a trial fit is essential at this point. Get the skin placed properly on the frame and clamp it down at several locations around the edge. Then draw the outline of the frame on the inside of the skin. Take the skin off the fuselage and lay a straightedge along the center of the outline of all the vertical and diagonal members of the frame. Place a mark on the edge of the skin where these extended centerlines intersect the edge. Turn the plywood over and draw lines between these marks so that a stick drawing of the frame will be reproduced on the outside of the skin. These single lines will be used to position the gluing nails once the skin is epoxied in place.

After the nailing lines have been made, the inside of the skin can be sanded along the double lines of the actual frame drawing. Because of Murphy's Law, don't restrict the sanding to just between the lines. Add about a half-inch of sanded area to the outside of each line, just in case you don't get the skin back on the frame exactly as you had it before. It might be a good idea to redraw the outline after the skin has been sanded, so that the ideal position of each crossmember can be checked as the gluing proceeds.

Before starting to attach the skins to the frame, locate something that can be used to hold the gluing nails while they are being hammered in. These nails are quite small, and can be controlled better by something other than the fingers while being driven. A good pair of tweezers works well here, or an old pair of needlenose pliers with the tips ground down to a width of about an eighth of an inch.

Fig. 5-2. Example of a poor scarf where the color lines are ragged and uneven. The rasp was held at too shallow an angle on the right end, and too steep toward the middle and left end.

Attaching Skins to Frame

Beginning with one of the sides, clamp the skin back in place on the frame, making sure that the outline on the inside lines up exactly with the structure members. Then unclamp just the front end to a point about three feet back, and place a clamp at this spot on each side of the frame. Keep this forward section of the skin away from the frame by propping it up or suspending it from the rafters. This setup makes it easier to apply the glue to both sides of the joint. Have the tack hammer and tweezers or needlenose pliers handy, and pour out a quantity of gluing nails where they can be reached easily.

After the epoxy has been brushed on, reclamp the skin to the frame and check once again for proper alignment. Then, using the lines drawn on the exterior of the skin, tap in gluing nails about every two inches or so. If the temperature is high, these nails should be put in as quickly as possible in order to establish an optimum bond. If clamps are at a premium, gluing nails should also be used along each longeron.

Needless to say, things would go a lot quicker here by using a staple gun. However, if this is placed a little off center near the edge of the structure member underneath, there is a risk of splitting out a portion of this piece. Also, staples will rust if left in place, whereas gluing nails are specially treated to preclude this. If you are using Aerolite to attach the plywood skins, it is almost inevitable that the hardener will come in contact with the glue brush as you work it into the junction of the skin and the longerons. Therefore, if you have a fair amount of glue made up, pour enough for the operation at hand into another container so that the whole batch isn't ruined.

The two clamps at the aft edge of the glued area are left in place, and all the other clamps are now removed. Prop up or suspend the skin from the rafters and continue the gluing process, working in sections from two to three feet long. As each section is glued in place, clamp the rear edge of the glued area and insert gluing nails as before.

After the entire skin is on and the epoxy has cured, trim off any excess with a saber saw and/or flat wood rasp. Then carefully inspect the entire glued area between the frame and the skin for any gaps, and FOG as required.

The same procedure for marking, clamping, and gluing is used for the other side. With both sides in place, a problem crops up with respect to clamping when the bottom skin is installed. No longer can clamps be attached to the longerons under each edge of the skin. This can be solved by gluing the center section of the bottom skin in place first. After the epoxy is applied, align the skin on the frame as before and clamp to the cross pieces under the front and rear edges of the skin. Then insert gluing nails into all structure members being joined at this time. Once secured, the clamps at the front can be removed and the plywood lifted up just enough to permit gluing of the required parts in this area. Nail this section in place as before, and attach the rear portion of the skin in the same manner. Because of the length involved here, it is probably easier to do this part in two or three steps. After everything has dried, trim, sand and FOG as required.

The two pieces that make up the top skin of the frame are the least troublesome to install, and do not require too much time. However, do not glue the top skins in place until you check with the FAA inspectors. Technically, one side of the fuselage should be left uncovered so that they can properly examine your work. But once the lightening holes have been cut, the interior of the frame can be viewed without difficulty. Because of this, they might allow you to install the top skins, if you brief them on what they will be dealing with.

Before these holes are cut, an outline of the area to be removed should be drawn on the outside of the fuselage skin. Here again, the lines drawn for the gluing nails come in handy. The plywood skin should extend about an inch an a half from the edge of each structure member of the fuselage frame in the areas where the plans call for these lightening holes. Once these sections have been outlined, the cutouts can be made easily with a saber saw. Since you'll be working through these holes quite a bit as the project wears on, give yourself a break and sand the edges smooth.

At this point in the game, the fuselage can be hung up from the rafters or stored out of the way, because at least half of the table will now be needed to work on the spars. The next chapter will discuss how the inner and outer wing spars are built and covered.

Chapter 6

Spar Construction

Building up the center spar section is where the Corsair project starts to differ from other, straight-wing designs. The double curve of the inverted gull wing creates a few problems in constructing the front and rear center spars. If you choose to make the laminations required for the rear spar and the front spar capstrips, the plans describe the work table setup necessary for this operation. It involves large, securely anchored blocking pieces around the top edge of the spar capstrip and corresponding blocking pieces along the bottom edge. The blocks in this latter group are extendable, with their position controlled by blocks and wedges, to allow for the insertion of each lamination in the structure being built. As you might guess, it is a fairly slow process to glue in each layer, let it dry, and then add the next. And, after each unit is finished, the glue squeezed out on each side from between the laminations has to be sanded smooth.

Even though it is a little more expensive, by far the easiest way to go in this area is to buy the laminated spars/capstrips already made up. The time and aggravation thus saved is well worth the extra cost. Carving the intermediate blocks in the front spar is the biggest time-consumer in this portion of the project. The one in the middle of the spar is relatively easy, since it is a straight cut on both edges. The main thing to be careful of here—

particularly if the piece is being cut by a saber saw—is to ensure that the edge being cut forms a true 90 degree angle with the sides. If the tops and/or bottoms of any of the intermediate blocks are not perpendicular to the sides, they will cause problems when these parts are glued in place. These difficulties can take one or all of the following forms: nonparallel surfaces on the front and back faces of the completed spar, gaps between the glued surfaces resulting in a less-than-perfect bond, and a pronounced tendency to slip out of position when clamping pressure is applied during gluing. Therefore, it's a good idea to use the light technique described above for fitting the gussets to check for a good match between the surfaces being joined on all intermediate blocks in the spars.

Fitting the blocks at the end of the center spar does present a few more problems than the one in the middle. This is because both the top and bottom of each must be trimmed to match the curved ends of the capstrips they will separate. They must also line up flush the the ends of the capstrips.

Probably the best plan of action to follow here is to initially cut them a little oversize, again making sure that the saw blade stays perpendicular to the sides of the block. Final trimming to the exact curved shape of the capstrip is done with a wood rasp. Go cautiously in this area, making frequent checks using the light technique to ensure a precise fit. Be particularly careful while using the wood rasp to make your cuts at right angles to the sides of the piece. Because of the many trial fits necessary for these blocks, it is recommended that both the top and bottom surfaces be carved before they are glued in place.

After all the intermediate blocks have been trimmed to shape, trial-assemble the complete center spar to see that everything goes together properly and that the resulting spar is of the correct depth.

This can be determined by placing both capstrips and the intermediate blocks over the plans in their assembled position. Clamp the pieces together, then line up the top capstrip with the drawing. Mark a line on the plans along the bottom edge of the lower capstrip and compare this with the desired line. This line will tell you how much material must be removed from the intermediate blocks to make the spar the correct depth.

After working so hard to get the curvature just right on the blocks, it's a heartbreaker to find that a substantial amount of the block must be removed to achieve the proper dimensions. Should this be the case, proceed slowly, making sure that you retain a surface that is perpendicular to the sides: use the light frequently to check your work.

If the line drawn on the plans as described above indicates that the spar is not deep enough, an overcut has been made on the intermediate blocks. Rather than make a completely new block, try laminating a piece of plywood left over from the fuselage skin on the top or bottom of the block. When gluing this piece of plywood to the block, clamp the latter to the appropriate capstrip with the lamination in between to ensure a good bond across the entire surface. It would also be advisable to cover the capstrip with a piece of wax paper so the parts can be separated easily when the epoxy cures.

If it's a "go" for final assembly, the easiest way to proceed is to glue one surface at a time. This means, as an example, that just the top capstrip and the intermediate blocks should be joined in the first gluing operation. After these are dry, the bottom capstrip is added at the next gluing session. Clamp the capstrip to the table to ensure that it will be kept flat when the furniture clamps are applied to it and the blocks. If any of the surfaces being joined are a little off from the vertical, they will have a tendency to slip apart laterally, with the glue acting as a lubricant. Since the capstrip is curved in this area, slippage will also occur in the direction of the long axis of the capstrip. Therefore, a couple of the blocks used for holding the fuselage frame during assembly should be nailed in place at both ends of the intermediate blocks.

As with all gluing that involves clamps, it is advisable to use pads to protect the wood from possible damage by the metal clamps. Small pieces cut from scrap wall paneling make excellent clamping pads. These are also very useful later on, when various structures/assemblies have to be raised a tad for leveling or alignment.

After lower capstrip has been added and the glue has dried, the bottom blocks can be carved and epoxied into place. The length, thickness, and curvature required for these pieces makes bending them into position almost an impossibility. The easiest way to handle this problem is to make each bottom block in two sections, one on either side of the cutout for the landing gear strut. While you are waiting for the glue to dry after installing the bottom blocks, the intercostals can be cut and glued in place.

Before these pieces are epoxied between the capstrips, make sure that the vent hole has been drilled in each. These are a necessity to prevent trapped moisture. Once the bottom blocks have cured, place the completed spar over the plans as before to see how much they must be trimmed—if at all—to achieve the exact spar depth.

Skinning the Spars

When all the epoxy has cured, the completed spar can be removed from the table and all excess glue trimmed from the sides and ends. Then, each joint should be inspected thoroughly for gaps and/or crevices, which should be FOGed as required. The plywood skins for the spars are made up from sections, in the same manner as the fuselage skins. Once again, trial-fit the individual pieces over the plans to make sure that they cover the entire spar, and mark accordingly.

After the complete skins have been put together, they should be trimmed to within a quarter inch or so of the actual spar outline. This will allow C-clamps to be placed around the entire perimeter. The outline of the area to be glued is drawn on the inside of the skins as before and given a light sanding. Be sure to prepare both skins in this manner before the first is glued in place. Applying glue to this relatively large amount of wood is a little tedious using a single acid brush. Things go a little faster here if two of the acid brushes are taped together to form one applicator.

Unless extra-deep clamps are available, the proper joining of the areas in the center of the spar cannot be assured. This is where the standard shop staple gun comes in handy. This can be used on the spar since the thickness of the wood precludes any splintering. Before any clamping pads and clamps are put in place, it's a good idea to drive at least one staple in the center of the spar, and one at both ends. this will keep the skin from slipping while the C-clamps are being tightened down. Then, after these are all in position, staples can be used to tack down the interior portions of the skin. When this has dried, the staples should be removed, the excess skin trimmed, and the entire joint FOGed as needed. While doing the latter, be sure to check the junction between the skin and the intercostals and the intermediate blocks on the inside of the spar.

At this point the complete interior of the spar, including the non-glued areas of the second skin, should be coated with wood sealer. This topic is covered more fully in Chapter 8.

Do not glue skins on both sides of the spar at this time, because the FAA will have to inspect the interior construction in this area. Once they have taken a look at it, the skin for the other side can be installed in the same manner. On this second skin, be a little generous with the glue—both in the amount used and the area covered. This will allow for some slippage from the desired ideal alignment and still provide a good bond.

The skins for the rear spar are made up and installed in the same way. Even though this spar is a solid lamination, it may be wise to check with the FAA inspector before putting on the second side. He may want to check the workmanship here, particularly if you made up the spar from scratch.

After both spars have been skinned, one final check on their size should be made: Place each spar on the plans and determine if the butt ends conform to the outline on the drawings. When making this check, be sure to line up the centerline of the spar with the centerline of the plans, and then trim each as required. Here again, try to make this surface perpendicular to the front and rear spar faces. This is important because it is used to position the main wing fittings on each spar later on.

Outer Spars

The construction of the outer spars involves a new wrinkle, which requires a little preplanning, and a lot of care when it's time to cut wood. The major components are all double or triple-tapered. The capstrips in the front spar are an example of the latter, where three sides must be tapered toward the wingtip.

The safest way to proceed for the measuring and the marking of the wood is to draw centerlines on each face of the blank, and on the plans for these components. Take the measurements from the centerline drawn on the plans

and mark the wood accordingly. If you know your way around a table saw, there is a jig that can be made to cut these tapers quickly. The details on building this jig are found in the Corsair manual. However, if you are not too familiar with table saws, this method of tapering spars could be a little risky. One slip or miscut and the whole spar blank is ruined.

An alternate way of attacking this problem takes more time, creates mountains of sawdust, and is a trifle tedious—but the chances of mistakes are a lot fewer because the tapers are made incrementally. After the spar blank is marked, the first cut is made with a saber saw and should be 1/8 to 3/16 or an inch oversize. Here again, it is *critically* important to ensure that the blade is making a cut that is perpendicular to the surface of the blank. Check the bottom side of the cut as you go along, and after the excess if removed, be certain that the blade didn't lean in a little toward the taper outline. The upright belt sander is used to trim the spar down to the required taper. This is slow going, but the possibility of sudden disaster is considerably reduced. A *true* vertical cut is once again paramount, especially when a good bit of material must be removed, and there is a tendency to use a heavy hand while holding it against the sander. Since the rear outer spar is not all that thick, it is easier to do the entire job on the sander.

The large intermediate blocks in the outer front spar must also be tapered slightly. Careful sanding on the belt sander, and frequent checks using the light technique, is the easiest way to go here. The remaining intercostals may have to be given a touch of sanding to taper them just a tad, and thus ensure a good joint when they are glued in place.

The procedures and sequence for gluing the outer spar components together are the same as for the center spar. Clamp and block the pieces in position to prevent slipping, and join one surface at a time. The intercostal at the tip of the spar should be blocked in place to make sure the capstrips are properly aligned during gluing. Here again, pads should be used to prevent the clamps from damaging the spars. After the intercostals are in and everything has dried, sand off any excess glue, inspect all the joints, and FOG as required.

The skins for the outer front spars are made and applied as before; since this is a built-up spar, only one side should be covered until it is inspected by the FAA. The double taper of the rear outer spars is marked on the blanks using the centerline reference as before. After they have been tapered, the plywood skins can be applied to both sides of these spars, because they are made from a single piece of wood. Since these pieces are relatively small and easily handled, a little time may be saved by tracing the outline of the spar on the prepared skin. These outlines are then cut a little oversize to allow for slippage during gluing. Because of the taper, it is recommended that the skins be stapled in place before the clamps are applied.

Hinge Alignment

While the rear spar skins are drying, it's a good time to cut out the aileron spars and trim them to shape. These too are double-tapered, and are made in the same way as the rear spars.

Then, using measurements from the plans, draw the aileron hinge centerline on both the rear spar and the aileron spar. Now is the best time to install these hinges on their respective spars because later on, when these latter units are attached to other components, they are considerably less manageable. The location of the pads for these hinges is such that the hinge mounting bolts will be approximately centered on the pads. Position the hinge pieces on the spars so that the holes for the hinge pins are over the centerline previously drawn. Mark the area for the pads around the hinges, then glue these pieces of plywood into position. Once again, line up the hinge pins over the centerline as before, and draw the outline of each one where it contacts the mounting pad. All pieces should then be temporarily secured in position using masking tape. Pin the two parts of the hinges together and rotate the aileron spar through a couple of cycles.

During this trial alignment of all three hinges, some—or possibly all—of the taped pieces may pop loose and have to be repositioned slightly. Resecure them in their new locations and try a few more cycles of the aileron spar. If the hinge works okay, mark the final position of each piece on both spars. Disassemble the hinges and untape each piece from the spar. Then epoxy all pieces in their final position, and tape each to the spar again. Do *not* use five-minute epoxy for this operation, because it will set up before the final alignment can be completed. Pin the two spars together again, cycle the aileron spar a few times, and then, holding the spars parallel, wrap tape around both to hold them in this position until the epoxy dries.

The final bolting of the hinges to the spars is easily done by drilling through the hinge pieces and the spar, using the previously drilled bolt holes in the former as a guide. The above procedure is essentially the one described in the Corsair construction manual, and affords a relatively easy and effective way of aligning all hinge installations.

An alternate design of the various control hinges is shown in Fig. 6-1.

Control Surface Rib Alignment

The control surface ribs should be glued in place after the hinge alignment has been completed. It is a lot easier to do this now than after these units are mounted on the airplane. The main thing to be careful of when attaching the ribs is to make sure that their trailing edges are lined up properly. A simple way of doing this is to use a flat surface for the final assembly and gluing of the ribs to the spars. Temporarily install the root or tip rib on the spar by tacking it in place with gluing nails or small brads. Ensure that the centerline of this rib is perpendicular to the rear face of the spar. Lay this assembly on the flat surface and trial-fit the other ribs so that the bottom edges of all ribs are against the surface, and the edge to be glued forms a good joint with the spar. This may require a little sanding of the top or bottom of the forward edge of the

Fig. 6-1. A different design of a control surface hinge incorporating a bushing on the center piece, which permits smooth, positive operation.

rib to make it parallel to the spar.

The angled ribs in the elevator also necessitate the use of a cardboard or plywood template to hold them at the correct angle during the gluing process. A good rule of thumb to follow on the placement of ribs in the control surface area is to allow 3/8 of an inch between all fixed and moveable surfaces. This will permit a couple of layers of fiberglass to be put on both sides of the opening, while still ensuring freedom of control movement.

While all these hinge and rib alignment procedures are still fresh in your mind, it's a good time to build up and install the tail surfaces of the bird. The next chapter will discuss a few items that need special attention in this area.

Chapter 7

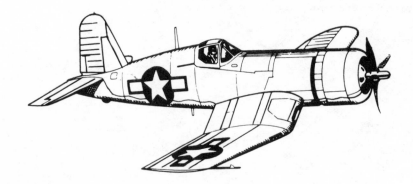

Tailfeathers

Before the fin spar is epoxied in the tail section of the airplane, its hinges should be bolted in place via the procedure described in the previous chapter. Again, ease of handling is the reason for this sequencing. The elevator hinges must wait until the stab spars are glued in. The easiest piece to install in this area is the rear fin spar; however, because it is the first to go in, it is a little tedious to ensure that it is truly vertical. About all you can do is rely on some carefully drawn centerlines and a large carpenter's square.

Draw centerlines on both sides of the fin spar, and on the web to which it will be attached. Trial-clamp the spar in place by matching up the centerlines on each piece. Lay a straight piece of wood a couple of feet long across the fuselage frame in front of the web supporting the spar. Make sure there are no glue bumps or other irregularities under this piece of wood when it is in place. This now can be used to measure for a true 90 degree angle between the fuselage frame and the spar. Check for the proper alignment of the fin, mark it, and then glue and clamp it in position.

After the rear fin spar and the rib connecting it to the tail web have been glued in place, there is the possibility of some more aggravation when working with the rudder

spar. If you utilize the hinge design shown in Fig. 6-1, it becomes a little difficult to install and remove the rudder spar. This is due to the design of the bottom rudder hinge and the rudder control horn mount, along with the requirement of having to work through the hole in the above-mentioned rib. This hole will most likely have to be enlarged by a small amount, after which the rudder spar can be worked into place by some judicious wiggling. This relatively slight inconvenience should not deter you from selecting this type of hinge, since its strength and smooth operation far outweigh the minor difficulties encountered here.

Forward Fin Alignment

The built-up forward portion of the fin must be aligned perfectly with the rear spar already installed. This can be accomplished by the centerline-and-carpenter's-square method described above. However, it's a good idea to check the accuracy of the alignment by another means. This is pretty much an eyeball procedure, but it does show if the top of the forward section is not lined up with the top of the spar. Make a mark on the upper front cross piece of the fuselage frame midway between the sides. Then, step-

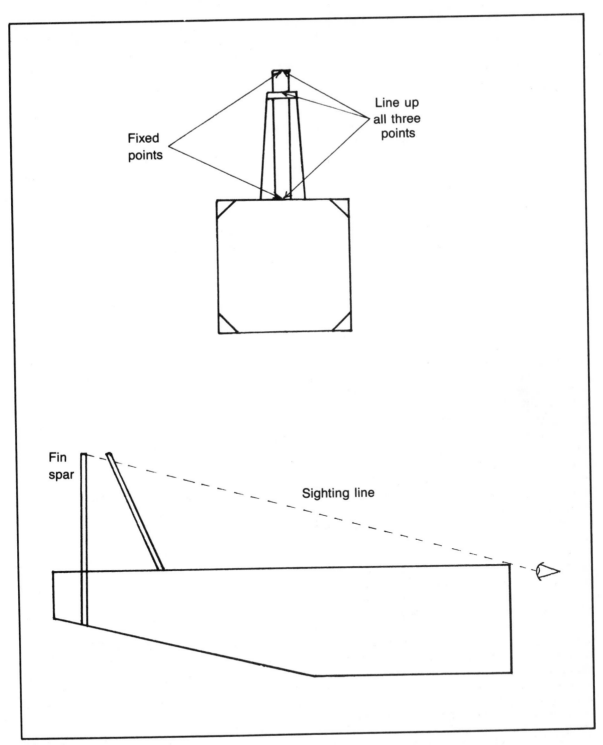

Fixed points

Line up all three points

Fin spar

Sighting line

Fig. 7-1. Fin spar alignment.

ping back a few feet, sight over this mark, through the centerline of the uppermost spacer of the forward section, to the top of the centerline already drawn on the rear fin spar (Fig. 7-1). The first and last of these marks are fixed reference points, and if the forward section is not in line with them, make appropriate adjustments.

Once the alignment is correct, the piece should be marked, glue applied, and then clamped into position. But before the clamps are tightened down fully, *recheck* the alignment to make sure that nothing slipped during the gluing.

Stab Spars

The two spars that make up the stabilizer are both double-tapered; therefore, the same precautions for measuring and cutting as previously described apply here. When they are finished, each should have a trial installation to determine what must be done to bring them into perfect squareness with the fuselage frame.

Place a mark on the bottom edge of the frame directly under the centerline of each spar on both sides of the fuselage. Place another pair of marks on the top edge of the frame, about 2 to 2-1/2 feet in front of the forward stab spar. Make certain that the mark on one side of the fuselage is the same distance from the tailpost as the corresponding mark on the other side. Also put a mark on both ends of each spar at the centerline. Then clamp the rear spar in position between the tail webs, making sure that it is centered properly. Measure the distance from the mark on the end of the spar to the one on the bottom edge of the fuselage. Repeat this on the other side. Both of these measurements should be the same, but if they are not, the spar must be tilted slightly until they are equalized (Fig. 7-2).

Once the spar is squared in a spanwise direction, take the same kind of measurements from the tip of the spar to the mark on the top of the fuselage. As before, these distances should be equal. If a disparity exists, shimming is necessary on the short side. Here the shims must be the full width of the joint so that a good bond will be formed. The shims should be made with a very gentle taper, similar to that used for a scarfed joint. If they are made deep enough, they can be tapped in until the desired correction is achieved. Then they are marked and cut so as to be ready for final installation.

Squaring the front spar is done in a like manner. Something that may have to be done here is to cut away any excess glue squeezed out from between the two webs and the top of the fuselage cross piece. This will allow the spar to be seated firmly against the cross piece, which

will result in a stronger assembly when glued.

When squaring either of these spars, it is not a good idea to sand a portion of the web so that the spar may be moved to equalize measurements. If too much material is removed, this will weaken the structure at a critical point. Therefore, the name of the game here is to use long, thin wedges as shims to accomplish any required movement of the spars.

After both spars are clamped in place and squared, a few other checks are advisable to see how things are lined up. Step out in front of the airplane a short distance and eyeball the structure as a whole. Do they look square and level when viewed from the front? From the side? Is the distance between the ends of the spars the same on both sides? Tack the tip ribs in place temporarily and check that both are level.

If everything looks good, mark the final position of the spars and webs in relation to each other. Glue only one spar in place at a time, and after all the shims have been added, recheck all the measurements for equal values on both sides. If these are okay, tighten down the clamps

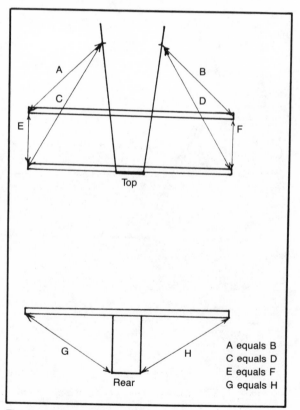

Fig. 7-2. Stab spar alignment.

Fig. 7-3. Control stops in front of the rudder horn, and reinforcing blocks mounted on the opposite side of the webbing.

and make one more check to be certain that nothing moved during the final clamping.

Control Stops

After the rear stab spar has dried, the elevator hinges should be installed according to the procedures described earlier. These must wait until this time because the cen-ter hinge is bolted through the tail web. Expect a few more problems with the elevator hinge than with the others. This is because *five* separate hinges must be aligned during this procedure, rather than the usual three.

While working in this general area of the airplane, it might be advisable to consider the installation of the rudder and elevator control stops. Admittedly, there are numerous other locations in the control system where these stops might be placed. However, putting them right at the control horns seems to be the easiest in terms of both design and time expended.

The rudder stops are simply two pieces of 3/4-inch square scrap from the fuselage frame. These are glued on the aft side of the web supporting the fin spar, and are placed so as to limit the forward travel of the rudder horn to 30 degrees. It is also recommended that reinforcing blocks be placed opposite the control stops on the front side of the web, in the corner formed by the web and the fin spar (Fig. 7-3).

The elevator stop is a U-shaped piece of .050 steel three inches long. It is mounted on the tail web under the center hinge, with the open end of the U extending back over the leading edge of the elevator. The arms of the U are bent appropriately to form up and down limits for the elevator (Fig. 7-4).

The aileron stops are set screws on the stick mount, and can be adjusted after that system has been installed.

The next chapter will be a short respite from the actual construction process, and will deal with some of the pros and cons of the various wood sealers on the market.

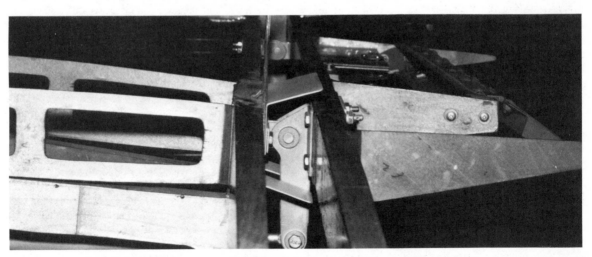

Fig. 7-4. Elevator control stop mounted behind the center elevator hinge. When installing this piece, make sure that this hinge is not moved out of alignment with the others. Recessing the tail web may be required. The final setting of this stop is achieved by the use of shims glued to the elevator spar.

Chapter 8

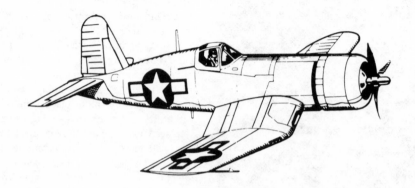

Wood Sealers

Just before the spars for the tail assembly are installed is the point in the project when some thought should be given to wood sealers. The frame becomes somewhat difficult to maneuver once they are in place, and even more so when the center wing spars are attached. Because of the restricted working space, it is a bit difficult to apply sealer to the inside of the fuselage, especially in the tail. Being able to roll the frame as the work progresses makes this job quite a bit easier.

Also, the wing spars are the next unit to be installed, and the interior of the front spar must be coated with sealer and the skin epoxied on before this sequence can proceed. Applying the wood sealer now will require that it be sanded off the joint area when other components are added in the future. Sanding is essential in these spots—preferably down to bare wood, since epoxy will not form a good bond with a semi-glazed surface.

There is a good deal of touch-up work and additional sealer applications to be done in any case, so it is advisable to get the bulk of the work out of the way while things are more manageable.

Kinds of Sealers

The purpose of wood sealers is to combat moisture,

trapped water, and fungi. These are the worst enemies of wooden airplanes, since they can produce dry rot, mildew, and a general breakdown of the structure of the wood.

Therefore, the main idea when putting a sealer on is to be *thorough*. Make sure you hit *every* nook and cranny in the framework, because even a pinhole will allow moisture to get at the wood and start trouble. In areas that are particularly prone to trapping water, or ones that will receive a lot of exposure to water, a second coat of sealer is advisable.

There are a number of wood sealers suitable for aircraft use available on the market. One of the oldest and most common is spar varnish. This is inexpensive, easy to apply, and will last indefinitely in areas not exposed to sunlight. Varnished surfaces that are exposed to the sun should hold up reasonably well for about six to eight years before cracking and peeling begin. There is no problem as far as working time is concerned when using varnish, and brushes and spills can be cleaned up easily by using the recommended solvent.

Another very popular sealer in use today is polyurethane. This is a synthetic varnish that is also inexpensive, but more durable than spar varnish. Its resistance to sunlight, gas, and oil is superior to varnish, and it is the easiest to work with and apply.

Epoxy sealers are also available from aircraft supply houses, but these are usually more expensive than varnish or polyurethane—some markedly so! Depending on their composition, they may be vulnerable to sunlight, but they do offer good protection against water, gas, and oil.

Two-part epoxy sealers that require mixing before use have some limitations. The working time, once the batch is mixed, is restricted and the entire batch must be used or the excess is wasted. The sealer offered by War Aircraft Replicas is this type, and has the added inconvenience of requiring brushes made of pure bristle. Since WAR does not list a solvent of this sealer, the brush must be thrown away after two applications that are separated by only a day or so. If a relatively large amount of a two-part sealer is made up, it becomes a little difficult to apply in an hour or so, due to curing action in the jar.

Some epoxy sealers also state that they strengthen the wood in addition to sealing it. This is possible only if the sealer penetrates *into* the wood, which necessitates the inclusion of a wetting agent in their makeup.

When considering all the advantages and disadvantages of these commonly used sealers, probably the best for the job—and the best buy—is polyurethane.

Sealer for Open Grain Wood

The sealers mentioned above are good for just about all woods used in aircraft construction. However, if an open-grain wood such as walnut or mahogany is used, they do not provide the required degree of protection. The relatively large pores and wide grain structure that typify the surface of these woods are difficult, if not impossible, to seal completely with varnish, polyurethane, or epoxies.

This type of wood must first be coated with a paste wood filler, which fills these voids and provides a base for additional coats of the conventional sealers. Paste wood filler is a putty-like substance that is held in suspension in a liquid so that it can be applied with a brush. After application, the surface is wiped off with a cloth, much like the procedure used for applying stain to new wood.

Ventilation and Sanding

As is true with any operation where volatile solvents are being used, sealers should only be applied in well-ventilated areas. This is particularly true of the WAR sealer, which becomes a little overwhelming in an enclosed space. When putting sealer on large sections of the bird at one session, it may be a wise move to transfer the framework to the garage for this job. If it is done in the cellar, the fumes will soon permeate the whole house, and you are almost guaranteed a few caustic remarks from the better half.

When additional casts of sealers must be applied, the entire area should be lightly sanded to remove surface fuzz and irregularities that become apparent with the first coat. After the second coat, sanding should not be necessary unless the wood is still rough to the touch.

Now that the fuselage frame is prepared for the installation of the wing spars, it's time for some of the preparatory work in this area. The next major item to be tackled is the manufacture of the metal wing fittings, and drilling the spars for their installation. These procedures will be covered in the next chapter.

Chapter 9

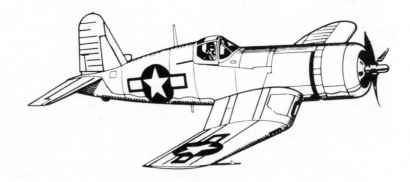

Wing Fittings

The wing fittings are the first components of the airplane that require a fair amount of physical work to build. They are cut from 4130 chrome moly sheet stock that is about 1/8 of an inch thick. Expect slow going here, regardless of how the steel is cut, because this metal is *really* tough.

The best way to proceed is to make cardboard patterns of all the fittings, and mark an outline of each piece on the sheet stock. Do *not* scribe metal to be used for aircraft work with a sharp pointed tool. A scratch thus made can develop into a crack later on. Also, 4130 steel has a grain, just like wood, and the "long way" of the grain is in the same direction as the printing on the sheet. Make sure that you align your pattern with the grain, since no aircraft fittings should be made cross-grain.

It is strongly recommended that these parts be cut out using a metal-cutting band saw. Trying to use a hacksaw for this job is like picking cotton—the first few rows aren't too bad, but after that, it's murder! The 4130 steel will wear out a regular hacksaw blade after it has cut only a few inches. Between changing blades and sawing, your arm will probably fall off before the first fitting for the front spar is completed. A saber saw with a metal-cutting blade does no better, and here again, the blades are worn smooth in short order.

Considering the effort required to cut out these fittings, it is well worth your time to locate a heavy-duty band saw that can do the job with the least difficulty. The machine shop instructor in your local vocational school may be a solution to this problem. As a last resort, the work could be done at a commercial machine shop, but this would be a relatively expensive course of action.

Because of the many curves on the inner front spar fittings, it might be advisable to have these cut a little oversize and then file them down to the exact dimensions. Once again this is slow, hard going, but it is the safe way to proceed, because you certainly don't want these critical parts to be less than the size called for.

If the oversized-cut-and-file-to-exact-size method is used to finish the wing fittings, you will most probably want to use a relatively coarse file for the majority of the work. If you don't own one, you'll be ready to sell your soul for one after about a half-hour on this job. A coarse file is a definite plus in this case, but you will find that it leaves a fairly rough edge. Therefore, once the fitting has been filed to shape, the entire edge should be gone over with a fine file to make it as smooth as possible. The idea here is to work out any grooves in the metal in order to minimize the chances of a crack forming, or giving rust a place to start. This same smoothing process should apply to any metal part whose edges or surface have been scored by filing, sawing, or grinding with a coarse-grit wheel.

From the scraps remaining after these pieces have been made, cut out the discs that will serve as doublers on the ends of all front fittings. Once these are trimmed to shape, they are welded in place as shown on the plans. Check the drawings carefully as to which face of the fitting these doublers are attached to, because once they are in place, the fittings become matched pairs for each end of the front spar.

Mounting Holes

Drilling the holes to mount the inner fittings is an exacting task that should be approached with planning and care. Trace the outline of the front spar inner fittings on heavy tracing paper, making sure that the centers of all the holes to be drilled are accurately marked. Cut this tracing out and tape it to either the front or rear inner fitting for one end of the main spar. The locations of the holes to be drilled are made using a centerpunch, tapping through the tracing to the metal beneath. Be particularly careful that the four holes that will be used to attach each of the landing gear mounting brackets are aligned vertically. This procedure is repeated for the corresponding inner fitting on the other end of the spar.

The next step is to stack on the spar both of the inner fittings and both of the plywood doublers that will be used for that end of the spar. These are stacked in the same order as they will be when permanently installed. Be sure to carefully measure where the end of the spar intersects the inner face of the fittings, and mark the latter accordingly so that they can be positioned correctly.

Once aligned properly, clamp the entire stack together and drill through it completely, using the centerpunch marks as guides. It is *very* important that these holes are perpendicular to the face of the spar; therefore, it is strongly recommended that a drill press be used for this operation. Here again, because of the toughness of the steel, expect that the drilling will take a little time. A technique that may help during this procedure is the drilling of small pilot holes through the stack before the final cut is made with the full-sized drill.

Something to consider when drilling the holes for the wing attach bolts in the front and rear fittings is to enlarge the size of these holes to 1/2 inch and 5/16 of an inch respectively. This permits a stronger bolt to be used in these areas, and there is plenty of metal in the fitting to accommodate the increased size with no compromise of strength.

While on the subject of drilling, there are a couple of points that ought to be remembered about the care and use of drill bits. Some drills are designed to be used *exclusively* in wood; these of course, should never be used for metal. The standard twist drill is made for metal, but can be used in wood as well.

A lot of aggravation can be saved in any drilling operation—particularly the wing fittings—if you ensure that the drill is always kept sharp. A good approximation of eternity can be simulated by trying to drill through 4130 steel with a dull bit. The sharpeners that fit in the chuck of a 1/4-inch drill do not do that great a job for drilling operations of this sort. If you have the time before getting too deep into your project, you will be way ahead of the game by having an A & P mechanic or a machinist teach you how to properly sharpen a drill. This can be done on a belt sander or a grinding wheel; it only takes a minute or so, once you get the knack.

If you are drilling through a piece of metal and don't seem to be making any progress, the solution is *not* to lean harder on the drill. Such an action will most likely lead to the tip of the bit getting overheated to the point where it turns blue. If this occurs, don't waste time trying to sharpen the bit, because it has now lost its temper and will not hold an edge.

Another good practice to use whenever the work area permits it is to use cutting oil to help keep the drill bit cool.

Compression Bushings

After the 1/4-inch holes have been drilled through the stack, they must be enlarged to accommodate the compression bushings. Only the holes in the spar and the doublers are to be made bigger. *Do not* enlarge the holes in the metal fittings.

There are two problems associated with reaming these holes for the compression bushings: ensuring that the new hole is centered on the old, and that it, too, is perpendicular to the face of the spar. Both of these problems are solved by using a drill press.

Perpendicularity is assured and centering is easily accomplished by using the following procedure: With a 1/4-inch drill in the chuck, position the spar and doublers, which have been clamped together, beneath the tip of the bit. Make final adjustments in the position of the wood assembly so that the bit can be lowered completely into the hole without the drill being in operation. Once positioned, clamp the wood in place, raise the drill, install the larger bit, and drill the hole for the bushing. Repeat this procedure for each hole requiring such an addition.

Despite such precautions, you may still run into some problems when the wing fittings are installed as a set. The gods of homebuilding are a perverse lot, and you will probably find that while most of the compression bushings line up with the holes in the fittings, a couple may be off just a tad. *Never* make the holes in the fitting larger to correct for such a misalignment. The recommended procedure is to plug the hole in the spar with a wooden dowel and epoxy, and redrill the hole. However, when redrilling the spar for the compression bushing, you stand just as good a chance of repeating the same error.

If the needed correction is large, the dowel method should be used, but if the bushing only has to be moved 1/16 of an inch or so, a little simpler process can be used. Determine which way the hole has to be moved, and after taking the fittings off the spar, cautiously use a round wood rasp to achieve the desired correction. Check your progress frequently to avoid an overcut, and remove just enough material so that the mounting bolt can be pushed through both fittings with a little effort. Remove the wing fittings and compression bushing, and apply a liberal amount of epoxy to the entire inner surface of the enlarged hole. Reinsert the bushing with a twisting motion to ensure that it is completely coated with epoxy, and then bolt the wing fittings back in place. Use bolts through other holes as well as the enlarged hole so that the epoxy will fill the newly created gap correctly, and the bushing in the modified hole will be held in the proper position.

It is not always possible to find stock tubing with the exact internal and external dimensions needed for compression bushings. Here again, the Corsair is a case in point. Tubing is available from the supply houses with the correct outside diameter; however, the inside diameter is a little small. The proper way to enlarge the interior of these tubes is by using a reamer in a drill press or lathe.

However, if this tool is not available, the job can be done using a standard metal-cutting bit. This is a lot more troublesome way to go, but after a few practice runs, the techniques required will become apparent. A piece of scrap lumber about 2 inches thick is needed to support the tube while it is being drilled out. This necessitates a hole in the block about 1 to 1 1/4 inches deep and the same diameter as the outside of the tube. Insert the tube in the hole and center beneath the drilling bit. A pair of vise grips will be needed here to keep the tube from turning while it is being drilled, and also to hold it firmly against the bottom of the hole in the block.

This job now becomes a two-man operation. While one person holds the tube with the vise grips and controls the feed of the drilling bit, the other keeps the bit and the tube bathed in oil. A good household lubricant, cutting oil, or motor oil can be used for this, its main purpose being the cooling of the entire operation—and hopefully minimizing seizing. But regardless of the amount of lubricant used, expect some seizing to occur, so be ready with a fast hand to shut off the drill press.

Using a slow feed rate, drill to about the center of the tube, and then turn it over and repeat the process. This will minimize the area of surface contact between the drill and the tube, which in turn will reduce the amount of heat generated.

After the complete tube has been reamed, the ends and the sides will probably have to be dressed up with a file to smooth them out before installation.

Outer Fittings

After all the work involved in making the main spar inner fittings, those for the rear spar and all the outer fittings will seem like a piece of cake. The procedures for drilling and installing the rear spar inner fittings, and for making the compression bushings, are the same as described above. Here again, careful measurement and placement techniques are required to ensure that the correct length of the fitting extends beyond the end of the spar. After the metal doublers have been welded on the front outer spar fittings, all of these outer units are then paired up. Each of these pairs is clamped together, and the wing attachment hole on the end is drilled through both fittings at the same time. These are then tied together, or otherwise labeled as a matched set.

The remaining holes in the outer fittings, which are used for bolting the fittings to the spar, are done a little differently than described above. Select the fittings that will go on the forward side of the front spar and on the aft side of the rear spar. The locations of the mounting holes are then centerpunched through a tracing paper pattern, as was done before. The holes are then drilled in this half of the matched sets of outer fittings. *Do not* drill mounting holes through the spar at this time. These latter holes—and those in the other half of the fittings—will be made when the outer wing assembly is attached to the inner spars. The holes drilled now will serve as initial guides that are easily accessible when these assemblies are bolted together.

The last thing that needs to be done to the outer fittings at this time is to bend a slight angle in those that will be mounted on the rear spar. This spar sweeps forward slightly so that a 5 degree bend must be made on the ends of these pieces. The easiest way to do this is to bend them in a vise until they match the outline of these fittings as shown in the top view of the wing plans. Approach this angle slowly with a series of small bends, rather than one large one, which may result in an overshoot. Bending this piece *back* to the correct angle may cause weakening of the metal in this critical area.

Prior to putting these fittings aside for a while, the cutouts for the landing gear struts can be made in the forward center spar. This is done by pinning the main wing fittings in place temporarily with a few bolts. Trace the outline of the cutout on both faces of the spar, remove the fittings, and cut out with a saber saw. This job could be done after the spar is joined to the fuselage and the fittings are installed. However, things become a little awkward now, and the procedure is more time-consuming.

Before starting on the next stage of construction, the airplane should be moved to the garage, or other large area, where just about all the remaining work will take place. The following chapter will discuss how the spars and the fuselage are glued together. Once this is done, your project becomes relatively immobile until it is removed from the table to sit on its own gear.

Chapter 10

Joining the Spars and Fuselage

Before this phase of the project can begin, the second skin must be glued in place on both spars. As mentioned earlier, this will require an FAA inspection before these parts are covered, so make the necessary arrangements ahead of time to preclude any delays.

Installing the spars for any straight-wing airplane will probably not require any special additions to the work table. However, the gull-winged Corsair needs some fuselage supports if it is to sit on a work table four feet wide. These supports will raise the fuselage sufficiently so that the bottoms of the spars will not touch the edges of the table.

If the wood kit with the pre-laminated spars was purchased, the shipping crate for the spars is perfect for this application. Saw the box in half and nail end pieces on the two open ends made by this cut. Make sure these boxes are fairly sturdy, since they will have to support the weight of the entire assembly plus *you* later on, when you start to crawl in and out of the cockpit. Additional height can be gained by adding 2×6s cut to a length that is just a little shorter than the distance between the two spars. You will also probably want to put some kind of support beneath the tail to keep the whole assembly from rocking.

Spar Slots

The first thing to be done in the spar installation procedure is to cut the slots in the fuselage skin. Here again, the gull wing introduces an anomaly. To allow the spars to be slipped through both sides of the fuselage, the slots must be cut 4 to 5 inches higher than the actual height of the spar. When cutting these slots, it might be advisable to undercut them slightly on both sides in the fore and aft directions. This will preclude the saw from hitting the vertical frame members and possibly enlarging the spar slot. Trim off any excess left by the undercut with a wood rasp, and also clean off any dribbles of glue or wood sealer that may be on the opposing faces of the spar slot.

The wooden shims at the bottom of the slot, used to set the angle of incidence of the wing, can be glued in place at this time. Check over all surfaces of both spars and sand down any irregularities that might cause problems when sliding the spars into position. This is a very snug fit, so pay particular attention to the overlap joints in the spar skins.

Before going any further with the installation of the front spar it would be well worth your time to pause at this point to consider saving yourself some heartburn later

44

on. This refers to drilling the holes in the spar for the control stick mount. The problems associated with trying to do this job *after* the spar is in place are discussed in Chapter 14 in the section dealing with the stick grip.

Installation and Alignment

The procedures for installing the spars in the fuselage are similar to those for just about every other component in that many trial fits are required. Wrestling the main spar in and out of position gets a little tedious after the first four or five tries. Therefore, mark as many spots as you can find where connections must be made each time the spar is in the fuselage. The shape of the spar and the tight fit through both slots make for a difficult task in sliding it into position—especially the first half-dozen or so times.

Above all, do *not* force it if the going seems to get a little tough. It is amazing just how little force applied to push it through will result in a jam. If this occurs, it will probably take a considerable amount of force to extricate the spar. Jams can be serious enough to require some heavy hammering on one end of the spar to back it out. If this must be resorted to, don't forget to use a block of scrap wood over the end of the spar to prevent damage to the latter from the hammering.

Any time a spar hangs up during installation, check the slot(s) and mark the areas to be sanded down to allow the spar to be inserted. Sand these high spots sparingly and check the fit frequently so that too much material will not be removed.

After the obvious irregularities have been removed from the inside faces of the spar slots, any further corrections should be made by sanding the spar. This will ensure that the slots are not made too wide to allow the ends of the spar to pass, only to have an unacceptable gap at the center section. An exception to this would be if you found that the slot width was too narrow along the entire length of the spar. In this case it would be a lot less work to sand down each face of the slots by a small amount until a snug fit is achieved.

Once the spar can be slid into position without binding, it and the fuselage should be marked for the alignment procedure. This is the same as that used for the stabilizer spars, and is well detailed in the construction manual. On both sides of the airplane mark the top longeron directly above the centerline of the spar, and the top edge of the end of the spar, again at the midpoint. The third alignment point will be the top front corner of the fuselage frame on each side of the bird.

Once again, corresponding measurements on both sides of the fuselage should be equal. If they are not, corrections are made by sanding and/or shimming the appropriate spots. If you find it necessary to use shims to obtain the proper alignment, do not glue them in position at this time. Mark the spot where each will go, and tap them into place when the spar is being glued to the frame.

When the correct measurements have been achieved, draw lines on both faces of the spar to mark the final position of its intersection with the slot in the fuselage frame. The lines are drawn on the inside and on the outside of the cockpit area.

Remove the spar from the slot and sand off any wood sealer between each of the four sets of lines just made. Also remove any sealer from the inside edges of the slot. Put the spar back in the frame but off-center it slightly so that all the lines are exposed. Spread the epoxy between the lines on the spar and slosh the hardener between the spar and the inside edges of the slot. It is recommended that more of these components be used here than with a normal joint. This is to ensure that a sufficient amount of glue is left in the interface after some is lost when the spar is moved back to its final position. If a one-part adhesive is being employed, make sure that an ample amount is worked in between the spar and the slot faces.

After the glue has been applied, slide the spar into its correct position as indicated by the lines. Make sure that it is firmly seated on the shims at the bottom of the slots so that the correct incidence will be obtained. Quickly tap in any other shims to bring the spar into alignment, and recheck all measurements for equal values on both sides.

In order to preclude a last-minute panic if some measurements are off a little after the glue has been applied, have some spare shims made up ahead of time. These can be coated with glue and inserted where needed for any last-ditch corrections. Carefully check all measurements again to make sure everything is aligned properly.

Mounting the rear spar is done in the same way, but now there is an additional measurement that can be made to ensure good alignment. The distance between the front and back spars should be the same on both sides when measured at the ends. When all the trimming and shimming have been done for the rear spar, slide it into position and step back to look at the bird from a distance. Are the lines of the rear spar parallel with those of the front spar? Does it appear to be sitting correctly with respect to the front spar, or is it too high or low? If everything looks okay and all the measurements check out, glue it into position as described above.

Slot Patches and Underspar Blocks

The extra large slots cut to allow the gulled spars to be inserted into the fuselage must now be attended to. Make U-shaped patches from 1/16-inch plywood that will extend at least one inch beyond the slot openings on all three sides. The arms of the U are tight against the front and rear faces of the spars, and reach to the bottom longerons (Fig. 10-1). If gluing nails were used for the fuselage skins, those under the patches should be removed or countersunk before the latter are glued in place. This will permit a better bond between the patch and the fuselage skin.

When the epoxy has cured after the spars are joined to the fuselage, the underspar filler blocks must be glued in place. These blocks are the full width of the spars, and complete the bond between them and the fuselage framework. Needless to say, these pieces should fit snugly in order to maximize the structural strength in this area. Therefore, make cardboard patterns for each block before starting to cut any wood.

You will find that this is an awkward area in which to check for the exact fit of the pattern. Thus, it may be a smart move to cut the blocks a little oversize and trim to final shape using a sander and wood rasp. If an overcut is made, and the resulting gap is too much to be filled by epoxy, drive a shim into this space during the gluing process.

This gluing operation is another where it is impossible to use clamps, and the fuselage skin may be warped just enough to prevent a good bond with the filler block. This problem can be solved by placing 2×4s across the width of the fuselage, just beneath the underspar blocks. Remove all other support for the fuselage and allow the weight of the structure to keep the gluing surfaces in good contact. Use plenty of epoxy when gluing these blocks in place to gap-fill as much as possible any irregularities between the two surfaces.

Installing the corner blocking between the spar faces

Fig. 10-1. Plywood patch used to cover the enlarged slot in the fuselage skin needed for spar installation.

and the fuselage skins is not as simple a job as it looks. The fuselage skin is curved slightly in these spots, and none of the angles are a true 90 degrees. Each piece of corner blocking must be individually trimmed to fit, and care must be exercised in mitering the corners. Gluing nails are used to hold these pieces in position until the adhesive has cured.

It's back to metal work for the next phase of construction, which will be detailed in the following chapter. This will involve the building and installation of the wing truss assemblies.

Chapter 11

Truss Assemblies

Building and installing the truss assemblies for the Corsair—*particularly* installing them—is this project's version of the Chinese Water Torture. The frustrations encountered in lining up the trusses, and the plates bolted on their sides, so that the retract system works satisfactorily is enough to test the patience of Job. Expect problems at just about every turn during this procedure.

The only way to minimize these difficulties is to be *meticulously* careful in taking measurements and checking levelness at each step along the way. These two areas are the keys to success when installing the trusses. Therefore, when leveling or measuring, check it, *recheck* it, and check it *again* to be absolutely certain of every value. Be super-critical of how you eyeball each measurement, and correct any variances down to at least plus or minus 1/32 of an inch. If the differences can be made even less, so much the better.

The *slightest* deviations from perfect alignment between the trusses will cause binding in the shaft used to retract the landing gear. The name of the game in this phase of the project is to go slowly and check constantly before any holes are drilled.

Building the Trusses

About 42 feet of the 3/4-inch square steel tubing will be required to build the trusses. Take the measurements for the individual pieces right from the plans, and cut them about 1/16 of an inch short. This gap is necessary because the metal will expand upon heating, and will not contract an equal amount after cooling.

Check all four sides of each joint to make sure that all surfaces match up evenly with no gaps. When it is time to start welding these parts together, it is absolutely essential that a *metal* jig be used to hold the pieces in place during this process. Do not use wood for this purpose, since it does not have the required strength. The heat of welding generates considerable forces, which must be counteracted if distortion of the finished product is to be avoided. Therefore, the metal jig for the trusses must be of greater mass and ridigity than the structure being welded.

While the parts of the truss are being prepared for assembly, bleed holes must be drilled inside certain joints. These 1/16-inch holes are needed to relieve the pressure caused by heated air and gasses inside a closed tube. Without them, these gases would have to escape through the molten portion of the weld, resulting in a less-than-perfect joint. They are required in either end of any tube that will be sealed at both ends, and are usually made in the piece to which the closed tube is being attached. Center this hole beneath the tube to be closed so that it will not be inadvertently welded shut (Fig. 11-1).

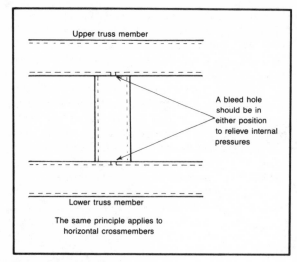

Fig. 11-1. Bleed holes.

The sharp angles at the rear of each truss pose a problem if TIG or MIG welding is to be used. The cup on the end of the torch is too large to allow the seam inside the angle to be welded. Therefore, a "butterfly" must be used to secure the inner edge of this joint. Four of these are cut from .040 4130 sheet stock, bent into a U shape, and welded in place around their entire perimeter. The pattern and dimensions for these butterflies are shown in Fig. 11-2. Once clamped into position, they effectively increase the angle between these two truss pieces to the point where they can be joined with a MIG or TIG welder. The two outside seams of the primary joint between these two parts are welded and then filed or ground smooth on the sides. The butterfly is then positioned over these welds, and thus makes the finished joint a lot stronger (Fig. 11-3).

Joining the two sides of the truss together with cross pieces is where the metal jig and careful alignment assume an even greater importance. The completed truss assembly forms a box when viewed from the front, and the sides of this box must be parallel, as well as being 90 degrees to each other. A little time spent to ensure these conditions when the parts are being set up in the jig will save a *lot* of heartburn later on.

A note that is worth repeating here applies to the welding to be done in this phase of the project: If the work is being done by anyone *but* a certified aircraft welder, weld samples should be prepared for the FAA inspector. The samples of tube welding should include both 90 and 45 degree junctions.

After these units are complete, the truss plates and all the gearing required for the retraction of the wheels

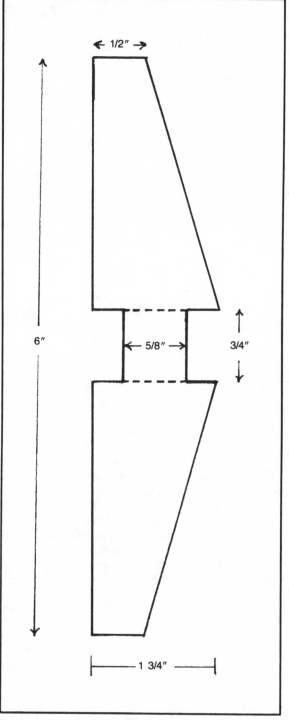

Fig. 11-2. Butterfly pattern.

Fig. 11-3. Rear end of wing truss showing the butterfly welded in place.

are added. The specifications and dimensions listed in the plans for the various gears in the retract mechanism are okay to use. However, the basic geometry of the retract system as shown in the plans results in an arrangement that *does not work*. This assessment is based on an almost universal complaint by WAR Corsair builders, indicating significant problems in this area. Therefore, it is obvious that some changes must be made if this system is to function properly.

No doubt there are many approaches to making an operable retract system for the Corsair. The changes to the plans that are necessary deal with the dimensions of the upper strut and retract knuckle arms. These modifications are discussed in the chapter on the landing gear, and offer one such solution to this problem.

There are a few things recommended in this system that are not called for in the plans. The first of these is an additional plate to be bolted on the outside of each of the outer truss assemblies (Fig. 11-4). The purpose of these plates is to give increased support to the shafts used to retract the gear, and spread landing and taxi loads over a greater area. It does add to the problems of aligning this shaft so that it rotates freely, but the additional strength it provides is well worth the extra effort. Other features—specified in the plans but suggested for deletion in this system—are the diagonal braces running between the torque tube and the upper knuckle arms, along with the

cross pieces between both sets of knuckle arms. Grease fittings should also be added to help make the whole mechanism work smoother. Once all the gears are installed in the truss boxes, it is desirable to "run them in" for a short while before the trusses are bolted in place.

The first things needed for the installation of the truss assemblies are the mounting brackets that will attach them to the front spar. The plans specify extruded aluminum angles for these parts; however, extrusions of the exact size and thickness are difficult to find. Sheet steel of the appropriate gauge is less expensive, more readily available, and will serve just as well. Steel brackets can also be used for securing the inner trusses to the rear spar instead of the plates that are shown in the plans. If you opt for brackets here, remember that the outer one is bent to more than a 90 degree angle to allow for the slanted part of the truss assembly (Fig. 11-5).

When making any of these brackets, it is best to initially cut them about 1/4 inch oversize in all dimensions. This will provide a little cushion to allow for positioning adjustments before the final mounting holes are drilled. Once these are made, the excess material can be ground off prior to the installation of the brackets. When grinding these down, *remember that the maximum distance a hole can be from the edge of a piece of metal is equal to twice the diameter of the hole.*

Fig. 11-4. Truss assembly showing suggested outer plate and bushing for the torque tube.

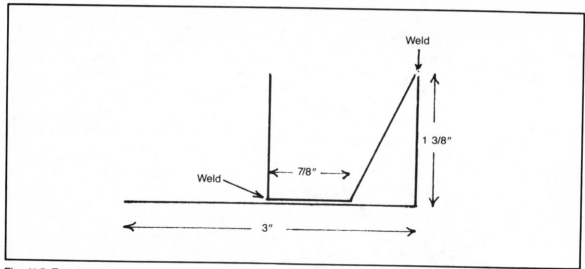

Fig. 11-5. Top view of inner truss rear mounting bracket.

Truss Alignment

Before starting the installation of the trusses, be sure that the plywood doublers and the main wing fittings are in place on the forward spar. This is also a good time to glue both sets of doublers in place on the rear spar. All of these items will affect the upcoming measurements, so they should be at least temporarily installed.

Truss Alignment

Locate the holes in the aft main wing fitting that will be used to bolt the brackets to the spar. Lay a straightedge through the centers of these holes and make a mark on the upper and lower edges of the wing fitting to indicate this centerline.

Using these marks as a guide, center each bracket over the holes and clamp it in place. Slide the truss assemblies down between the mounting brackets and clamp them in position here, and also to the rear spar. Then level the airplane in both fore-and-aft and spanwise directions. Block the structure quite securely during this leveling process so that it is firmly supported, particularly in the tail section. Place a level across each truss assembly in a spanwise direction, and level them by adjusting the position of the mounting brackets against the main wing fitting.

During this process, do not remove the clamp that holds the brackets and the truss together. Also, keep checking the reference marks on the edges of the wing fitting to make sure that the brackets stay approximately centered during these adjustments. Because the structure

will be bumped and handled during this alignment, make frequent checks on fuselage levelness in both directions—especially before a reading is taken on the levelness of the truss assembly. Once the trusses are square away in this direction, reclamp the brackets in place and loosen the clamps holding the truss assemblies in the brackets. Then adjust the trusses vertically within the brackets to their approximate positions, and level each in a fore-and-aft direction. Again, before this measurement is taken, recheck the fuselage for levelness.

With these preliminary alignment procedures in hand, it's time for a trail installation of the torque tube that extends between the two trusses in each wing. Slide this tube through all three bushings to its final position. On the first couple of tries, expect some small misalignment problems in getting this shaft in place.

When this occurs, make the required corrections by moving both trusses by small amounts, rather than moving either truss by a large amount. Such a procedure will minimize the deviation of the final position of these trusses from the idealized location called for in the plans. Be cautious in making these adjustments, since you don't want to move the trusses to an extreme in any direction. This could result in a situation where there might not be enough metal left on the truss or the bracket to properly bolt them together.

Since the corrections made here will be strictly in the up-down or the fore-aft directions, do not loosen the clamps holding the forward brackets to the main wing fittings. Once the tube can be inserted, make small vertical ad-

50

justments of the trusses to bring the shaft to a level condition. After this is done, the trusses are reclamped in position.

Critical Measurements

The next step in this operation is the amount of truth—and also marks your introduction to frustration and tedium on a *grand* scale. This is where the critical measurements are made on the alignment of the trusses and the retract mechanism. The first of these is to ensure that all trusses are square with the rear face of the main spar. This check requires a carpenter's square with one arm at least 24 inches long; however, the length of this arm should not exceed the distance between the front and rear spars.

The sequence for squaring the trusses is to start with the outer one on each side. This is necessary because you are somewhat limited in how far you can move the rear end of the truss to achieve squareness and still stay within the bolting pattern of the rear wing fittings.

If you find that the rear of the truss must be moved excessively to bring it into alignment, a somewhat drastic course of action may be called for. (This usually happens on one of those days where if it wasn't for bad luck, you would have no luck at all.) What must be done here is to move the forward brackets to the right or left to lessen the amount of movement required at the rear of the truss. This procedure is not a guaranteed cure-all for this problem, since you are again limited on how far you can move the brackets. Too far in either direction will result in not enough room being left between the hole and the other face of the bracket for the stopnut on one side, and possibly drilling a hole too close to the edge of the bracket on the other. Of course, once this adjustment is done, the whole alignment and leveling process as described above must be reaccomplished for that truss. If you must go through this drill, be sure to include leveling the torque tube.

The actual placement of the carpenter's square for this check does present a small difficulty. The truss should be square with the spar face; however, the brackets that are clamped to the main wing fitting interfere with the proper placement of the square. Therefore, a short piece of *straight* wood must be clamped to the spar face, between the trusses, and level with the top of the outer assembly. A section from the handle of a broken hockey stick is perfect for this, since it is straight, hard wood of the required thickness. With this piece in place the square can be laid along it and along the top outer member of the truss assembly.

Be critical of how the rear of the truss lines up with the square, because this is where small errors in the front become magnified. When this truss has been squared with the front spar, clamp the rear mounting plate to the back spar. This assembly now becomes the primary reference for setting the final position of the rear mounting of the inner truss.

The second critical measurement is the distance between the rear main wing fitting and the front of the torque tube. This value must be the same when taken at both ends of the shaft near the truss plates. If this is made by laying the tape measure over the top of the shaft and eyeballing the front edge, care must be taken to line up your eye over the shaft at the same spot each time a measurement is taken to avoid parallax error.

An alternate procedure can be used here by making a mark at the center of the torque tube near each end, and a corresponding mark over the center of the mounting hole for the shaft. Then line up the two marks when the shaft is installed, and measure from the wing fitting to the center marks on the ends of the torque tube.

Because the rear mounting plate of the outer truss is welded on, any corrections needed to equalize these measurements should be made by moving the inner truss backward or forward, if at all possible. Having the capability to move the inner truss for these fine adjustments is sufficient reason for using brackets for the rear mounting of this assembly, rather than the plate called for in the plans. If the plate is used, then shims must be placed behind one or the other trusses to achieve equal measurements at the torque tube. Once everything matches up, clamp the trusses to the brackets and recheck the entire assembly for levelness.

The third critical measurement is the distance between the truss assemblies to ensure that they are parallel. Once again, a pair of measurements are taken and adjustments are made to make them equal. These checks are made between the widest parts of the two trusses at the following points: directly over the torque tube, and at the extreme rear end. As before, any required adjustments should be made by moving the rear end of the inner truss. Constantly cross-check these measurements, since a relatively large movement of the rear of the truss will make a change in the value taken over the torque tube. When these two distances are the same, clamp the back of the inner truss in position. A schematic of the critical measurements is shown in Fig. 11-7. Figures 11-8, 11-9, and 11-10 show where these measurements are taken, and Fig. 11-8 also shows the setup for determining if the outer truss is perpendicular to the main spar.

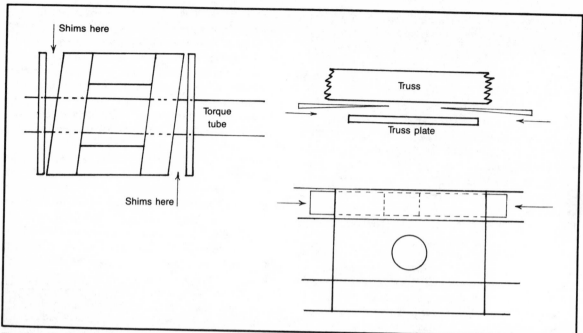

Fig. 11-6. Truss plate shims.

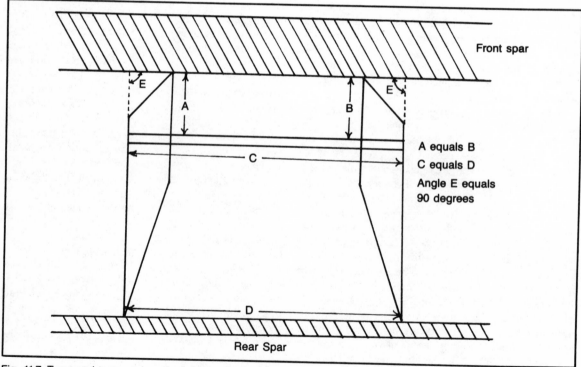

Fig. 11-7. Truss and torque tube alignment.

Fig. 11-8. The first critical measurement, using a large carpenter's square along the outer edge of the truss and up against a section of hockey stick clamped between the truss brackets.

Fig. 11-9. The second critical measurement to ensure that the torque tube is parallel to the front spar. The area is less cluttered than pictured here when this measurement is actually taken, since the aileron push-pull tube and the gear door close bulkhead will be installed at a later point.

Now begins the merry-go-round of rechecks on distances, squareness, and levelness that will test the dedication of the most ardent homebuilder. Start by making sure that the fuselage is level in both directions, and continue by doing the same with each truss and the torque tube. When all have been leveled as required, recheck each pair of measurements and the squareness of the trusses with the forward spar. Remember, if *any* of these need readjusting, the required movement may throw off some other value. Therefore, the name of the game here is to recheck everything constantly while making these corrections.

When all of these values are correct, clamp all units down tightly. Then, before starting any of the following checks and adjustments, trial-fit the large gear on the inside end of the torque tube. Make sure that this gear meshes snugly with the vertical worm gear. If not, the

Fig. 11-10. The third critical measurement to align the inner truss with previously squared outer truss. Note that the tape measures go from the lower section of the inner truss to the upper section of the outer truss in order to remain horizontal.

Fig. 11-11. Gear on end of the torque tube with wheels in retracted position, showing the notch in the bottom truss plate that may be required.

plate on this assembly must be moved fore or aft slightly to allow these gears to come together properly.

After this plate is positioned correctly, rotate the gear to see if it clears the lower plate in this truss assembly. If it doesn't, a notch must be filed in this plate to provide the proper clearance (Fig. 11-11). At this point, get ready to face another moment of truth.

Torque Tube Installation

Slide the torque tube into position, and determine if it rotates freely in the bushings. The upper retract knuckle arms should be welded on the shaft at this point, and this assembly should be checked for freedom of movement over its intended arc of operation. It would seem that if the alignment procedures were followed carefully, this shaft should rotate without difficulty, right? *Wrong!* There are three reasons why things could go amiss in this area. The first is inaccuracies in the critical measurements, but for the time being, let's assume that these are correct. The most probable cause of binding in this shaft are truss plates

that are not parallel, and/or not in line, and a torque tube that was warped slightly when the upper knuckle arms were welded in place. This latter problem is caused by a very slight bowing of the shaft in the direction of the knuckle arms caused by welding on only one side of the tube. This can be corrected by careful rebending with the aid of some pipes and a heavy vise.

If the truss plates are the source of the trouble, the corrective action is a little more involved. Since the torque tube was able to be positioned through all three truss plates during the alignment procedure, the variances between the plates that keep it from rotating must be slight. To make things easier, consider the inner truss plate as being correct, and make all adjustments to the outer two plates.

Remove the outermost plate and see if the shaft can be rotated when supported by just the other two. If binding still occurs, move the other plate backward or forward and/or up and down to determine if some new position will free it up. Before settling on a new location as the answer, clamp the plate tightly to the truss and see how the shaft will work under final conditions. If problems still exist, it's a good bet that the difficulty is caused by the plate not being perpendicular to the torque tube.

Another trial-and-error procedure is resorted to in this case. Make up a pair of long, thin wedges from scrap wood, much like those used to help align the fuselage frame in the jig. Each of these shims should be at least as long as the length of the truss plate. Slide the shims between the plate and either the top or bottom structural member of the truss. They are inserted as pairs, one from either end, with their points facing each other. Push them in a short distance, clamp the plate, and try the shaft. If it still binds, tap the shims in a little farther, reclamp, and try it again. If it's still no dice after the shims are fully inserted, or if things are only getting worse, try the shims on the *other* edge of the plate. Once a position is found where the shaft works okay, mark the shims, cut them as required, and epoxy them to the inside edge of the plate.

Temporarily install this modified plate and the torque tube on the truss assemblies. Slip the outermost plate over the shaft and clamp it against the truss. This will be its final position as far as fore-and-aft and up-and-down directions are concerned.

Should the shaft still bind upon rotation, try another pair of shims on one edge of the outer plate. In all probability, the binding problem is being caused by a truss assembly whose cross section in the area of the plates more resembles a parallelogram than a rectangle. Therefore, try the shims on the edge of the outside plate that is diagonal from where the shims on the inside plate are located (Fig. 11-6).

If the problem *still* persists even after trying the shims, the warp in the torque tube from welding may not have been removed entirely. Check this piece with a straightedge and carefully bend out any curvature, particularly near the ends. Even a very slight bow in the center will be magnified quite a bit at the ends of the shaft, resulting in considerable binding difficulties.

If an A & P mechanic made the trusses and gear plates for your bird, it's a good possibility that the corner mounting holes will have already been drilled through the plates and the truss. Should this be the case, some care will have to be exercised if the plates have to be moved to allow the shaft to rotate freely. It will be necessary to enlarge the holes in the *truss plates only* by using a small round file. Again, be aware of the limits on holes close to the edge of a piece of metal. After these holes have been enlarged and everything is working okay, the plates can be rebolted to the truss, using standard nuts instead of stopnuts for the time being.

If for some reason new holes must be drilled in the truss assembly to properly mount the plates, the easiest way to go would be to remove the truss and drill it from each side. However, after making all the measurements and adjustments on these components up to this point, most builders would take a whipping in the public square and give you an hour to draw a crowd rather than disturb the trusses.

The most practical course of action to follow in this case would be to purchase a 1/8-inch drill at least six inches long. The reason for the 1/8-inch drill rather than the 3/16 of an inch called for is as follows: Working from the outboard side of the truss, there is no problem in drilling through both walls of the outer section. However, when the tip of the drill hits the inner section, it cannot be controlled precisely, and it may have a tendency to walk slightly before biting in. If this occurs, the new holes will not line up exactly with those in the truss plate on that side. Therefore, these holes must be enlarged in the proper direction by using a small round file. Starting with a 1/8-inch drill commits you less positively on the inside member of the truss than would a 3/16-inch drill in case of a misalignment.

There is of course the possibility that with the increased size of the holes in the truss assembly, the plates may be jarred out of alignment by taxi and landing loads. To counter this potential problem, bolts are placed through the plates and the top and bottom truss members about midway between the front and the back of the plate. The holes for these bolts are not drilled until you are *absolutely* sure that no further adjustments will be made on the gear. Therefore, it is highly recommended that this operation be done *after* both the gear retract system and the gear door close mechanism are installed and working properly.

Drilling Truss Mounting Holes

Now with all the brackets, trusses, and plates clamped in their final positions, and the shaft working freely, it's time to start drilling some mounting holes. Once this is done the die is pretty much cast, so before firing up the drill, one last recheck is in order. Go back to the first step and make sure that the fuselage is level in both directions. Then retrace all the other measurement, squareness, and levelness checks described above, and make any corrections that may be necessary. If anything has to be moved a tad, don't forget to recheck the torque tube.

The first mounting holes to be drilled are those that attach the forward brackets to the main wing fittings. Make sure that the clamps holding the brackets in place do not cover the exit hole of the drill as it comes through the bracket. Push the drill through the compression bushing from the front side of the spar until it hits the bracket, and start drilling.

You might find it handy to put a bolt with a standard nut in each hole as it is drilled. This will allow that particular clamp to be removed, and thus ease somewhat the interference to drilling succeeding holes.

While everything is still in place, mounting holes are drilled in the rear plate of the outside truss. These are made like those in the front brackets—that is, through the compression bushings from the opposite side of the spar. If any type of bracket is used to secure the aft end of the inner truss, the location of its mounting holes should now be made on the forward face of the rear spar. These can be marked by using a nailset, awl, or by just dimpling the wood with a light touch of the drill through the holes in the bracket.

While the holes through the rear plate of the outer truss are being made, there is a better-than-even chance that a nasty little problem will surface. If perhaps you have recently angered the gods of homebuilding, you may find the drill emerging inside a truss tube, or into one of its walls. If it's the latter case, you'll get your first clue that something is wrong when the drill seems to be making no progress at all. What has happened is that you have hit a weld, and drilling through this material makes chrome moly seem like soft butter by comparison.

If the drill hits a wall, or so close to it on the outside that a nut cannot be put on the bolt, proceed as follows: Drill a hole through the affected side of the tube just in front of the weld, and even with the bolt hole through the plate. Then, using a small round file, enlarge the hole to *just* the point where a washer and a locknut can be slid in over the bolt hole. This is slow, knuckle-busting work, but proceed cautiously and do not remove any more material than is absolutely necessary.

Should the drill come through inside the truss, eyeball it to see which side the hole is closest to, and then proceed as above. If things *really* turn to worms and you hit a corner, it would be best to consult an A & P mechanic before cutting into two sides of a truss member.

The next step in drilling the mounting holes requires a bit of care or a large amount of tedious work will be undone. Remove the torque tube from between the truss assemblies and place a clamp at each spot where the front brackets intersect a truss member. If rear brackets are used on the inner truss, these should be clamped also. Cinch all these clamps down quite firmly. Next, remove all the mounting bolts through the spars that support one of the truss assemblies.

Then carefully lift the truss, with its clamped-on brackets, *straight up* from between the spars so as not to disturb the position of the brackets on the truss. Clamp the truss to the workbench, remove one of the clamps holding the brackets, and drill a perpendicular hole through the brackets and the truss arm. Replace the clamp over the hole just drilled, or temporarily bolt these pieces together. Then remove the other clamp and drill the second mounting hole.

This procedure is duplicated for each set of brackets used with the truss assemblies. When all the holes are made, temporarily bolt everything in place between the spars and check that the torque tube still rotates freely. If any binding occurs, it is probably better to try to correct it by moving the plates rather than by enlarging any of the holes just drilled.

The average builder will probably be on the ropes after wrestling the truss assemblies into position, so the upcoming segment of construction provides a bit of much needed relief. The next chapter will cover the building and installation of the seat back and cockpit floor.

Chapter 12

Seat Back and Floor

The installation of the seat back and floor is a relatively easy job, but don't skimp on the quality of workmanship in this area. There are a couple of important reasons why these pieces should be fitted into position as carefully as possible. First of all, these units are important structural additions to the strength of the fuselage frame, and secondly, they will be visible when the cockpit interior is completed. Shoddy workmanship here will stick out like a sore thumb.

The need for strength in the floor and seat back becomes particularly apparent after the first few times you crawl in and out of the cockpit. About the only way to get out of any WAR design is to wriggle your feet back till they clear the spar, plant them on the slanted floor section, and push. This action will slide you upward along the seat back until your elbows clear the canopy rail, and you can get your arms into the act. This exerts considerable pressure on the back of the seat, so make sure that both it and the support frame behind it are fitted exactly—and don't spare the glue.

The framework that supports the seat back is the first to be cut out and installed. When making the notches in the vertical pieces so that they will clear the top of the rear spar, remove just enough material to allow them to

fit snugly against the spar when in position. Gluing these pieces to both the spar and the framework will give them added rigidity.

While the support frame is drying, cut out and install the two small sections that make up the rear floor. These must have support blocks glued beneath them, and it's a lot easier to get at this area now than after the seat back is put in.

Before cutting out the seat back and main floor, measure the inside width of the cockpit, *from skin to skin*, where these pieces will be installed. Wherever possible, these two units should extend the full width of the cockpit in order to maximize the gluing surface, and thus the strength of these joints.

A pitfall to be avoided when installing the seat back and frame is to glue the frame to the back of the seat and then put them both into the airplane as a unit. Doing it this way will allow a good glue joint to be made between all parts of the frame where it touches the seat back. However, compromises must be made on the fit of the frame pieces at either end so that the completed unit can be worked into position. Another problem with proper fit arises when the vertical frame pieces must be notched where they intersect the top edge of the rear spar. It is a lot easier—and a much better fit is obtained—if these vertical pieces are trimmed and installed by themselves as the frame is being built.

Seat Back and Floor Installation

Trying to work the seat back into position against its support and inside the fuselage framework will bring back the unpleasant memories connected with installing the webs in the tail section. Undoubtedly, both top corners will have to be notched down the sides before this piece can be slipped into position. Do this notching in small increments to keep from making it any larger than necessary. Once again, after a procedure is found to maneuver the seat back in with a minimum of difficulty, remember how it was done to expedite things during the gluing operation.

When the final trimming and fitting is accomplished, trace the outline of the support frame on the rear face of the seat back. This will be the area that is lightly sanded before gluing. Also sand down any glue bumps and irregularities on the support frame so as to provide a good flush joint.

Before removing the seat back after drawing the outline of the frame, try experimenting with some braces to hold the seat back and frame together while the glue dries. These would be made from scrap pieces of fuselage frame stock, and are wedged against the seat back and any other convenient spot inside the cockpit area. Another brace may be placed behind the seat frame to hold it from that direction. It is bet to have these braces cut to the exact size needed—and know where each will go—before the gluing process begins. Scrambling around trying to find the right length of wood, and then figuring out where it will go, while the epoxy is curing may take so much time that an imperfect joint will result.

Another way of approaching this problem is to use gluing nails. However, if you opt for this method, don't forget to draw the frame centerlines on the front of the seat back to act as nailing guidelines.

After the seat back has been glued in place, the main floor section can be fitted for installation, but do not glue it in at this time. Cut a length of piano hinge to go along the front edge of this floor part; however, make it short enough to clear the inside of the fuselage frame on both sides.

The slanted floor section comes next, but only the front and rear edges are cut to the final dimensions. When measuring for the front of this piece, put the main floor and hinge in position, along with the slanted floor. Mark the front of the latter just forward of the point where the

bottom surface rests against the top edge of the spar. The rationale here is to let the top of the spar support the slanted floor, rather than making a bevel cut and having the floor rest against the aft face of the spar. This situation would result in a jammed floor the first time any weight was put on it. The sides of this floor section are just cut to clear the inside of the fuselage frame at this time. The size and location of the throttle quadrant, console panels, and rudder cable covers will determine how this piece must be trimmed later on. With everything in place, you should be able to open this hinged section of flooring to the maximum in order to gain access to the controls beneath.

After all the parts have been trimmed, clamp the main and slanted floors to the workbench with the hinge between them in the position it will be when everything is installed. Drill holes through the hinge and floor sections every couple of inches or so along both sides. Then pop-rivet the hinge to the main floor section, after which this assembly can be glued in place. The slanted floor is not attached to the hinge at this time, because it will be easier to make the final trimming cuts to the sides if it can be taken out and laid on the workbench. When all these cuts have been made and the slanted floor is pop-riveted in position, it will be necessary to dimple the gearbox mounting block underneath to make room for the rivets in this area.

With the seat back and floor installation completed, it's time to think downstream a little—and possibly make things easier for yourself later on. The area just finished will be highly visible when the airplane is completed, and poor craftsmanship will be apparent. Therefore, *now* is time to sand smooth all of the glue joints associated with the seat back and floor, since the cockpit is easily accessible and relatively unencumbered at this point in the project. If a few of the joints turned out a little ragged and are in plain view, some sort of filler should be used to smooth them over and make them less obvious.

Forward Cockpit Floor

The forward cockpit floor, in front of the main spar, is best tackled by making a pattern from paper or cardboard beforehand. The numerous cutouts and bevels required to get around the fuselage frame members and corner blocking for the spar are more easily located with a pattern, and the risk of ruining a large piece of plywood is considerably reduced.

This floor, too, should extend over both bottom longerons to the fuselage skin. It will be necessary to glue a wooden strip in front of the underblocks of the main spar to support the aft end of this floor. Later on, you may have to cut short sections out of this strip and the floor in order to gain access to the nuts on the bolts used to mount the control stick assembly. These holes do not have to be of minimum size, because not too much stress is exerted on the back end of this floor. In addition, these holes can be used to route wiring and fuel lines, and also allow for the installation of an auxiliary fuel tank mount, if one is desired.

After this floor has been epoxied in place, gluing nails can be used at the front and back edges, and around the rudder pedal mounting blocks, to hold things in place. Getting these nails tapped in along the sides is a little difficult, so weight may be the answer here.

Before the forward floor gets cluttered up with the rudder pedal assemblies, openings should be made for the brake line connections. These are centered on the floor and even with the brake cylinders when the pedals are in the neutral position, which is approximately straight up and down. Holes are made in the forward floor on both sides of the centerline for firewall fittings. Beneath these, a rectangular opening is cut in the fuselage skin large enough to allow a wrench to be used on the fittings coming through from above. Since there fittings will be mounted in a relatively unsupported area, it's a good idea to pass both of them through a single metal plate measuring about two by three inches. This will add some rigidity to the plywood around the holes for these fittings.

Now that the cockpit floor is in place forward of the spar, the rudder pedal assemblies can be attached. The next chapter will go over a few of the problems that can crop up in this procedure.

Chapter 13

Rudder Pedal Assemblies

Another task that is not too difficult is the installation of the rudder pedal assemblies—but this job is easy *only* if a few preliminary details are addressed and corrections made if required. In these discussions, the rudder pedal assembly is considered to be made up of the mounting brackets, the pedal support brackets, brake cylinders, and the rudder pedals themselves.

Some other givens to be kept in mind are: The brake cylinders referred to are Gerdes A-110-14, and the pedals are the standard "Cessna type" called for in the plans. Both of these things are stock items that are available from Aircraft Spruce and Specialty Co., Wag Aero, and other parts supply houses. If you decide on the "store-bought" pedals, they will have to be drilled for both pivot tubes and the bolt holes for attaching the brake cylinders. This is a somewhat awkward job, because they do not lend themselves to clamping to a drill press or workbench.

Problem Identification

The first thing that needs to be done in this phase of the project is a trial assembly of all the components in the rudder pedal assembly. Clamp the mounting bracket to the workbench and build up the whole unit from there.

One of the initial things to look for on this dry run

is the compatibility of the pedal and the brake cylinder. Is the actuating shaft on the latter long enough to reach the attach arm on the rear of the pedal? Can these two be connected when the attach arm is more or less horizontal?

If these items cannot be bolted together without the pedal being at some oddball angle, extensions are necessary on the actuating shaft of the brake cylinder. This is a rod of sufficient length to reach the attach point on the arm when the pedal and the entire assembly is in the vertical position, or nearly so (Fig. 13-1). They are threaded onto the actuating shaft and slotted at the other end to fit the thickness of the arm on the back of the pedal. Make this slot deep enough so that the arm does not hit the bottom of the slot through the entire range of operation. The aft side of this slot will probably require more trimming than the front because of the tapered arm on the pedal. It is more advisable to file the bottom of the slot than to trim the end of the pedal arm in case of a restriction of movement. This type of correction keeps the strength of the thinnest part of the arm at a maximum.

The other end of the brake cylinder can also cause some problems as far as freedom of movement of the entire assembly is concerned. If the attachment lug on the bottom of the cylinder is square, its corners might hit the

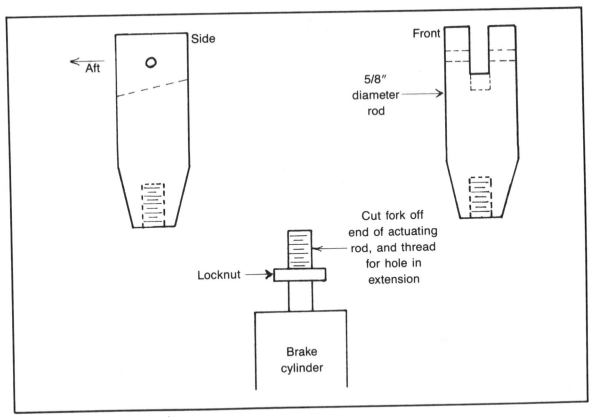

Fig. 13-1. Brake cylinder extensions.

top of the rudder pedal assembly mounting bracket as the cylinder is rotated fore and aft. About the only corrective action that can be applied here is to file off the corners of this lug just to the point where it clears the bracket. Again, to preserve the strength of this lug, do not remove any more material than is absolutely necessary.

When all these small items have been taken care of, reassemble the entire rudder pedal assembly and see that it operates freely throughout a complete cycle, backward *and* forward.

Checking Rudder Cable Clearance

Before drilling holes for the rudder pedal mounts, mark their position on the forward cockpit floor, as per the dimensions given in the plans. Then check to see if these marks line up with the holes in the mounting bracket. If they do not, be cautious as to what direction you move the bracket, and how far. The marks represent the ideal position with respect to the side frame and the

rudder pedal mounting block between the floors. Drilling a hole too close to the edge of this block could possibly produce a weak spot in this assembly that would go undetected.

After the holes are drilled, temporarily bolt the entire rudder pedal assembly in place. For the following check it is necessary to attach the rudder cables to the pedal support bracket. The cables should be swaged to the mounting tabs, because their bend around the thimbles effectively widens this assembly in an area where space is at a premium.

Holding the cable parallel to the floor, move the pedal assembly back and forth over its intended arc of operation. While the pedal is being moved, make sure that there is adequate clearance between the cable and the side pieces of the fuselage frame (Fig. 13-2).

Mounting Bracket Shims

If some adjustments are necessary to move the cable away from the frame, a very thin wedge must be made

61

Fig. 13-2. Arrow indicates minimal clearance necessary between the rudder cable swagged around a thimble, and the side fuselage frame members.

Once these units are in place, the return springs can be installed between the pedal assembly and the firewall. These springs are relatively light, since there only function is to hold the pedals in the upright position. Strengthwise, they should be about the same as a screen door spring, or slightly lighter. Their length should be an inch or so shorter than the distance from the firewall to the pedal support bracket when the latter is in the upright position. One end is attached to the same tab that anchors the front end of the rudder cable. Then, while holding the pedal in the vertical position, stretch the spring forward to the firewall, making sure that it is parallel to the longitudinal axis of the airplane. Mark this spot and drill a 1/8-inch hole through the plywood firewall. Secure the forward end of the spring to the loop in the head of a cotter pin, push the latter through the firewall, and spread the open ends flat against the engine side of the plywood. See Fig. 13-3 for the completed installation.

Having completed one segment of the control system, it is appropriate that things continue in that vein. The next chapter will go over some of the more-or-less uncommon items associated with finishing off this installation.

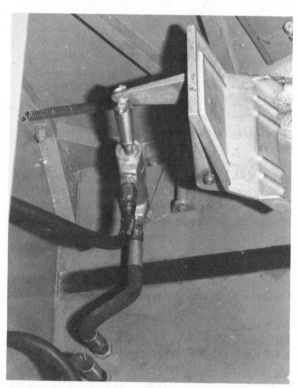

Fig. 13-3. Rudder pedals and brake assemblies plus extensions, with return springs and brake hoses attached.

and placed beneath the mounting bracket. Trace the outline of this mounting bracket on a scrap of plywood no more than 1/8 of an inch thick. After it is cut out and trimmed to the size of the bracket, this piece is beveled toward its inside edge with a wood rasp or on a sander. The reason this wedge is used, rather than some washers under the outside edge, is to provide a firm support under the entire mounting bracket. This setup is much more sturdy than the somewhat limited support afforded by the washers. Since a movement of the bracket by a small amount will be multiplied at the level of the rudder cable, the finished wedge will most likely not be very thick on the outside edge. The taper should be such that it is almost paper-thin on the opposite side. Make sure that this wedge still provides adequate clearance when the mounting bolts are tightened down quite securely, as will be the case on the final installation.

After all these adjustments have been made, the rudder pedal assemblies can be permanently mounted. During this procedure, spacers and washers should be used to take up any slack where these units are attached to each other. These are used only to ensure a snug fit between all moving parts while still allowing the components to rotate freely.

Chapter 14

Control Systems

Before installing the various rods that make up the elevator and aileron control mechanisms, the other components of these systems should be bolted in place. After careful measuring and careful drilling, attach the transfer crank, idler arms, and bellcranks as indicated in the plans. Make sure that the holes for the aileron bellcranks are centered in the intercostals inside the outer wing spar. If the midpoints of these pieces were not marked on the spar skins before assembly, locate the edges of each intercostal by tapping a thin brad through the plywood to determine where the solid wood is. These nail holes should then be sealed with epoxy.

Something else that should be done before installing the control rods is to protect their interiors from corrosion. This is accomplished by drilling a small hole near one end and inserting enough boiled linseed oil or varnish to coat the inside. These rust inhibitors can be introduced into the control rod by a hypodermic needle or a thin tube connected to a funnel; you will find that the former is considerably easier. The hole in the rod is then sealed by a plug to keep the oil or varnish from dripping out.

You have a choice as to the method of constructing the ends of the control rods. The drawings indicate that a rod end insert is welded in the end of each tube, on which is mounted a female rod end bearing. If this procedure is used to construct the control rods, then the preservative must be introduced through a hole as described above.

However, some consideration should be given to another type of construction, which results in a control rod with greater strength in these critical areas. Instead of welding an insert in the ends of the tubes, use a nut in its place. This is a bit sturdier than the assembly just described, and will also require the use of male rod end bearings in place of the female. If you decide on this latter option, then the linseed oil or varnish can simply be put in through the nut in the end of the rod.

Stick Grip

The following is another option that is not absolutely essential, but it does add a nice touch to the cockpit. (Also, anyone building a fighter replica is bound to have just a little bit of fighter replica is bound to have just a little bit of fighter pilot's blood in his veins,and would most likely want to go this route.) The item in question here is the stick grip, and a rubber handlebar grip stuck on the end of the control stick just doesn't seem to hack it. A grip carved from wood, equipped with microphone and trim switches, is a lot more authentic and isn't that hard to make. (There are surplus stick grips from fighters available in the various supply house catalogs, each with a multitude of buttons and a trigger. However, these items are just too massive to be used in a half-scale replica, and really look out of place in the cockpit.)

Trace the side and back views of your grip design on a scrap block of wood and rough-cut it out, retaining the more-or-less rectangular shape of the blank. This will make it a lot easier to clamp in place for drilling the mounting hole in the bottom. Since this will be a custom-made grip, you might want to drill this hole at a slight angle-off from the true vertical axis of the blank, allowing the grip to sit at an angle that conforms to the natural angle of your hand as it lays in your lap.

Carve the drilled block down to the outlines with a wood rasp, making sure that you don't go too deep where the top rear of the mounting hole is close to the surface. In order to make the carving a little easier, the section used to mount the microphone switch is made as a separate piece and epoxied to the grip.

Admittedly, an elevator trim system is not absolutely essential on an airplane of this size. However, it is a convenience that is not too difficult to install, and can be made to replicate the "beep trim" system used on modern fighters. The details of the trim system will be covered in a later chapter; therefore, only the installation of the switch will be discussed here.

Drilling and carving the mounting holes for the two switches on the stick grip requires some careful planning and measurements. First, a hole must be made to accommodate the body of the switch and the wire terminals underneath. Then a smaller hole must be drilled connecting this opening with the top of the stick mounting hole in the center of the grip. These will be used for the two sets of wires that connect the switches to the appropriate units. The switches themselves are mounted on small, thin aluminum tabs that are recessed into the surface of the stick grip and held in place by epoxy and/or small wood screws. This is why care must be exercised when drilling the switch holes, because enough material must be left around the hole to accept the wood screws and provide adequate strength for this mounting.

The wire used to hook up each of these switches is one pair cable, with the wire being stranded rather than solid. This will provide the protection and flexibility needed for this installation. Because the solder lugs for attaching the wires to the switches are fairly close together, and things will become even more cramped when the switches are pushed into their mounting holes, be sure to

slide spaghetti tubing over each lug after the wire is attached.

A small exit hole for these wires is drilled in one side of the control stick at some point below the level of the slanted floor. This hole should only be large enough to fish the cables through, and its edges should be filed smooth to prevent chafing. About a foot of each cable should extend beyond the exit hole, and knife disconnects should be soldered to the end of each wire. This type of connector provides a reliable junction when together, yet the entire assembly can be unhooked quickly without disturbing the bus bars, if the stick has to be removed.

Before the switches are finally mounted on the stick grip, install the latter on the stick and drill a hole through the grip and the stick for a 1/8-inch machine screw. Here again, to make the grip conform to the natural angle your forearm and hand make with the stick, twist the grip slightly on the stick from the true fore-aft alignment before drilling the hole. Countersink this hole on both sides of the grip so that the head and the nut for the bolt are recessed. The grip can be given a touch of realism by adding crosshatching grooves on each side with the edge of a small triangular file. (This is easy to mess up, though, you might want to ask at your local gun shop if they—or anyone in your area—does custom gunstock checkering.) Then the entire grip and the switch mounting tabs are given a few coats of high-gloss black enamel (Fig. 14-1).

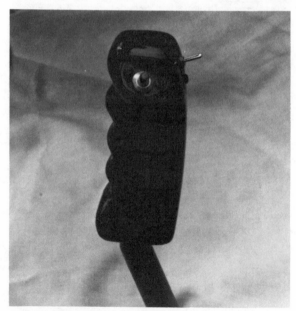

Fig. 14-1. Stick grip showing microphone button and beep trim switch.

After the grip and the stick have been bolted together, lubricate the moving parts of the control stick mount, assemble the complete unit, and bolt in place.

This is one more point in the project where you should be ready for another one of those small but aggravating problems. The two lower holes for attaching the control stick mount are fairly close to the bottom of the fuselage. The plans also call for these to be perpendicular to the face of the spar. However, given the bulk of most 1/4-inch drills, you will probably find that the fuselage skin prevents the drill from being lined up at a true right angle to the spar. Check out the variance; if it is small, you may be able to live with it. But if it is significantly out of line, the exit hole may be too close to the bottom of the spar to provide adequate support for the washer and nut. In this case it would be best to borrow a right angle or flexible shaft drill attachment for this job. Either of these should allow you to get a much better shot at drilling a more perfectly aligned hole.

Of course, the skillful homebuilder, who plans ahead, would drill these holes in the spar *before* it is installed in the fuselage. This is the easiest and preferred way to go, and the only caveat here is to make sure that the centerline of the spar is positioned over the centerline of the fuselage when it is glued in place.

If you are planning to install an external tank mount, such as that shown in Chapter 20, use standard nuts on the control stick mount. These will undoubtedly have to be removed many times before the tank mount installation is finalized, so hold the stopnuts until everything is accomplished in this assembly.

Aileron and Elevator Controls

The inboard part of the aileron control system is the next item to be addressed. Cut holes in the fuselage skin just aft of the main spar slot, and a little above the bottom longerons, that are only large enough to accommodate the inner aileron tube. These holes will have to be enlarged, but a few trial fits are necessary to determine the amount and direction. Slide the aileron tube with its rod end bearing through the hole and pin in place on the control stick. Then, with the aileron idler in position on the end of the wing fitting, eyeball how the hole must be enlarged to bring these two pieces together. Most likely, these will not be able to be joined at this time because of interference from the truss brackets.

Once you can see that the control rod will attach to the idler properly, mark where each truss bracket must be notched to allow the control rod to function correctly

Fig. 14-2. Notch required in truss brackets to permit installation of the aileron control rods.

(Fig. 14-2). The easiest way to make these cutouts is to use a drum-shaped grinding wheel about an inch in diameter in a 1/4-inch drill. Grind out only enough material to allow the control rod to move freely without scraping. Do *not* solve this problem by making a standoff to move the aileron idlers further to the rear in an effort to clear the truss brackets. Such a procedure will move the control rod aft to the point where it will interfere with the knuckle arms as the gear is retracted.

Another difficulty that may crop up during this installation is the control rod hitting the upper member of the outer truss when the stick is full throw to that side. This may not be a problem after the control limits are set, but it is best to eliminate it as much as possible at this time. Try moving the rod's attach point at the control stick down a hole or two. If this doesn't provide the necessary clearance, the rod may have to be bend slightly. Either of these solutions will most likely require the notches in the truss brackets to be enlarged. When the rod can be installed, temporarily pin it in place to check that it is of the proper length. Here, the aileron idler should be slanted inboard about 15 to 20 degrees when the stick is centered.

The installation of the elevator push-pull rods is quite

straightforward. Temporarily pin these components in place to check for proper length and freedom of movement. It may be necessary to enlarge the opening at the tailpost slightly to permit the rearmost rod to be connected to the elevator horn without rubbing. Make sure that when the stick is in the neutral position, the elevators are streamlined. Small adjustments in this neutral position of the stick to make it more comfortable can be made by moving the rod end bearings on each unit in or out. If this is done, remember to leave sufficient stick throw to reach the elevator control limits.

Achieving these limits may require deepening the cutout in the slanted floor and/or shaving some wood off the top rear edge of the main spar. Do not use locknuts at this time when installing either the aileron or the elevator control system. These rods will probably have to be removed and replaced a couple of times when working on other parts of the aircraft. But this is as good a time as any to add whatever washers are necessary to the bolt at each moving joint to take up any slack that may be present.

Although it is a little premature at this point in the project, there is a check that has to be performed later on that will cause considerable worry and work if delayed until after the framework has been foamed. When the outer wing panels and ailerons have been completed, it's a good idea to pin these in place and connect all the push-pull rods of the control system from the stick to their respective control surfaces. Once everything is hooked up, a problem may become apparent in that the control surfaces are not lined up with the airfoils when the stick is in the neutral position. Both ailerons may be deflected up or down, and/or they might exhibit unequal deflection in either direction.

The most probable cause of these anomalies is the incorrect initial positioning of all or some of the rod end bearings throughout the system. From here on out it's pretty much a trial-and-error procedure to align the control surfaces properly. Put the stick in neutral and then adjust as many rod end bearings on one side as are necessary to bring the aileron into adjustment.

There are a couple of things to keep in mind while making these alterations in the length of the actuating rods on either side. If it turns out that the total length must be reduced—that is, the rod end bearings have to be screwed down closer to the control rod—make sure that enough threads are left to put a locknut between the rod and the bearing. This may require that a given adjustment must be made by moving many bearings a small distance,

rather than changing one or two bearings by a large amount.

Should the problem be that the total length must be increased by screwing the rods and the bearings farther apart, another general rule applies: The minimum overlap between the two threaded parts should be equal to the diameter of the bolt, plus one thread. As an example, a 1/4-inch bolt must be screwed into the other piece for a distance of at least 1/4 of an inch, plus one more thread.

If, after making all the adjustments and following the above rules,the ailerons still cannot be streamlined, about the only course of action left is to remove one of the rods and shorten or lengthen it accordingly. Then the above procedures will have to be redone for that side.

There is the possibility that even after getting the ailerons to line up properly at this point, they may be a little out of kilter when the bird is assembled after foaming and glassing. However, any adjustments needed at that time will just amount to some fine-tuning on the ones made earlier. After running through one set of these changes in the aileron system, the merits of doing it when all the components are readily accessible will be seen clearly.

Rudder Cable Holes

Running the rudder cables from the pedals back to the pulleys behind the rear spar does get a little more involved than the aileron or elevator systems. The problem here is to determine just where the holes should be made in each face of both spars to ensure a straight line from the bottom of the pulley to the cable attach point on the pedal assembly.

The first step in the procedure is to clamp a piece of wood across the front of the fuselage frame, level with the cable attach points when the pedal assemblies are in the vertical position. Then stretch a piece of string from this cross piece, over the cable attach points, over the front spar, to a point on the top of the rear spar that is in line with the long axis of the pulley below. Make sure the string is taut, and draw vertical lines on each face of both spars directly below the string.

Measure the distance of both ends of the string from the top of the fuselage frame, and, using these measurements, draw the position of the string on the plans. Then, on the plans, measure the distance from this line down to where the rudder cables pass through the front and rear faces of each spar. Transfer these measurements from the string down the vertical lines drawn on the spar faces, and mark accordingly (Fig. 14-3).

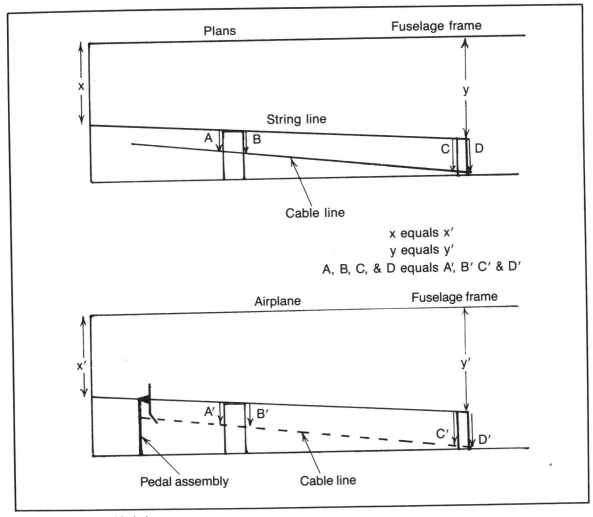

Fig. 14-3. Rudder cable holes.

Drill holes slightly larger than the diameter of the cable at each mark, ensuring that the aft hole in the rear spar lines up with the pulley. Thread the cable through the holes and under the pulley, and pin the front end to the pedal assembly.

Work the pedals back and forth to see where the cable rubs at each hole, and enlarge it accordingly. When the cable run freely throughout the full travel of the pedals, they can be swagged to the attachment tab and pinned to the rudder horn.

Unless you hit each measurement perfectly on the first shot, and everything lined up correctly, you will probably have holes of varying sizes in the spars. To make things a little neater, phenolic or plastic disks are epoxied over the holes after the cables are permanently installed. These are made in halves, a little larger than the hole, with each piece having a semicircular cutout for the rudder cable. Space around the holes in the rear spar may be limited; therefore, these cable guides will have to be cropped accordingly.

The next phase of construction provides a real test of nerves for the first-time homebuilder. Because of its cost, and the fact that one slip could ruin the whole thing, cutting and installing the canopy on its frame is a tricky job. The procedures and techniques for handling this task are covered in the next chapter.

Chapter 15

Canopy and Windshield

Before starting work on the actual canopy and frame, there are a couple of preliminaries that are recommended for the Corsair. Although not called for in the plans, these additions will shore up an otherwise weak part of the structure.

The thin plywood specified for the rear canopy guides and support needs some beefing up to handle the continued operation of the canopy, and the loads imposed on it. This is done by making doublers from .063 aluminum that cover the entire area above the guide slot, and 1 inch below it, for the full length of the rear canopy support. These doublers are pop-riveted to the plywood, making sure that they don't interfere with the guide washers on the canopy bolts that ride in the slot.

After the doublers are in place, install sway braces from the canopy guides to the centerline of the fuselage (Fig. 15-1). This latter attaching point for the sway braces must have a supporting block glued under the fuselage skin.

Once the sway braces are put on the bird and the metal doublers are attached to the canopy guides, the slots must be trimmed to make sure the canopy bolts will move back and forth smoothly with a minimum of excess room. This will ensure that the canopy will be held snugly to the rails,

and lessen the chances of vibration when it is in the open position.

Find a bolt that is the same size as those welded to the canopy frame, and run this back and forth in the guide slots to check for any binding. This is a lot easier than wrestling the canopy frame on and off the fuselage during the initial sizing of these slots. Trim very sparingly, with frequent checks, only in those spots where a problem exists. After you have smoothed down any irregularities so that the bolt moves freely, secure the canopy in place and see how it operates along the full length of its travel. Trim any rough spots as required until the canopy can be opened and closed easily while seated in the cockpit.

After this has been accomplished, the final job is to give the guide slots one last touch-up with an extra-fine file or sandpaper. The purpose of this is not to enlarge the slots, but merely to make the track as smooth as possible for troublefree operation.

When installing the windshield bow, be certain that the mounting brackets that go around the top longeron fit very snugly on all three sides. Twist and bend these brackets as required for a good joint, and don't spare the epoxy in this area.

Fig. 15-1. Canopy sway braces and metal track doublers. Note clearance of the pop rivets from the track to accommodate the washers on the canopy attach bolts.

Don't forget to drill the numerous holes in the windshield bow mounting flanges as called for in the plans. These are necessary for good epoxy adhesion, and care should be taken to ensure that the epoxy is stippled into these holes, and is also spread on the outside of the flange. Slow-curing, two-part epoxy may be preferable to use for these joints instead of Aerolite, since the metal can't absorb the components and strengthen the bond as with wood. The consistency of this type of adhesive also makes it easier to work with in this situation.

In order to ensure the best bond possible, use a couple of C-clamps to secure the inner face of the flange against the inside of the longeron. After these are in place and tightened down, use another pair of clamps to hold the top and bottom of the flange tight against the longeron. When the epoxy cures and all the clamps are removed, it will be necessary to FOG each of the spots where the clamps were attached. Once again, this area will be highly visible when the cockpit is finished off, so sand down all the excess epoxy and make the entire joint as smooth as possible.

The windshield bow takes a lot of abuse during construction because it is a very handy place to grab onto for any number of reasons. Therefore, be particularly careful to make this a strong, solid junction.

The next items to be made up are the aluminum angles for the inside edge of the canopy rails, and the Teflon guides that fit over these angles. Be sure to use flathead wood screws that can be countersunk for attaching these angles to the wooden rails. File down any part of the screw that projects above the angle strip to ensure smooth canopy operation.

Something els that is not called for in the plans—but is just about a must—is a good solid block glued between the canopy rail and the top longeron on both sides. Because of the varying angles encountered here, fitting this piece is a little tricky, but after using the canopy rail to lever yourself out of the cockpit a few times, you'll see why it is necessary.

Fitting the Canopy Frame

When the canopy frame has been welded together, temporarily install it in the rear guide slots and on the Teflon guides mounted on the canopy rails. This is a trial fit in the closed position to see if the frame lines up with the windshield bow and sits properly on both rails. *Gently* bend the frame in whatever direction required to achieve a good fit all around when the bolts are in the rear track and the attach tabs are pinned to the Teflon guides. Twisting or corner-to-corner bending may even be necessary to get the frame positioned properly.

When this is accomplished, none of the mounting points will be under tension in any direction, and the forward canopy arch and the windshield bow should match up as close as possible. If any bending of the forward arch is indicated, do this first, since changing the arc will affect the position of the sides. Then, after it lines up with the windshield bow, work to get the bottom sections of the frame flat against the rails.

When all the bending is done, carefully inspect each weld joint on the frame for cracks. If any have to be touched up, the frame must be refitted, although the second time around it is much easier.

If things are really going right and the front canopy frame and windshield bow line up quite well, and are very close together in the closed position, your good fortune may mask a future problem. If you plan to utilize a rubber strip around the windshield bow to act as a seal against rain and/or air noise, be sure to allow sufficient space for it to be installed. If the canopy frame and windshield bow are just fairly close to each other, this rubber strip may be advantageous in producing a good tight seal. However, should the two pieces of framework fit *very* close together, it may be necessary to enlarge the forward end of the canopy track at the bottom, where it starts to slant upward, in order to accommodate the rubber seal.

But if the windshield and canopy bow have turned out to be an excellent fit, and since it would be equivalent to asking for a pound of flesh to suggest modifying the tracks to allow for the rain seal, an alternate solution is available. This involves using a length of the sponge rubber weatherstripping material used as a seal around doorways. Used as-is, this is relatively flimsy stuff and would not stand the gaff very long if just glued to the windshield bow. A better tack to follow would be to enclose this weatherstripping in a piece of thin but strong fabric, such as balloon cloth, and attach it with the same screws that mount the windshield plex to the bow. A thin strip of aluminum is placed over the cloth strip, and this is held in place with the same screws. The strip extends back over the weatherstripping, and just a little over the front edge of the canopy in the closed position. This type of installation provides an effective rain/air noise seal that is fairly well protected against damage caused by using the windshield bow as a hand hold. A cross sectional view of how this weatherstripping and metal cover are mounted is shown in Fig. 15-2.

Sealing the rear of the canopy against the turtledeck is a little more involved procedure. First of all, for appearance's sake, the blunt rear edge of the plex should be faired smoothly to the fuselage. This can be done by attaching to the back of the canopy a strip of metal bent into a sharp V, with the open end being as wide as the thickness of the plex. This strip is not unlike the preformed trailing edge material sold by many supply houses, except that it has a sharper rear edge. The strip is carefully bent to conform to the back arch of the canopy, and then attached to the rear bow by the canopy mounting screws in the same manner as the strip over the windshield. Another piece of sponge rubber weatherstripping is sewn into a strip of balloon cloth, which is then fastened to the underside of the metal strip by means of flush-mounted rivets.

Before this piece can be bent successfully, the lower surface will have to be notched every inch or so with a deep V cut, reaching almost to the rear edge, if you are making it out of relatively hard aluminum stock. This will permit the top surface to be bent without the bottom surface buckling. If very soft aluminum is used, the notching may not be required.

Cutting the Canopy

Canopies and windshields ordered from WAR will

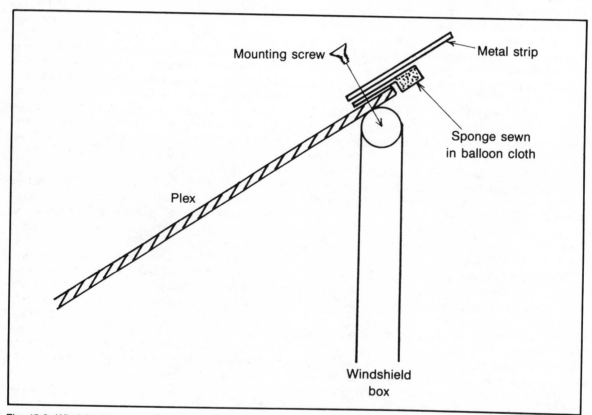

Fig. 15-2. Windshield/canopy weather seal.

most likely be manufactured by Gee Bee Canopies Inc. When these are fabricated, they are made with quite a bit of excess material, which is used to mount them in the shipping crate. Also, the canopy is oversize on the sides and in length. Removing this extra plex requires careful planning and execution, because one slip here and that's all she wrote.

Support the canopy frame with lengths of 2×4 under each side piece. Position the canopy over the frame, making sure that it is centered properly and the front of the plex is parallel with the front arch of the frame. Check that the frame pretty well touches the plex all the way around both bows. The rear of the frame will have to be raised slightly with blocks to do this, and the canopy may have to be moved slightly to get it to touch all parts of the frame.

Draw a cutting line on the plex with a grease pencil, allowing 1/4 to 1/2 inch beyond the size called for in the plans for the final trim. If you feel lucky and want to make this cut right to the actual dimensions, a strip of masking tape should be placed along the line of cut, and the actual line is then drawn on the tape. This will prevent chipping along the edge of the plex when the cut is made.

Remove the plex from the frame and place it over a padded sawhorse for cutting. This operation calls for an extra body, since someone must hold the canopy steady while you *carefully* make the cut around the lines. A disk-shaped cutting wheel especially designed for plastics works very well here. This is available in most hardware stores and is mounted in a 1/4-inch drill. The cutting instructions that come with the canopy specifically state that a saber saw should *not* be used for this operation. The cutting wheel is easy to use and the cut goes fairly rapidly, but by all means take your time here because any mistakes caused by hurrying or forcing the cut will really water your eyes.

Mounting the Plex to the Frame

When all the flash is removed, mark the top center of the canopy on the front and rear edges. A corresponding mark is also made on both canopy frame bows. Reposition the plex over the frame and align the marks as closely as possible while ensuring a snug fit around the entire frame.

The next phase of the operation will require about three dozen Cleco fasteners—and the tool needed to insert them. Starting at the top front centerline, drill a 3/32-inch hole perpendicular to the plex surface, through the plex and just *one* side of the canopy frame. Then secure the plex to the frame with a Cleco fastener. Repeat this procedure at the top rear centerline mark. These two holes determine the alignment of the canopy and the frame, so make sure that they are lined up with the marks on the frame as closely as possible when starting to drill into the metal. Continue drilling these holes about two inches apart down each side of both canopy frame arches, alternating between sides and between ends as each hole is drilled. The alternating procedure will ensure that the canopy is progressively fitted to the frame while minimizing the chance that a small error introduced on the front end will be magnified at the rear. After the plex is Clecoed to both frame arches, drill the holes along the bottom frame members, continuing to use Clecos as before.

When all the mounting holes are drilled, remove the Clecos and lift the canopy from the frame. Each hole in the frame is then threaded for the mounting screws with a 6-32 standard tap.

This brings up another touchy job where a small miscalculation could mean big problems. The holes in the plex must be countersunk from the outside to accept the 6-32 machine screws used to fasten the canopy to the frame. Either AN or MS screws with a 78-degree head are suitable here. This job will require a 78-degree countersink to be used in your 1/4-inch drill, and these are also available at most hardware stores for only a few dollars. Before using this tool, it might be a smooth move to drill a few practice holes in the flashing cut from the canopy. Then see just how much pressure is required to make the countersink in each hole. These should *only* be deep enough to flush the top of the mounting screw with the canopy surface—any deeper and you are effectively diminishing the strength of this joint.

Fasten the canopy to the frame with the mounting screws, but before doing this, check each hole in the frame for rough edges caused by the tapping. These should be filed smooth to prevent scratching the canopy while it is being positioned.

Once in place, the final outline of the canopy is marked on the plex with a grease pencil (if some excess was allowed for the first cutting). A better finish will result if this final trimming is done with a cylindrical grinding stone in a 1/4-inch drill, rather than the cutting wheel used previously. It is also a little easier to do this trimming if the canopy is removed from the frame and held steady by someone else while it is being ground down.

Installation Checks

Since the plex extends below the canopy frame on

Fig. 15-3. Front quarter view of the canopy rail support block, showing how it may have to be dished to provide clearance for the bottom of the plex.

edge of the windshield will be held in place and sealed by the layers of fiberglass.

Although this procedure is called for in the plans, you might want to hedge against the eventual possibility of having to replace the windshield. However, with the windshield epoxied to the skin, it doesn't take much imagination to realize what a messy and extensive job *this* could turn into. Skin would have to be cut away and the entire area reglassed, to say nothing of priming and painting. A better solution to this potentiality would be to proceed with the fiberglassing as directed, but only after placing Saran Wrap (or a similar material) around the bottom edge of the windshield. The resulting mounting base for the plex can be made watertight by the application of automobile windshield sealer around the bottom.

Once the canopy is in place on the bird and is working properly, it might be a good idea to see how it operates from *inside* the cockpit. Use whatever cushions you plan on flying with, and try opening and closing the canopy while seated with the safety belt and harness on. Even an average-sized person will find that the lack of elbow room mentioned earlier will prevent the easiest and most obvious method for opening the canopy. You will probably determine that the quickest way to start the canopy back is to work cross-handed until it is open far enough to get your elbows and hands up; then it can be pushed straight back.

Whatever method you come up with that works should be practiced a few times to get the technique down pat. You never know when you'll have to climb out of the bird in a hurry, and that's no time to start developing egress procedures.

both sides, the complete assembly should be checked for proper clearance by mounting it on the aircraft. There are two possible sources of interference here: The first is the support blocks between the top of the longeron and the bottom of the canopy rail. These may cause some binding with the bottom edge of the plex, and will have to be dished slightly for the canopy to operate properly (Fig. 15-3). The half-round side of the wood rasp described earlier is excellent for this job. Make sure that enough material is removed from these blocks to allow for the prescribed layers of fiberglass to be put in place later.

The second problem area is the front of the canopy rails where they are attached to the windshield bow. Rather than cutting away any wood at this point, which would materially weaken the joint, a small portion of the plex is removed. This amounts to a slight bevel being ground into the front corners of the canopy. Don't take off any more material than is necessary to get the canopy to close tightly against the windshield bow. The cutting, fitting, trimming, and mounting of the windshield must wait until the styrofoam has been applied to the top of the fuselage between the cockpit and the fuel tank. However, the procedures used for this operation, as far as the plex is concerned, are the same as described above. The forward

Canopy Lock

The device called for in the plans to lock the canopy utilizes a sash window lock. While this is adequate, it can be improved upon. A better idea is one that will hold the canopy in two or three open positions as well as full closed. However, if this type of installation is desired, you will have to make the decision before the canopy frame is finished and the plex attached. Otherwise, a lot of disassembly, brazing, repainting, and reassembly will be required.

The first thing that needs to be done if the multi-position canopy lock is to be installed is to braze a section of 1/4-inch copper tubing to the rear of the front canopy arch. The ends of this length of tubing are about 3 inches above the side frame pieces, and the one on the left is angled about 30 degrees to the rear in the last 1 to 1 1/4 inches. When attaching this tubing, make sure that it is below the top edge of the canopy arch so that it does not interfere with the mounting of the plex to the frame.

Once this tubing is in place, the remainder of the canopy frame can be built and the plex attached. The other parts of the locking mechanism can be made and installed later, after the frame has been fitted to the airplane and the plex has been cut and mounted to the frame. Given all the handling, bending, and drilling involved in these latter operations, it is probably advisable to hold off on the final installation of the other parts of the locking device, since they would only be in the way during this process.

The next items to be fabricated are the locking pin assemblies. These are small pieces of sheet steel with a 3/8 inch tube welded on one face. Inside the tube is the locking pin itself, which is made from a 3/16-inch bolt with the head cut off and that end rounded. A washer is brazed on the bolt 3/8 of an inch from the rounded end, and is then ground down so that the bolt and washer will fit inside the metal tube.

Three evenly spaced vertical cuts, about 1/8 of an inch deep, are made across the diameter at the top of the tube. The small tabs formed by these cuts are then bent in slightly, to reduce the size of the hole at the upper end of the tube to just a little greater than the diameter of the locking pin. In this fashion, they not only act as a guide for the locking pin, but also serve as a retainer for the compression spring that keeps the pin in the extended

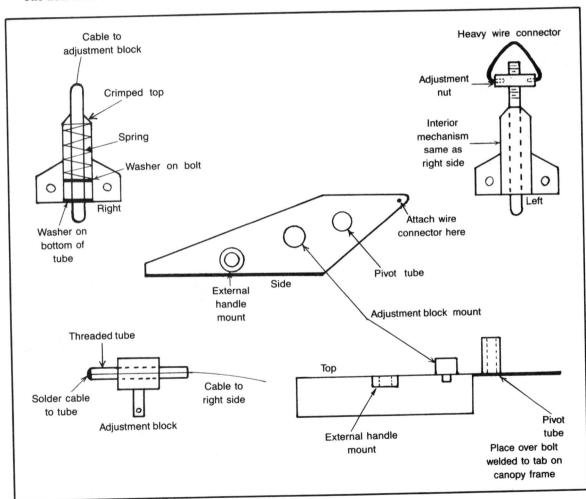

Fig. 15-4. Canopy lock mechanism.

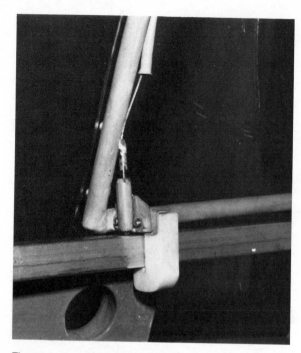

Fig. 15-5. Canopy locking mechanism, right side, showing the pin pulled up to allow canopy movement.

Fig. 15-6. Canopy locking mechanism, left inside, showing how the handle is attached to the adjustment nut on the locking pin. The external control is secured to the rearmost nut welded to the handle, and extends through a slot in the canopy, just visible between the handle and the frame.

position. This spring, which must fit inside the tube, is placed over the flat end of the pin and down against the washer. The flat end is then inserted in the tube from the bottom, and the spring is compressed fully by pulling the pin out through the top and clamping it in that position.

With the pin retracted, a similar washer is brazed to the bottom of the tube to act as a guide for the locking pin, and also as a stop for the spring extension. A thin cable is brazed to the flat end of the pin that will be installed on the right side of the canopy. This cable should be long enough to be threaded up through the copper tube attached to the canopy bow, plus an extra four or five inches on the other side. The threaded end of the bolt that will be the left locking pin will be used for an adjustment nut that will be connected to the unlocking handle. Each of these assemblies will be attached to the front side of the bracket on the canopy frame, used to mount the Teflon canopy guides.

The unlocking handle is really a double acting lever that is mounted on a bolt welded to the tab on the left side of the front canopy bow. The bushing in the handle is of such a length on the outboard side so as to align the handle with the top of the locking pin. Pushing down on the handle lifts the left locking pin, and at the same time

pulls down on the cable, which raises the right pin.

In order for these actions to be accomplished simultaneously, the left end of the cable is secured to an adjustment block. This device is only cotter-pinned to the handle so that it is free to rotate, and incorporates a threaded tube with which small adjustments can be made. This tube is placed midway in the block, the cable passed through it, which is then soldered or brazed to the bottom end. The front of the handle is connected to the adjustment nut by a piece of heavy copper wire, bent as shown in Fig. 15-4 and inserted into small holes drilled in the sides of the nut. The dimensions of the handle are such that the bottom portion does not hit the canopy rail when it is depressed.

Fig. 15-7. Canopy locking mechanism, left outside, a simple T-handle that is held in the horizontal position by a locknut on the inside end. Just to the left of the handle is the adjustment block.

After installing the locking mechanism and reattaching the plex to the frame, a slot for the external access handle must be cut in the canopy. To mount this handle, a 1/4-inch hole is drilled in the side of the internal unlocking handle, and a nut welded on the inside face.

Using a grease pencil, draw on the outside of the canopy the arc that this hole makes when the unlocking handle is depressed. Carefully drill a series of holes along this arc using a 1/8-inch bit. These holes are then enlarged with a round file until the 1/4-inch mounting bolt moves freely over the full travel of the unlocking handle.

To keep this hole from being a source of cold air in the winter, the outside part of the handle could incorporate a small plastic or sheet metal flap as a cover.

Another feature that could be easily added to this system is a warning device showing when the pins are not fully seated. This would take the form of a red stripe painted around the locking pin, which would show above the top of the tubes if the pins were not in the full locked position. Pictures of the completed canopy locking mechanism are shown in Figs. 15-5 through 15-7.

It's back to Heartbreak Hill and Frustration Ridge for the next phase of the project. This is the installation of the outer spars—and, more particularly, the setting of the dihedral and incidence of the outer wing panels, which will be described in the next chapter.

Chapter 16

Outer Spar Installation

The installation of the outer spars is another part of the project where caution, and careful measuring that is rechecked frequently, are the keys to success. The process here is identical to that used when the truss assemblies were being bolted in place—that is, be *absolutely* sure of *every* measurement before drilling any holes. Keep in mind that important stability characteristics will be determined by just how close you can come to the dihedral and incidence values specified in the plans.

This is also a phase of the project where the space requirements will almost double, since at least one outer wing panel will be attached at all times. If the alternate procedure to be described later on is used to support the aircraft during this process, the space needed will more than double. The first technique to be discussed should be considered when space is a problem, since the alternate procedure will require at least a two-car garage.

Preliminaries

The initial step is to swing the fuselage frame 90 degrees so that it is positioned across one end of the table. The front face of the main spar should be very close to the long edge of the table so that it may be clamped down later on. Level the table in both directions, again employ-

ing the techniques for using the level described earlier. If the table legs have to be blocked up to achieve levelness, make sure everything is fairly sturdy, because you'll be leaning on and crawling over the table quite a bit during this procedure.

Since measurements will be taken at various locations, be certain that the levelness is constant from the fuselage frame to the far end of the table. A way to check this is to stretch a string along the edge of the table from the fuselage to the other end. Check the levelness of the string by using a line level, and adjust the attach point at the end of the table accordingly. Then compare the surface of the table with the string, looking for high points or low points.

Once the work table is squared away, the fuselage is also leveled fore-and-aft and spanwise. When this is done, install bar clamps from the top of the spar to underneath the edge of the table on both sides of the airplane. Use pads between the clamps and the top of the spar, and cinch things down quite securely. Then recheck the levelness of both the table and the aircraft, but particularly the latter. The clamping pressure may be just enough to throw the previous leveling out of kilter. If anything has changed, use shims as needed to level the entire assembly, then clamp it back into position.

Measure on the plans the distance from the centerline of the attachment bolt holes in the outer wing fittings to the end of the spar concerned. Draw a line on the inside face of each fitting to indicate the position of the spar. Then pin each matched pair of fittings to the inner wing fittings with the wing attachment bolts.

Before the rear outer fittings are put in place, they will have to be bent to achieve a 5 degree forward sweep of the rear spar, as described in Chapter 9. The mark just drawn on the fittings is the bending point. Again using dimensions from the plans, draw lines on the face of each spar to indicate the top of the upper fittings and the bottom of the lower fittings. These will be used as general guides for positioning the wing fittings on the outer spars.

In order to make correct measurements for the dihedral of the outer wing panel, it will be necessary to draw a centerline on the front face of the outer spar from the root to the tip. The double taper of this spar precludes accurate measurements being taken from anywhere but this centerline. Slip the outer spars between the two bottom sets of fittings, and line up the latter with the guidelines on the spar faces. It will be necessary to use blocks under both outer spars to bring them up level with the inner spars. Clamp these lower fittings in place and block up the tips of both spars until the root ends of the outer spars are parallel with the outer ends of the center spars. It is sufficient just to eyeball this, since the following check is made only to point out a relatively large misalignment of the spars.

Clamp the upper fittings in place temporarily, and see how they line up with the guidelines. If they are way off, it may be necessary to raise or lower the outer spars slightly to equalize the distance from the edges of the fittings to the edges of the spars. After this check, reclamp the lower fittings in place if any movement had to be made, and unclamp the upper fittings and fold them back out of the way for the time being.

Setting the Dihedral

Draw lines on the tip rib to locate the position of the front and rear spars, and glue the compression strip to the rib as indicated on the plans. Then tack this rib to the ends of the spars with a few small brads.

Place blocks under both spars to raise them to the proper dihedral of 9 degrees. Rather than use a protractor to measure this angle, it is easier and more accurate to convert it to inches that can be measured at the tip rib. This conversion uses the sine of the angle, which requires that the length of the spar be known. This measurement is taken along the centerline drawn on the outer spar from the tip to a point directly above the center of the bolt that pins the lower fittings to the main wing fittings. The extra distance from the end of the spar to over the bolt center is the same as that determined earlier to mark the spar position on the outer wing fittings. Simply add this to the actual length of the spar, and you have the value required for the conversion. Multiply this total length by .1564 (the sine of 9 degrees) and you have the number of inches that the tip of the spar centerline must be raised to achieve the correct dihedral.

The perpendicular distance that the inner end of the extended centerline is above the table is the next measurement that must be taken. Add this value to the one just calculated, and you now have the total height above the work surface that the tip must be to give you a 9 degree dihedral. Use a large carpenter's square when checking for this distance at the wingtip, to ensure that you are measuring along a true perpendicular from the table (Fig. 16-1).

When the dihedral is set properly, adjust the outer blocking under the rear spar until the tip is level when checked along the compression strip. This will produce the zero-degree incidence at the wingtip as called for in the plans. Then carefully recheck the levelness of the table and the aircraft in both directions, and the dihedral measurements as well as the levelness of the tip rib. These values cannot be reviewed too often because, with the outer spars just being blocked up, there is a good chance that any jarring or bumping will throw some measurement off.

When everything rechecks okay, rotate the upper spar fittings into position on the outer spars as indicated by the guidelines. Clamp these in place, and then run through the levelness and measurement checks again in case something moved while the clamps were being tightened down. If everything is on the mark, remove the wing attach bolts holding the fittings together and take the tip rib off the ends of the spars. The mounting holes for the fittings can now be made, using the holes previously drilled in half the fittings as guides.

When making these holes, the drill should be tilted slightly toward the butt of the spar to compensate for the tapered sides. The hole should be perpendicular to the spar *centerline,* not the spar face. If a drill press is used for this operation—which is the preferred way to go—block up the far end of the spar to make the centerline level, then drill the holes. Once the spars have been drilled, the process for enlarging the holes for the compression bushings is the same as described earlier.

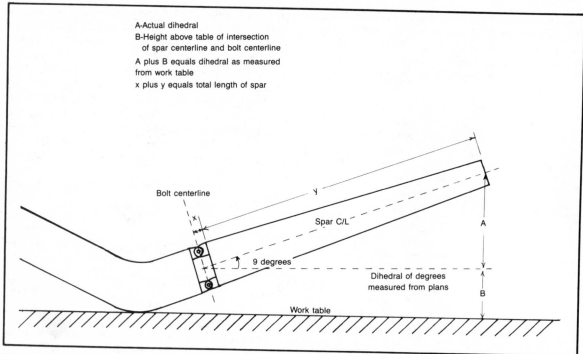

A-Actual dihedral
B-Height above table of intersection
 of spar centerline and bolt centerline

A plus B equals dihedral as measured
from work table

x plus y equals total length of spar

Bolt centerline

Spar C/L

9 degrees

A

Dihedral of degrees
measured from plans

B

Work table

Fig. 16-1. Setting dihedral.

Correcting Dihedral and Incidence Problems

When these bushings are in place, attach the wing fittings to the outer spars, and once again pin the complete assembly to the inner spars. Tack the tip rib back in place, and recheck all levelness and all measurements to see if they are still correct. If both the dihedral and incidence are off, correct the dihedral first, then work on readjusting the incidence. The dihedral is corrected by moving the front outer spar, which of course will necessitate a similar change in the rear spar, if dihedral was the only problem. *Do not* enlarge the holes through the spar to accomplish this, because a serious weakening of this critical assembly would result.

Remove both upper fittings of the front outer spar, weld the spar mounting holes shut, and then grind the excess weld from the faces of these fittings to make them smooth again. This welding and grinding operation should only be done by an experienced A & P mechanic. This is not a job for the usual first-time builder, since too many undesirable problems could develop if it is not done properly. Pin both upper fittings to the main spar fittings and reaccomplish the table and aircraft leveling procedures. Block up the front spar to obtain the proper dihedral, and clamp just the rear upper fitting in place

using the guidelines. Recheck levelness and the dihedral measurement, after which the drill is pushed through the compression bushings from the front side of the spar until it hits the fitting, then drill the new holes. Put mounting bolts in these holes to keep everything in place while the clamps are removed and the front upper fitting is rotated into place along the guidelines. Clamp everything down securely, remove the bolts, push the drill through the existing holes from the back side of the spar, and drill the front fittings.

Alternate Method for Outer Spars

If space is not a problem, there is an alternate method for setting up the frame and attaching the outer spars. However, as mentioned earlier, this will require the area of a two-car garage as a minimum. The advantage of this procedure is that it allows both outer wing panels to be attached at the same time. This will result in less variance in the measurements on one side as compared to those on the other, since the center section does not have to be moved.

This method requires the installation of four vertical posts from the floor to the ceiling of the shop. These are arranged in a pattern that will allow the entire airframe to be supported by clamping the inner spars to the posts. Naturally, these should be positioned so that they are as close to the true vertical as possible. Clamp the fuselage frame in place, and level in both directions. Use sawhorses or other posts to support the outer spars while setting the dihedral and incidence. Establish a *level* reference line on the posts from which to take measurements, and from then on, the procedure is the same as that described above.

If space is not a problem, about the the only drawback to this setup is the time it takes to put in the posts. Also, if the shop floor is concrete, some method of securing the lower ends of the posts with lag bolt anchors will have to be devised.

Your tour on Heartbreak Hill isn't over yet, because the next item on the agenda is the installation of the landing gear. The following chapter will detail one such procedure for this major phase of the project, as well as covering the retract mechanism, wheels, tailwheel, gear door close mechanism, and gear retract motor.

Chapter 17

Landing Gear and Retract System

An operable retract system for the Corsair requires that a few changes be made in the basic geometry of the landing gear. One of the most important deviations from the plans is moving the attach point for the retract knuckle arm to further down on the strut. This of course requires that the upper strut be longer than called for in the drawings, which in turn necessitates lengthening the lower knuckle arms. The key dimensions of this revised system are shown in Fig. 17-1. This longer upper strut, however, does not increase the overall length of the landing gear. It just amounts to more of the lower strut being covered in order to achieve a workable retract mechanism.

Any one of the many problems that can—and most probably *will*—occur during the installation of the landing gear and retract system may necessitate corrective action that alters the geometry of the retraction mechanism. For example, if it becomes necessary to change the size of the landing gear mounting brackets (by means of a procedure that will be described later), it is obvious that this will change the dimensions shown in Fig. 17-1. The measurements that will be particularly affected here would be the length of the lower knuckle arm and the distance from the torque tube to the centerline of the retract shaft.

However, the measurement that is the key to success in this arrangement remains unchanged—that of the at-

tach point on the gear strut up to the retract shaft. In reality, the final length of the lower knuckle arms cannot be determined until all modifications and adjustments have been made to the landing gear, and you have a completely operable retract system. Once this is achieved, and the gear is plumbed to make sure that it is parallel to the spar face, the size of these lower arms must be altered to retain this alignment. New, longer arms may be needed, or the existing arms might have to shortened to line the gear up properly; however, small, final adjustments can be made with the rod end bearings.

If someone is building the metal components of your gear and retract system, be sure to mark all the changes on the plans before he starts work. The checks made later on will also require an assembled wheel, consisting of at least the hub, rims, spacer, bearings, tire, and tube. These will be needed to establish the proper clearance between the retracted wheel and the truss framework, and therefore should be ordered well beforehand.

Gear Mounting Brackets

Similar to the wing fittings, the mounting brackets for the landing gear should be drilled as a set for the gear retract shaft. Line up each pair carefully, clamp them to-

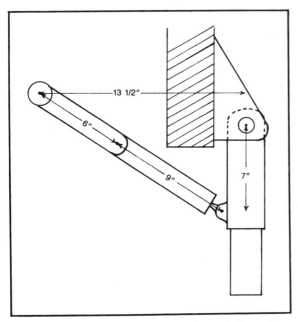

Fig. 17-1. Schematic of gear attach and retract dimensions.

gether, and drill this large hole in both as a single operation. Do not drill the four 1/4-inch mounting holes in the bracket at this time. Draw lines on the front main wing fittings that go through the center of the four holes that will be used to mount each of the gear brackets. These lines should extend from the top of the fitting to the bottom.

Taking only one side at a time, position a bracket over each line so that the face to be bolted to the fitting is centered laterally over the line. Level the airplane in both directions and temporarily install the retract shaft in the mounting brackets. Then, using a level that will fit inside the brackets, check to see if the shaft is level. If it is not, move one or both of the brackets to correct this situation.

When making these adjustments, remember to average out the moves between the brackets so that neither is moved to an extreme position. If this were to happen, there might not be enough metal between the mounting hole and the edge of the bracket, resulting in less-than-optimum strength in this *very* critical assembly.

There is another reason for averaging out the adjustments if these brackets have to be moved to level the retract shaft. If there is even a little play between the shaft and the holes in the brackets, it is possible for the shaft to be level while the brackets are not aligned with the true vertical. This slight misalignment of the centerlines of these holes will play havoc later on, when you are trying to push the retract shaft through the brackets *and* the gear strut trunnion.

After all the corrections have been made, recheck the levelness of the airplane and the retract shaft, and the plumbness of the mounting brackets. Also make sure that each bracket is still pretty well lined up over the centerline of the mounting holes drawn on the wing fittings. When everything looks good, drill the mounting holes in the brackets from the back side of the spar, through the previously drilled holes in the wing fittings. The gear mounting brackets are then bolted in place with regular nuts rather than stopnuts. These are used because there is a good possibility that the brackets will have to be removed and replaced a few times before all the dust settles. This same procedure is repeated for the other gear.

Trunnion Mounting Holes

The next step in the process is the drilling of the mounting holes in the trunnions attached to the top of the gear strut. It will be necessary to mount the wheel on the strut for the second set of measurements in this procedure. Level the aircraft in both directions and clamp a strip of wood across the top of the fuselage frame, above and in line with the retract shaft on both sides. This strip should be long enough to reach a point directly over both gear struts (Fig. 17-2).

Using measurements from the plans, locate and mark the center of the retract shaft holes on the outside faces of the trunnions. Drill a 3/16-inch pilot hole at each of these locations. Then suspend the complete gear strut by a 3/16-inch rod through the holes in the mounting brackets and the pilot holes in the trunnion. The rod will be resting on the bottom of the large holes in the brackets.

Hang a plumb bob from the wood strip so that it falls along the side of the gear strut. The string will be parallel to the front face of the spar, and should just barely touch the 3/16 rod holding up the gear assembly. Check the side of the strut with the plumb line to see if the gear leg is parallel to the spar face. If it is not, move the bottom of the strut forward or backward to line it up with the true vertical, and use blocks at the wheel axle to hold it in position.

Next, move the plumb line to the front of the strut to check that it is not tilted in or out. Mark the center of the retract shaft as a reference point, in front of which the plumb line should pass. If some adjustment is required here, one or the other of the pilot holes in the trunnions must be enlarged to align the gear with the vertical in this dimension.

Recheck levelness and plumbness all around, begin-

Fig. 17-2. Setup for aligning gear struts with a plumb bob.

By this time you have probably found that the cutout in the spar for the gear strut is not the easiest place in the world to check for clearances between the trunnion and the wood. Using a trouble light on the opposite side of the area you are interested in helps considerably. However, because of the restrictions to seeing the space between the parts clearly, this is not the perfect answer to finding out where the high spots in the wood are located. This is particularly true when there is just one small point that is preventing the gear from retracting fully.

An easy solution to this dilemma is to copy a technique used by dentists, when they are finalizing the surface of a new filling, to ensure that it meshes with those on the opposing tooth. Cut out a small square of carbon paper large enough to cover the undersurface of the notch in the spar. Place the carbon side of the paper next to the wood, and fold the gear up into the well as far as it will go. Then bang the gear against the upstops two or three times, after which it is put in the full down position. (As

ning with the aircraft. Then, working through the large holes in the gear mounting brackets, make short marks on each outside face of the trunnions at both ends of the horizontal diameter of the large hole (Fig. 17-3). Then fold the gear with the wheel and tire installed into the full retracted position. The gear will have to be supported here by wedging a board beneath it, or by using a rope sling between the trusses. If your choice is the latter, make sure that the rope is tight enough to keep the gear full up.

This position can be determined by making a template from scrap wood that duplicates the curve on the upper edge of the rear spar. The template should extend from the false rib over the inner truss to the end rib on the center section. Clamp these ribs in place temporarily while the gear is retracted, and run the template back and forth over the ribs in the area of the tire. There should be at least a 1/2 inch clearance between the tire and the template to allow for the foam in the upper wing surface. Adjust the full up position of the gear to achieve this clearance. This may require hollowing out the notch in the front spar for the strut and/or grinding off some of the wing fitting on the top of this notch.

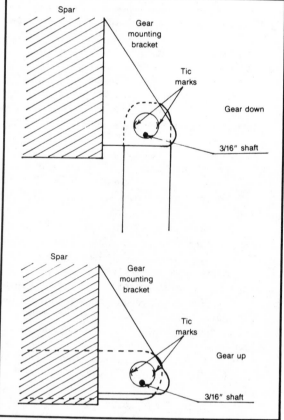

Fig. 17-3. Marking the gear trunnion.

you might guess, it is a lot easier to use this method when the knuckle arms have been disconnected from the strut and rotated up out of the way.) Once the gear is back down, remove the carbon paper and inspect the inner surface of the notch. All the high spots in the wood will be smudged black, and can be easily identified for grinding down with the high-speed hand drill utilizing a round burr.

Wheel Well Clearance

The first thing to check for when the gear is retracted is the amount of clearance between the bottom of the tire and the rear spar. If it is about an inch it is okay, but should it be much more, a correction is indicated that will save you quite a bit of time and effort later on. Excessive clearance here means that the wheel is too far forward in the well, which could present problems during the normal retraction cycle.

If this is the case, weld shut the pilot holes in the trunnion faces and redrill them closer to the top of the trunnion. When repositioning these holes, remember that they will be *approximately* the center of the holes for the retract shaft. Therefore, their new location should not be so close to the top of the trunnion that there will be insufficient metal left after the holes are enlarged. There should be at least 1/2 inch between the top of the shaft holes and the top of the trunnion.

If, however, you should find that you will not be able to move the pilot holes upward and still have the 1/2 inch of metal above the enlarged hole, all is not lost. There is an alternate method available to move the wheel farther back in the well—but, as you might imagine, it is a lot more difficult procedure than correcting the problem by moving the pilot holes. This other method involves removing the landing gear mounting brackets, cutting them apart, and grinding off the rear edge of the piece that contains the retract shaft mounting holes. The particulars of this procedure are fully described later on in this chapter under the heading of Retraction Problems.

With the gear supported in the retracted position, move the wheel to the right or left until it clears the truss assembly on each side by an equal amount. Then make two more marks on each trunnion face exactly as described above. Take the gear assemblies from between the mounting brackets and remove the wheels, which will make them easier to handle for the following operations. Cut out a round cardboard pattern slightly smaller than the diameter of the retract shaft. Center this between the four marks on each trunnion face, and draw a circle that connects these marks.

The next job is a little tedious, but it is best to go slow here because this hole must fit the retract shaft exactly. Using a round file, enlarge the pilot hole in each trunnion face by filing to the circular outline. When the hole is near completion, try the retract shaft frequently to ensure a snug fit all around. If either of these holes is overcut, it will cause the gear to wobble. Also, as the last bit of filing is being done, make certain that the cut is at right angles to the trunnion face. After the two holes are finished, check that the retract shaft can be pushed through both without too much difficulty.

If problems are encountered here, do not force the shaft through by hammering. In all probability, one of the holes is not at right angles to the face of the trunnion, and its edge may have to be filed accordingly. Here again, do not make the entire correction on one side, but take small amounts from both holes until the shaft fits tightly. These holes will be a prime wear point due to landing and taxi loads, so as much supporting material as possible should be left in each.

There is another general rule of homebuilding that comes to the fore when discussing the problem of forcing the retract shaft through a pair of holes that may not be perfectly aligned: In any case like this, where a shaft needs a little extra push to get it in or out of its mounting holes, always place a wooden block over the end of the shaft to protect its edges from the hammer. Failure to do so will probably result in the ends of the shaft being peened outward slightly, which will actually worsen the problem, and cause considerably more difficulty in the long run.

There does seem to be some loss of impetus, however, when using a wooden block, and if you are faced with a particularly "tight" situation, another, more direct approach may be tried. Find a carriage bolt whose head is a little larger than the diameter of the hole in the shaft that is stuck. Place the head of the bolt on the end of the shaft, and hammer gently on the other end of the bolt. Using this technique, any peening of the edges as a result of hammering will be on the inside wall of the shaft, and this will not present any problems.

Bevel Gear Installation

Although the plans call for a full circular bevel gear on the top of the strut and on the retract shaft, the system works just as well with half a gear in each place. Less than half a gear is required to rotate the wheel 90 degrees upon retraction, so why carry around the extra weight?

The diameter of the half bevel gear mounted on the top of the strut should be along a 45 degree line drawn

Fig. 17-4. Half bevel gears on the top of the right main gear strut.

required. If the gear on the retract shaft must be moved outboard for the set to mesh properly, large diameter washers of the correct thickness must be used as shims. These are placed on the retract shaft between the tab welded on the outboard end and the outer gear mounting bracket.

When the gears mesh correctly, clamp the one on the shaft in position and drill a 3/16-inch mounting hole through the cylindrical body pieces of the gear and the retract shaft. After all the final adjustments have been made, this hole will be redrilled and reamed for a 1/4-inch bolt.

Temporarily pin in place the retract shaft, both bevel gears, and the gear strut with the wheel attached. If there is any space between the outside trunnion faces and the gear mounting brackets, large washers should be placed on the retract shaft to fill these areas and prevent any lateral movement of the trunnion assembly.

Then check that the gear folds correctly, and the wheel rotates 90 degrees into position, by pushing on the bottom of the strut. The main thing to look for on this

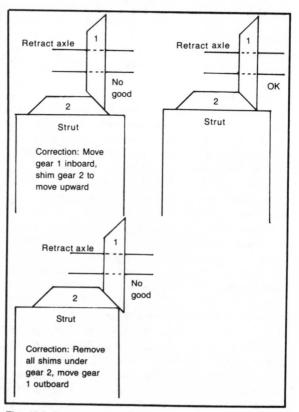

Fig. 17-5. Proper meshing of bevel gears.

through the center of the strut cap. The 45 degrees is measured from the fore-and-aft diameter of the strut, toward the centerline of the airplane, with the front end of the line pointing toward the nose of the bird. The gear is placed on the fuselage side of this line. The top of the half gear mounted on the retract shaft is tilted to the rear just enough to engage the first few teeth of this gear with the one on the top of the strut (Fig. 17-4). These gears should mesh together tightly, because any play here will allow the wheel to shimmy. Make sure that the gear on the shaft is outboard far enough so that the gear teeth are in contact across their full width (Fig. 17-5).

If some play still exists, it may be necessary to raise the gear on the top of the strut just a tad. This is done by removing the gear, drawing its outline on material of the proper thickness, and cutting out a full-sized shim to be mounted beneath the gear. Do *not* use washers for this operation, since they will not provide the overall support trial run is the smooth operation of the bevel gears. Make sure that the gear teeth do not jam or bind through the entire arc of retraction. If any of these hang up, the outside edges of the teeth may have to be smoothed down with a file so that they will engage without problems. There is a good possibility that any number of other difficulties will become evident during this test; the remedies for these will be discussed after the retract system has been installed.

The positioning of the remaining parts of the retract system is determined by the gear box mounted near the center of the fuselage, beneath the slanted floor of the cockpit. One comment on this gearbox is necessary at this point: The large gear on top of the shaft going down through the subfloor has been changed from that shown in the plans. In order to work properly in the retract system described here, this gear is 3 1/2 inches in diameter and has 48 teeth. The worm gear is the same as in the plans.

Bolt this unit in place and cut a metal rod long enough to reach from where the universal shaft attaches to the gear box to the gusset mounted in the fuselage frame. Since the gear box is not exactly centered in the fuselage, make sure you do the long side first. This rod is used to locate the hole for the bearing that supports the universal shaft. Therefore, when marking this spot, be certain that the rod is level and that the end by the gusset is the same distance from the main spar as the end in the gear box.

Drill a pilot hole first, and cautiously enlarge it until the bearing fits tightly. Try the universal shaft through the bearing and see if it will attach to the gear box properly. If it is slightly out of line, the mounting hole for the bearing must be enlarged in the proper direction to bring this end of the shaft into alignment with the gear box attach point. Any space left around the bearing as a result of this adjustment must be filled in by wooden shims epoxied in place.

After both of these bearings are installed, and the shafts are working freely, the former can be epoxied in place. Getting the rest of the universal shafts into the system on both sides will necessitate unbolting the inner trusses so that they can be moved out slightly to allow the coupling to be slipped over the gear shaft in the truss.

Chain and Sprocket Assemblies

The chain and sprocket assemblies are the next items to be installed, and the latter are another departure from the plans. The hand-cranking system is much more efficient if an eight-toothed sprocket is used on the end of

the crank, and one with 17 teeth is installed on the universal shaft.

The positioning of the upper sprocket for the hand crank is very important, because the chain, when finally in place, must be tight between the two sprockets. If you purchase new bicycle chain for use here, you will find that it will "stretch" just a little after cranking the gear through a couple of up and down cycles. This system must be problem-free, and a loose chain could be the cause of serious difficulties at the worst possible time. The stiffness of a new chain is considerable, and the "stretching" does not amount to a full link. Therefore, the problem is to position the upper sprocket so as to compensate for the "stretching," but not to the point where things will be so tight as to make installation of the chain impossible.

If the sprockets are in place and the chain is cut accordingly, the stiffness may prevent its being pulled together sufficiently to allow the ends to be bolted to each other. Probably the best course of action to solve this dilemma is to first make the chain, and then position the upper sprocket to take the stretching into account. Using the plans as a guide, mark the position of the upper sprocket on the skin over the gusset in the fuselage frame. Hold the crank sprocket over this spot and wrap the chain around both sprockets to determine the ideal length required. Cut the chain, place it around the universal shaft, and rivet the ends together. Then wrap the completed chain around both sprockets, stretch it as tight as possible, and draw the outline of the hole to be drilled for the upper bushing. However, before drilling any holes, the center of the bushing should be moved up about 3/32 to 1/8 of an inch. This should compensate for any lengthening of the chain once it is put under load.

When drilling the hole for this upper bushing, it is advisable to make it a little undersized, and then gradually enlarge it with a round wood rasp to the final, tight-fitting size. At times, this bushing takes a considerable load; therefore, it should be seated securely.

It will probably be a little difficult to insert the bushing in the mounting hole with the chain installed on the first few tries. About all that can be done here is to run the chain back and forth around both sprockets a fair number of times to loosen it up a little. Once the upper sprocket is installed and working, epoxy the bushing in place. Then this entire chain and sprocket assembly should be covered by a sheet metal guard to keep foreign objects out of the retract mechanism.

Connect the various parts of the universal shaft together by drilling 1/16-inch pilot holes through the couplings and the shafts and inserting a steel nail as a temporary pin. Do not use cotter pins for this, since the loads encountered in cranking the gear up and down will shear them very quickly. (The colored nails used for wall paneling are excellent for this purpose.) The retract knuckles are then bolted to *one* landing gear strut, and the rod end bearings in the lower knuckle arms are adjusted to make the gear leg vertical.

After all the adjustments that have been made on the landing gear and retract system up to this point, do not be surprised if the lower knuckle arms do not line up perfectly for attachment to the gear strut. One side may fit very snugly against the strut mount, while the other might be wide by an 1/8 or 3/16 of an inch.

Before jumping to any conclusions and filling these spaces with washers, pin the knuckle arms to the strut with a bolt and a standard nut, but without any washers. Do not tighten this nut down to force the rod end bearing up against the strut mount, since the lower knuckle arms should stay in their natural alignment with the upper knuckle arms. Crank the gear to the up position and see what happens to the original spaces between the rod end bearings and the strut mount. If any of the parts involved are in anything but perfect alignment, these spaces may change from the full down to the full up position of the gear. If this does occur, it is pretty much of judgment call as to how many washers will be used to fill up these spaces and yet not exert a binding influence when the gear is in the opposite position. If it boils down to a tossup as to whether a washer will be used in the up or down position, choose the latter. This will ensure greater rigidity of the gear when it needs it most. Recheck to make sure that all gears and shafts are at least temporarily pinned in the retract system.

Retraction Problems

The time for another moment of truth has arrived. Crank this one gear slowly into the retracted position, watching carefully for any binding and a failure of the wheel to rotate. The gearing in this retract system can exert considerable force, so if any problems are encountered, stop the retraction immediately and determine the cause of the difficulty. As the tire nears the wheel well, check for the proper clearance between it and the truss assembly. While the wheel may have fit okay when the trunnions were being marked, it still might not clear the truss while being retracted. The reason for this is that during retraction, the wheel is tilted out of the horizontal, and thus is effectively wider than when it lies flat in the well. Again, if a problem develops between the tire

and the truss, do not try to force things by continued cranking. Note the spot where the tire hits, and the distance it must be moved to clear the truss member. Then crank the gear back down so that work can begin on any retraction problems that may have cropped up.

Problems in this part of the retract system usually involve one or more of the following areas: The wheel doesn't rotate, the tire hits one truss assembly, or the tire barely clears or hits both truss assemblies. The fact that the wheel doesn't turn a full 90 degrees upon retraction is no big thing. In actuality, it is probably beneficial if it stops a little short of 90 degrees when the gear is up. This will allow the long axis of the wheel to line up more closely with the angle of the gull wing at the wheel well. This, in turn, will minimize the need for bumps in the gear doors to accommodate the retracted gear.

Rotation problems during retraction are caused by two things: the bevel gears not meshing properly, or the inner gear strut being too tight inside the upper gear strut. The first can be solved by shimming up the bevel gear on the top of the strut. If it is determined that the bevel gear on the retract shaft must also be moved inboard to make these gears work properly, then a more drastic action must be resorted to,

This fix is the same as that used to adjust the upper wing fittings to achieve the correct dihedral. The mounting hole for the bevel gear in the retract shaft must be welded shut, and the hole redrilled in the proper location. As before, the welding and smoothing down of the shaft should only be done by an experienced A & P mechanic. This is another one of those critical junctures where everything must be *absolutely* correct. If this procedure must be used, expect some difficulties on redrilling the mounting hole for the bevel gear. You will undoubtedly be hitting part of the weld, which makes for tough going, so a pilot hole would be a good idea here.

An inner strut that fits too snugly inside the upper gear strut presents a problem that is more difficult to correct. The gear must be disassembled and each surface inspected for signs of binding. If these can be found, concentrate your first efforts here; if not, then the entire barrel of the upper strut must be worked on. This job will require making a wooden drum with a diameter of a little less than the inside of the upper strut. The drum is about three inches long, and is mounted securely on a metal rod that will fit in the chuck of an electric drill. A narrow slit is then cut lengthwise in the surface of the drum. A piece of medium to fine grade sandpaper is wrapped around the drum, with the ends tucked down into the slit. Using this tool, work over the interior of the upper strut until a slightly looser fit is obtained. Check this frequently, since removing too much metal here will allow the inner strut to wobble slightly.

If it hasn't been done already, it is a good idea to install a grease fitting in the upper strut while these two units are apart. This will allow these surfaces to be lubricated occasionally, thus preventing corrosion from causing rotation problems in the future.

While speaking of grease fittings, it should be mentioned that there are a few other spots on the metalwork in this airplane where they are recommended. These places would be: the bushing for the cog gear in the inner truss that operates on a vertical shaft, the bushing for the torque tube in the inside plate on the outer truss assembly, the lower part of the upper gear strut so as to lubricate between the lower shock strut and the upper strut assembly, and at the tailwheel swivel point. Since these parts are all fairly tight-fitting, this is the easiest and most practical way to ensure they are greased regularly.

If the retraction problem is the tire hitting one truss, the solution depends on the amount of correction needed. When the tire only has to be moved a relatively small amount (about 1/4 inch), it may be accomplished by the use of shims. These are made from .032 aluminum, using the back side of the landing gear mounting brackets as a pattern. One or more of these full-size shims are placed under the mounting bracket that is on the *opposite* side from where the tire hits. As an example, the most likely spot for the tire to hit is the lower part of the outer truss assembly. In this case, the shims would be placed under the inner gear mounting bracket.

Moving the tire any more than 1/4 inch makes the use of shims impractical. Corrections of this magnitude are made to the mounting bracket itself. Remove the bracket from the *same* side that the tire hits. Reference marks should be made on both pieces of the mounting bracket so that the same relation between the mounting holes and the retract shaft hole can be maintained. This bracket is then cut along the weld joining the two pieces that make up this part. Since you are cutting along a weld, expect that this job will be a little difficult, and a heavy-duty band saw is recommended for this task. Then grind off a small amount (about 1/8 inch) of the rear edge of the piece that contains the retract shaft hole. Both pieces are then put in a jig, the reference marks realigned, and the seam rewelded. This entire operation is one where accuracy of alignment and strength of the modified bracket are paramount. Therefore, it is strongly suggested that this work be done by an experienced A & P mechanic who is current and proficient as an aircraft welder.

Before installing these pieces on the bird, save yourself a lot of heartburn later on by checking the weld bead on the face of the gear bracket that lies against the wing fitting. If this bead has any irregularities that project above the flat surface of the rear piece, they must be filed smooth before the bracket is installed. This surface has to be perfectly flat in order to provide a firm support for the entire gear assembly. This procedure moves the retract shaft back toward the spar face on that side, which in turn will swing the tire clear of the truss. Should the tire still hit the truss after this modification, it may be necessary to repeat the procedure. However, if the new correction needed is small, try using shims as described above before going to the trouble of cutting the bracket again.

If it has just been one of those days, when you run the initial retract check and the tire hits, or barely clears, the angled portion of both trusses, your work has just doubled. The fact that the tire is hitting both trusses indicates that it must be moved farther back in the wheel well. Assuming that the strut is of the correct length, the problem lies in either the mounting brackets or where the holes were drilled for the retract shaft in the trunnions. It would not be advisable to try moving the holes in the trunnions by enlarging them and welding over the opposite side. This would undoubtedly create more problems than it would solve. The best course of action is to cut, grind, and reweld *both* gear mounting brackets as described above. The primary thing to keep in mind is to grind down the bracket pieces from both sides by an equal amount. If these do turn out a little unequal after rewelding, the difference can be made up with shims.

Should the worst happen and the tire does not have adequate clearance from the angled parts of both truss assemblies, as well as being offset to one side, the same procedure as just described must be used. However, in this case the bracket on the side where the tire hits must be ground down more than the other bracket. How *much* more will be a judgment call based on the distance the tire has to be moved. But there is one factor that should be considered when estimating how much metal to take off the rear of the bracket piece. Since the truss assemblies diverge toward the rear, some of the necessary correction will be achieved when the tire is moved aft by grinding both mounting brackets. Therefore, the amount of extra grinding on one side may not be as much as that needed simply to swing the tire without moving it rearward. Once again, when everything is back together, small corrections can be made by inserting shims behind the mounting bracket on the side opposite where the adjustment is needed.

If grinding off some of the rear edge of the gear mount must be resorted to, anticipate that the cutout for the gear strut in the spar will most likely have to be enlarged. If the strut had to be moved rearward a fair amount, the front wing fitting may also have to be notched at the top of the cutout to accommodate the bolt in the strut cap. It is probably best to angle the outboard side of this notch so that the bolt head will clear the fitting in the last phase of retraction. If such alterations must be made in this area, don't forget to touch up the affected spots with primer and wood sealer.

After the wheel folds back into the well correctly, crank it to the full down position and disconnect the retract knuckles from the strut. Then connect up the retract system for the other gear and repeat all the checks and procedures described above.

The procedures just talked about will hopefully solve the major problems associated with getting the gear to go up and down correctly. However, before considering this job done, there are some minor adjustments that will undoubtedly have to be made in order to fine-tune the combination of the gear assembly and the retract system.

The first check is made by grasping the fore and aft sides of the tire and trying to twist it back and forth. This is just the same as checking the front wheels of a car for a loose suspension. Any movement here indicates that the bevel gears on the top of the strut are not meshed tightly enough. The fit here must be fairly exact to prevent any movement in the wheel, but not so tight that the gear cannot be retracted. Given the undesirable consequences of wheel wobble during takeoff and landing, a little stiffness in the retraction can be lived with, if a choice has to be made here. If a looseness is apparent between the gears, apply the shimming and movement procedures described earlier to achieve a tight fit.

The next check is to try moving the gear strut in the fore-and-aft direction. If the strut can be moved, inspect both the attach points of the lower knuckle arms at the strut and the hinge point between the knuckle arms. Any looseness in these areas must be corrected by the use of bushings. It would probably be inadvisable to redrill the affected holes and go to the next larger size bolt, since this would weaken the connection and also add weight.

When both gears are retracting properly into their wells, it's a pretty safe assumption that there will be no more modifications to be made to this system. This being the case, all the steel nails used as temporary pins for the parts of the universal shaft can be removed. The 1/16-inch holes are then enlarged to 1/8 inch so that roll pins can be installed. Although these devices fit in place

very tightly, it is a good building practice to also secure them with safety wire.

Before putting the roll pins in the universal shafts, a few decisions have to be made along with a couple of checks, all of which will save you a lot of aggravation later on. Once this shaft is installed from truss to truss, it cannot be removed without an awful lot of work. To make matters worse, this task involves removing the torque tube along with the inner truss—and, after thinking about all the trauma involved in getting these components installed and aligned properly in the first place, most builders would rather take gas than go through that drill a second time. Therefore, *now* is the time to decide whether you want to have an electric retract system or not.

Regardless of the method of retracting the gear, the size of the sprocket on the shaft coming from the bottom of the gear box must be determined. Once you have the numbers, it's a good idea to make a cardboard cutout that will be the same size as the actual gear involved. Slip this on the shaft extending from the gear box down through the bottom of the fuselage skin. If the proposed gear is relatively large, there is a good chance that there will be interference between it and the elevator push-pull rod. If this is the case, some drastic modifications will have to be made in the gear box; if an electric retract system is definitely decided upon, other changes will have to be accomplished in the universal shaft.

The whole idea here is to get your plan of action down pat before finalizing the installation of the gear box and universal shaft by the insertion of bolts and roll pins. If either of these alterations must be made, put the paneling nails back in the shaft to keep things tied together until the work in this area has been completed. Although it is not impossible to reverse your field after the roll pins are in place, it is quite a bit easier to preplan your work on these systems and save yourself at least a little extra effort.

Wheel Assemblies

The first thing to be aware of when starting to shop for the various parts needed for the wheels is a precaution that has been brought to light about certain designs of wheel rims. If possible, it is best to avoid wheel rims whose bolting surface is similar to that shown in Fig. 17-6. There have been reports that cracks have developed in the small semicircles of metal going around the inner side of the bolt as a result of landing loads. The preferred choice in this area is a wheel rim whose bolting surface is a little more sturdy, such as that shown in Fig. 17-7.

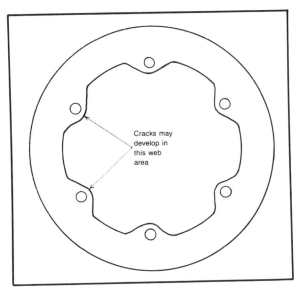

Fig. 17-6. Wheel rim, satisfactory.

Wheel rims for the Corsair do take a little shopping around to locate, and the recommended style may not always be readily available. For this reason, it may be advisable to start looking for your wheel rims well before they are due for installation so that the right design can be obtained.

The buildup of the wheel assemblies is quite straightforward, and follows the plans very closely. There is, however, one additional feature that should be added to each wheel. These are dust covers for all four wheel bearings; they are cut from a piece of felt and held in place by an aluminum disk. The felt and the disks are trimmed so that they just fit inside the two-inch diameter flange around the axle hole in the wheel hubs. The fit should be such that the edge of each disk does not brush against the hub when the wheel is in place and the tire is spun.

The spacers that go on the axle between the strut and the inner wheel bearing also demand some special attention. The proper length for these parts must be determined for each side individually. The way to check for this is to support the strut on the table with the axle pointing up. Put the spacer on the axle followed by the dust covers, bearings, and wheel. Then screw down the wheel retaining nut until snug, but so the wheel can still be spun. You should not be able to wobble the wheel on the axle when this nut is tightened properly. If the nut is at the bottom of the axle threads and the wheel is still loose, a longer spacer is needed. If the bearings and wheel are nice and tight with no wobble, but the retaining nut is not far enough on the axle to allow the cotter pin to be inserted,

the spacer must be ground down a little. Once these spacers are properly sized, label them as to which strut they are to be used with.

The installation of the brake disks and calipers is also according to the plans. As with other metal components, it is a good idea to attach the calipers to the wheel with standard nuts initially. Until all adjustments are made on the landing gear and retract system, the wheels may be on and off the struts any number of times. Therefore, don't use locknuts on these bolts until everything is ready for final assembly. In order to get the calipers over the disk, the bolts holding the thinner outer section of the former will have to be removed. Since the bolt holes in these outer sections also act as locknuts, try to minimize the number of times these must be taken apart.

When it is time to permanently install the wheels on the axles, make sure that all standard nuts are replaced with locknuts. Also pack each of the bearings with wheel bearing grease before final assembly.

Before leaving the subject of wheels and brakes, it would be appropriate to touch on the lines that will run from the fitting on the bottom front of the fuselage frame to the brake units themselves. The first part of these lines that start at the fitting is made from 1/4-inch, .035 wall, 2024T3 aluminum tubing. Bend them carefully so that the outboard end winds up close to the intersection of the inner truss and the lower part of its front mounting bracket. This will be connected to a flex line going to the

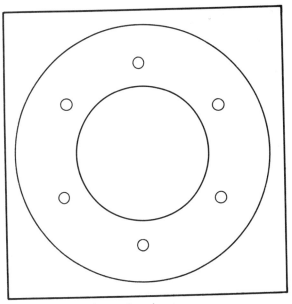

Fig. 17-7. Wheel rim, preferred.

89

top of the gear strut, and the idea is to position it so that a clamp can be placed around the flex line and bolted to the truss or main wing fitting. The purpose of this clamp is to support the hose, particulary while it is being bent during the retraction process. This is best accomplished by positioning the clamp over the metal socket on the end of the hose, close to the nut that connects the hose to the line fitting.

This flex hose will be used for the remainder of the brake line down the strut to the brake unit. Since this will be a relatively long, one-piece hose, its length will have to be determined fairly accurately, because it will most likely have to be made to order. In addition, the points where this line attaches to the truss and the strut must be found by a series of trial-and-error experiments using a Teflon tube or other material that approximates the flex line in stiffness. The quickest way to do this is to secure the practice line in its various locations with plastic electrical tape, and then retract the gear to see what happens to the line during the cycle. Things to be on the lookout for as the line is bent are interference with the aileron push-pull tube and/or looping over the knuckle arms at about the midpoint of retraction. This latter condition could seriously strain or rupture this line as the knuckle arm carries it upward and rearward.

Another factor that must be determined during these checks is how much of a loop to build into the line to allow for the rotation of the lower strut. This loop must be between the point where the line is attached to the trunnion and the upper scissors mounting bolt. Once the trunnion mounting point is found, an easy way to fix the length of the loop is to put the gear in the up position, then clamp the line to the upper scissors bolt. This would also be a good time to clamp the line to the lower scissors bolt and thus finalize the size of the loop required in this area. Once all these points are determined, they should be marked on the practice line so that the clamps can be located accurately when the real brake line is installed (Fig. 17-8). The pressure developed at the brake cylinder is not all that great; therefore, the expensive high-pressure type of hose need not be used for these lines. Rather, a 1/4-inch flex line that has a working pressure of 400 psi would be adequate.

Electric Retract System

By the time all the retract system adjustments have been made, you have probably found out that it takes quite a few turns of the crank to get the gear up and down. An electric drive system is certainly the answer here, and one such approach to the problem is described below.

If you decide to incorporate an electric motor to operate the gear, the upper sprocket assembly, through which the crank works, must be changed. The normal operation of the gear will be electric; therefore, the crank must be made removable so that it won't be spinning around inside the cockpit when the gear is cycling—but it must be available for an emergency manual gear extension should the motor fail. The easiest thing to do in this case is stow the crank in a clip on the cockpit wall, and make it attachable to the upper sprocket by means of a thumbscrew. The modification for the crank and the upper sprocket shaft are shown in Fig. 17-9.

There are many kinds of electric motors that can be used to drive the retract system. The main requirements

Fig. 17-8. Brake line from the truss to the brake assembly. Experiment with the attach point on the truss to minimize any tendency to hit the aileron tube, or loop over the knuckle arms during retraction. It may be necessary to use a clamp about one-third of the way up the lower knuckle arm to better control the hose flexing while the gear is being cycled.

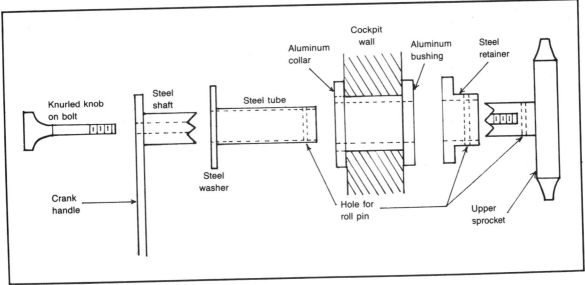

Fig. 17-9. Upper sprocket shaft and hand crank attach.

are that the motor develops a fair amount of torque, and is of the correct voltage for your system. Motors scrounged from wrecked airplanes that were used for the gear or flaps will work very well, if they can be mounted and adapted to your system. Another way to go that is probably a little cheaper is to use the motor that raises and lowers the top on a convertible. The Corsair described throughout this book used a top drive motor from an LTD convertible. The driving shaft of this unit is at right angles to the armature shaft of the electric motor. This allows it to be mounted on the bottom of the fuselage frame, with the driveshaft projecting up to the universal shaft running across the cockpit below the slanted floor. The relatively flat profile of this installation can be housed in the styrofoam around the fuselage frame, with no bulges required in the aircraft skin.

Regardless of the source of the motor to be used for the retract system, all unnecessary metal should be removed from the unit housing before installation. Retain any of the mounting tabs on the motor that can be used for your particular setup. If none are conveniently placed, it is probably easier to bend a wide aluminum strap around the motor to bolt it to the framework. This would undoubtedly be stronger and less trouble than building up mounting pads on the fuselage. Wherever you plan to mount the drive motor, a 1/4 inch plywood stiffener should be glued to the frame to provide better support (Fig. 17-10).

The motor—particularly if it is an auto part—will most likely have numerous electrical connections leading from

it. Before it is mounted on the bird, hook up a car battery to the unit to determine what combination of wires runs the motor the fastest. Also find out those that reverse it at the same speed. Mark all the wires that will be used in your system, than tape over the rest and tie them out of the way.

This brings up another general procedure to be used throughout the project with respect to labeling various parts for connection later. Masking tape is quick, easy and usually satisfactory; however, if a component sits around for a few years, the tape has a tendency to dry out and fall off. This is particulary true with the wiring system in the bird, since it gets handled frequently while being moved out of the way when work has to be done on other

Fig. 17-10. Electric retract motor mounted beneath the cockpit floor before being wired into the system.

parts. To preclude having to retrace a lot of circuitry, or bench test the gear drive motor once again, draw a diagram of all the electrical connections on the motor and number each one. Make sure that the numbers used correspond to the ones used in the electrical schematic outlining the hookup for this unit.

There are probably quite a few places where the drive motor can be attached to the retract system, and you will have to select the one that fits your requirements the best. The things to keep in mind when deciding on a spot to mount the motor are: (1) the gearing mechanism needed to connect it to the retract system; (2) accessibility to the motor, wiring, and gears once the aircraft is fiberglassed; (3) weight and effect on CG of the total package; (4) a method of declutching the electric drive to permit manual gear operation.

This last item deserves a little further elaboration. If the motor you select has its own set of internal gears, it may be impossible to manually crank the wheels up or down by trying to work through this gear train from the wrong end. There is also the possibility that the electric motor may seize, regardless of whether it has gears or not. Either of these situations dictates the need for a mechanism to separate the electric drive motor from the retract system so that manual operation can occur. The possibility of an in-flight electrical failure is another reason for such a device.

When designing this declutch feature, remember one of the basic precepts of homebuilding—keep it simple. This is an emergency system that has to work *every* time, so the less complicated it is, the better. With this in mind, some thought should be given to building a one-shot system that will separate the motor from the retract mechanism, and then has to be reset on the ground. The details of such a system are shown in Fig. 17-11, and Figs. 17-12 through 17-14 are pictures of the complete setup.

Since this is not the easiest of installations, perhaps some elaboration of the procedures involved would be in order. The first thing that has to be done is to cut a one-inch section out of the universal shaft on the left side of the gearbox. Some work can be saved later on in this operation if the section to be removed is located approximately where the rear of the drum will be in the final installation. If this spot is estimated carefully, only the sleeve will have to be cut to accept the key, rather than both the sleeve and the universal shaft.

Next, remove the roll pin that holds the remaining part of the universal shaft to the gearbox, if one had been installed previously. This will allow the shaft to be taken off, to permit the drum and sleeve to be worked into place

a lot more easily. It is also greatly facilitates the innumerable trial fits that must be made in this sequence.

The sleeve is made next, and its length is such that it will overlap the outer section of the universal shaft that goes through the bushing in the cockpit wall by at least an inch, and will extend beyond the front of the bevel gear on the drum by the same amount. The only purpose of the sleeve is to reconnect the two pieces of the universal shaft once the mechanism has been installed. When reaming the sleeve to fit over the shaft, do not make it an extremely tight fit like that required for the gear retract shaft and its mounting brackets. Work toward a comfortable-but-loose fit that will allow the sleeve to be slipped on and off the shaft easily.

When making the drum, it may be advisable to leave a little extra material on the front face where the bevel gear will be bolted. This will give you a cushion to work with, in case some adjustments have to be made once the fork is installed, to achieve the proper amount of travel of the drum. Actually, it doesn't have to move all that far—only about 3/8 inch—to positively disengage the gears. The distance that the fork will move is determined by the moment arms involved in all the pieces of the declutch mechanism from the fork back to the handle inside the cockpit. Temporarily pin all the parts in place and see just how much movement of the drum is possible when the cockpit handle is moved through its full travel.

If the width of the groove in the drum where the fork rides is too great, the latter may not have enough movement left, after it contacts the drum side of the groove, to move the two bevel gears far enough apart to effectively separate them. Since the travel of the fork is limited by the rods and levers involved, the only solution is to narrow the width of a groove. This is done by disassembling the bevel gear from the drum and removing the appropriate amount of material from the face to which it was bolted. However, do not make too deep a cut on this face initially since regardless of the corrections needed, the groove must remain wide enough so that the fork can function as a lever.

Once the groove is optimized, any further corrections needed must be made in the linkages. If you are planning to start out with a fairly wide groove, it may be a good idea to drill extra-deep holes for the bolts that will hold the bevel gear. Then, if the groove has to be narrowed, the holes can be tapped deeper as required.

The arms of the fork should contact the rear face of the bevel gear approximately at its midpoint, and the ends should be rounded across their width from front to back to provide a smooth bearing surface. The inside distance

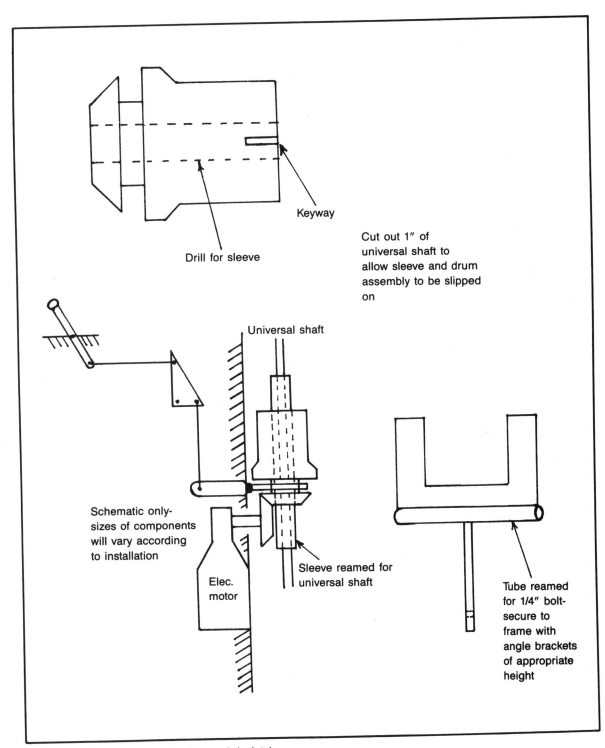

Keyway

Drill for sleeve

Cut out 1″ of
universal shaft to
allow sleeve and drum
assembly to be slipped
on

Universal shaft

Schematic only-
sizes of components
will vary according
to installation

Elec.
motor

Sleeve reamed for
universal shaft

Tube reamed
for 1/4″ bolt-
secure to
frame with
angle brackets
of appropriate
height

Fig. 17-11. Electric retract mechanism and declutch.

Fig. 17-12. Declutch mechanism installed on the universal shaft for an electric retract system. Wooden blanks are used to simulate the bevel gears in this picture. The width of the groove behind the gear on the shaft may be varied according to the throw available with the fork, and the movement necessary to disengage the bevel gears.

between these arms is just a little more than the diameter of the bottom of the groove. Here again, the idea is to have these parts fit together easily while still maximizing the width of each arm for strength purposes. When you cut the slot through the fuselage skin for the bottom arm of the fork, you will probably see that an installation prob-

lem is surfacing because of the half-inch-square frame member running across the cockpit. If the fork is not too wide, this difficulty can be circumvented by reversing the angle bracket on that side of the fork so that it points to the tail of the airplane.

The actuating handle is made in the shape of an L that has been opened up to about 120 degrees. The pivot hole at the junction of the arms is a little larger than the bolt used to mount it. This allows the handle to be moved from side to side, so that it can be positioned into a locking detent in the cover of the handle mount. When building this cover, some thought should be given to making the locking action effective by pushing the handle outboard. This would preclude an accidental unlocking of the handle as you squirmed around in the cockpit if the locking motion was to the inboard side.

Another small safety feature that could be added to the detent is a very slight angle to the notch so that wear and vibration will not cause the handle to slip out of the locked position. The oversized pivot hole does have a drawback in that it contributes to a looseness in the entire mechanism. However, this can be counteracted by compressing a fairly hefty spring between each side of the handle and the wall of the mounting box. As with nearly all such installations, the final adjustments cannot be made until all the components are bolted in place. For this

Fig. 17-13. Declutch shift lever mounted on the cockpit floor next to the seat back. The notched cover has been removed to show the spring arrangement on the hing pin that allows lateral movement of the handle.

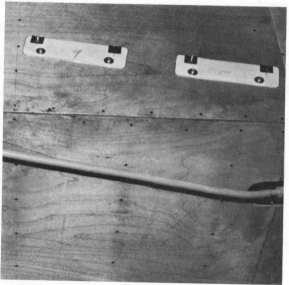

Fig. 17-14. Declutch bellcrank mechanism mounted on the fuselage frame under the cockpit.

94

reason, make sure that the arm connecting the handle to the bellcrank has a threaded end that can be used to fine-tune the system should any changes be necessary. Also, don't forget a locknut to secure everything once it's working properly.

Before putting the drum on the sleeve for the final installation, a light coat of grease would be advisable to make sure these parts slide smoothly. A liberal application of grease should also be put in the groove, since this will be a prime wear point.

Tailwheel Installation

The tailwheel on the Corsair is another area where it is advisable to end up with a little more than the plans call for. The extra feature needed here is a lockable, full-swivel mechanism for the wheel. This replica of the Corsair is short-coupled, which gives it very squirrely ground handling tendencies with a nonlockable tailwheel.

This problem is solved by cutting a detent in the plate where the tailwheel fork attaches to the leaf spring. In the fixed portion of this assembly is a spring-loaded pin that drops into the detent and locks the wheel in position. The pin is raised out of the detent by means of a Bowden cable to a T-handle in the cockpit. When installing the Bowden cable, make sure it is positioned so that it does not interfere with the retracting action of the tailwheel assembly.

The holes in the fuselage frame gussets, in which the retract shaft supports are mounted, must be made very carefully. These holes are perpendicular to the longitudinal axis of the airplane, *not* the fuselage frame. Mark the position of the retract shaft supports and start with small holes. These are enlarged slowly with frequent trial fits until the shaft supports fit snugly, and the mounting plates are flat against the gusset. The bolt holes to mount these supports are at right angles to the frame.

After the entire retract mechanism is in place, check that the overcenter arms break properly, and the tailwheel comes up without any binding. The spot where the folding retract arms attach to the leaf spring is adjusted so that the tailwheel axle is four inches below the frame in the retracted position. It may even be necessary to bend the leaf spring slightly to bring the wheel up to this point.

The next step brings up another change from the plans that is a result of making the large gear in the retract system gearbox bigger. The 30-tooth sprocket using #25 roller chain noted in the plans to actuate the tailwheel retract mechanism is replaced by one with 17 teeth which uses bicycle chain. After it is installed, fit a

length of chain around the sprocket so that the loose ends are even with each other. Line these ends up in the approximate direction they will be when finally installed. Then pull on that end of the chain that retracts the tailwheel until it is in the full up position. Now measure the distance between the two ends of the chain, halve it, and jot this number down for reference later. This figure will be used to calculate the diameter of the gear that will go on the bottom end of the shaft from the retract system gearbox beneath the slanted floor of the cockpit.

The calculations necessary to build this gear start with finding out how many degrees the shaft turns while cranking the wheels from the full down to the full up position. This can be done by making a mark on the large gear attached to the top of the gearbox shaft and seeing how far it travels during the retract cycle. The formula then becomes: $D = 360y$ divided by $3.1416x$, where D is the diameter of the new gear, y is the distance between the ends of the chain determined above with the tailwheel retracted, and x is the number of degrees the large gear moves during retract cycle.

While making the check on the amount of bicycle chain used to retract the tailwheel, make sure that the folding retract arms do not catch on the chain. If they do, or if it looks close, the sprocket may need to be moved outboard slightly, or a sheet metal divider must be placed between the arms and the chain. Do not offset the cables attached to the ends of the chain, since this may pull the chain out of alignment with the sprocket. This could cause the chain to jam or jump the sprocket entirely during a cycle.

While moving the tailwheel sprocket outboard slightly is the best solution to interference in this area, such action may generate another problem. The chain going around this sprocket must act in the plane of the sprocket; any movement outboard may cause some misalignment of the cable with the pulleys under the cockpit floor. If such a situation develops, and there is no way to line up the sprocket and the pulleys while at the same time preventing interference between the chain and retract arms, two other sets of pulleys must be installed. The forward pulleys in this arrangement may even have to be put in separately in order to obtain the two changes of direction required, as well as spreading the cables to meet the next set of pulleys by the gearbox, straight on.

As mentioned earlier, if the gear calculated by the above formula turns out to be fairly large (about three inches in diameter), there is a good possibility of a problem developing because of interference with the elevator controls. Before doing anything to finalize this installation,

Fig. 17-15. Gearbox with the windlass drum attached to the top of the shaft. The diameter of this drum will vary according to each builder's particular installation.

use a cardboard disk as a mockup of the gear to see how it will fit in relation to the push-pull rod. If these parts conflict with the movement of each other, it is probably best to start a plan to follow the alternate procedure described below. The feasibility of this entire process rests on the following check: With the gearbox in position, lower the slanted floor until it is in its normal position. Then, using a trouble light, look along the underside of the slanted floor to see how much clearance exists between the floor and the top of the shaft in the gearbox. If this distance is at least 3/4 inch, enough space exists to use this alternate procedure.

The first step is to remove the gearbox from its mounting. This will require extracting the roll pin from the universal shaft on the right side of the gearbox, and may necessitate enlarging the left side of the hole in the bottom fuselage skin. This will permit the gearbox to be moved laterally to the left until it clears the right universal shaft and can be lifted out. The vertical shaft is then removed and reinstalled with the long end projecting upward.

If the original problem was that the large sprocket interfered with the elevator controls when installed on the bottom of the shaft, the same trouble will exist if you try to relocate the sprocket to the top of the gearbox. Another factor that compounds the problem even further is that bicycle chain cannot be used when the sprocket is on top of the gear shaft. The reason for this is that the space between the aircraft skin and the sprocket is insufficient to accommodate the straight travel of chain needed to retract the tailwheel, plus the pulleys that change the direction of the cables attached to the chain. Therefore, with these given, the use of a large sprocket and chain is just about ruled out.

Working around these restrictions necessitates

substituting a windlass for the sprocket, and dispensing with the chain entirely by using cables for the complete system. Construct the drum of the windlass so that it has the same diameter as was calculated for the sprocket. The thickness of the drum is 3/8 inch, and the plates on either side are made from .063 aluminum. When making the drum, remember that the surface between the plates is flat, not grooved like that found in a pulley. See Figures 17-15 and 17-16 for views of this new assembly. Fit the windlass over the shaft in the gearbox temporarily, and clamp the entire unit in position as it will be when finally reinstalled. Once again lower the slanted floor and check the clearance between the front of the windlass and the bottom of the floor. If the gearbox shaft is not perpendicular to the slanted floor, and tilts fore or aft by a relatively small amount, the back or the front of the windlass respectively may rub against the floor. If this occurs, the problems associated with changing the shaft are too complex to consider at this point. Therefore, the easiest solution may be to block up the slanted floor, or recess it slightly where the windlass hits.

After these adjustments have been made, drill two holes for the cables through the fuselage framework to the rear of the windlass. The drilling line for these holes should be in the same plane as the windlass, and their extended centerlines should be tangent to the windlass drum at the 90 degree and 270 degree points, as viewed from above. Make these holes small at first, and enlarge them as required to prevent the cable from rubbing as the installation of this system progresses. Run a piece of string through one hole, around the windlass, and out the other hole, and work it back and forth to make a preliminary check on clearances. The large pulleys that were mounted

Fig. 17-16. Gearbox and windlass drum installed. This picture also shows the universal shaft cut for the declutch mechanism, over the slot in the floor where the fork will be bolted.

on the belly of the fuselage for the cables coming from the small sprocket called for in the plans should be removed. Then move the stick from side to side and determine the least amount of clearance between the bottom fuselage skin and the elevator push-pull rod. In all probability it will also be necessary to keep the stick in the full aft position when taking these measurements, since at these extremes the clearance beneath the skin is the smallest.

This distance is important since it determines the maximum size of the pulleys needed to turn the cables coming off the windlass back toward the tail. You will most likely find that this figure is not too large—something on the order of 3/8 or 1/2 inch. Choose a radius for the pulleys that will ensure some clearance between the inboard one and the elevator rod. Plan on mounting the axle for these pulleys flat against the bottom of the fuselage skin.

An easy way to do this is to weld or braze bolts with the heads cut off—or short pieces of threaded rod—to a small rectangle of metal cut just wide enough to line up the pulleys with the edges of the drum in the windlass. If this plate measures about 2 to 2 1/2 inches from front to rear, you will probably be able to use the holes drilled for the large pulleys just removed to mount this new assembly.

Draw lines on the fuselage skin leading rearward from the center of the slanted holes drilled for the windlass cables. The string wrapped around the drum can be used as a guide for this as long as it is not touching the sides of either hole. Then take a small block of wood about the same thickness as the radius of the pulleys, and place it between the string and the skin at a point where the string will clear the top and bottom of the slanted holes. Mark this spot on the centerline just drawn. Using this intersection as a centerpoint, draw a rectangle around it that is large enough to enclose the upper half of each of the small pulleys. This is the area that must be hollowed out, using a high-speed hand drill with a burr, until the pulley will rotate freely within it when the mounting plate is bolted in place.

Do not drill the bolt holes in the plate at this time, since some minor adjustments may be needed before the final installation. The best way to do this is to tape the pulley plate in its approximate position and thread the cables around the windlass, out both holes, and over the pulleys. Then have someone work the cable back and forth while you make the final adjustments of the pulleys to ensure that the cable works easily and doesn't touch the sides of the holes. Mark the final position of the mounting plate, and, while someone holds it in place, drill down through

the old bolt holes from inside the cockpit. If the pulley plate had to be moved slightly to achieve the final alignment, it may be necessary to touch up the recess holes to ensure freedom of rotation (Fig. 17-7).

There is one final check that must be made on the windlass assembly before this installation is complete. This involves the placement of the clevis pin used to anchor the cable to the drum in such a position that it does not take the direct strain of the pulling action when the windlass moves in either direction. The idea here is that if the windlass is moving in a clockwise direction as seen from the top, the pulling point will be at the 270 degree position initially. Therefore, for maximum effectiveness, the clevis pin should be between the 30 and the 90 degree position or greater at the start of the movement.

A good method of assuring that such a positioning is obtained for both the up and the down cycle is as follows: Manually crank the gear to the half-retracted position and leave it there. Then twist the windlass around on its shaft until the clevis pin points to the tail of the airplane. A line is now drawn across the mounting shoulder of the windlass through the center of the shaft in such a way as to avoid any rivets or bolts that are holding the parts of the windlass together. This guideline will be used to drill a hole through the mounting shoulder and the shaft for a roll pin that will hold these components together.

When it is time to install the cable that runs between the windlass and the chain from the tailwheel sprocket, there is a definite procedure for putting it on the windlass. After the cable comes up through the floor and first contacts the windlass, it should follow the drum around until the locking pin is reached. The cable is passed over the locking pin and then looped around behind it so that it

Fig. 17-17. Pulley plate mounted on the underside of the fuselage frame. Note that the fuselage must be recessed for the upper half of the pulleys. The plywood patches on either side of the pulley plate are reinforcements for the rear external tank mount.

emerges from the locking pin recess, going in the same direction as before. Continue on around the windlass until you encircle it once and then on until you reach the exit side, where the cable is threaded through the hole in the skin.

You will probably notice that as the cables go rearward from the small pulleys to the tailwheel, they are close to, if not touching, the bottom of the fuselage skin. To preclude any undue wearing of the cables because of this, some Teflon rubbing blocks or guide blocks may be in order. These are simply thin rectangular blocks placed between the skin and the cables to keep the latter clear of the fuselage for the length of their travel. Small grooves can be cut into the block to stabilize the cable more securely, and mounting can be accomplished by using pop rivets (Fig. 17-8).

Despite all the calculations to arrive at the optimum sized windlass that should guarantee synchronization between the main and tail wheels during retraction, there is, as always, the potential for things not working out exactly right. If the windlass does not travel far enough during retraction to bring the tailwheel to the full up position, about all that can be done is to build a windlass with a larger diameter. However, if the tailwheel is fully retracted and the windlass still has a *small* amount of travel to go before the main gear is up, the solution may be a little easier.

In this case, a relatively heavy spring is placed in each cable line at one end of the turnbuckle. This spring will extend slightly to permit the windlass to complete its last bit of travel, and thus prevent jamming of the system. This spring should be strong enough to activate the retract or extend mechanism of the tailwheel without expanding, and only come into play when the tailwheel hits the up or down stops. You may have to experiment with springs of different sizes to find one that is suited for this particular installation. It is suggested that an Ajax Wire Specialty Co. number 10 spring be tried initially, then work up or down from that. These items should be obtainable at just about any hardware store.

After looking over all the procedures and envisioning the vast potential for problems connected with an automatically retracting tailwheel, most builders would ask: "Is it worth all the trouble?" Of course, each homebuilder will have to answer that one for himself, but having all the gear come up together—either manually or electrically—is certainly the preferred way to go. However, if it looks like too much of a hassle, an independent, manual system could be designed to work from a lever in the cockpit area, connected to cables back to the tailwheel sprocket. The biggest drawback to such a device would probably be the requirement for a relatively long handle to get the necessary leverage to actuate the tailwheel retract mechanism. This in turn would tend to create additional problems in an already overcrowded cockpit. But, like most problems in homebuilding, a solution could no doubt be found by the application of some skill and cunning—followed by a healthy dose of greenbacks.

Gear Door Mechanism

The gear door mechanism is yet another area where the plans must be altered somewhat to obtain a workable system. First of all, the plywood gear door bulkhead for the door close actuating device should be replaced by one made out of metal. A suggested pattern for this stronger unit is shown in Fig. 17-19, and the pieces should be cut from 1/8-inch aluminum. These should be trimmed so that they slide down between the truss plates just aft of the torque tube mounted in the plates. Next, make up the two arms that extend from the door close mechanism to the

Fig. 17-18. Teflon guide block for the tailwheel retract cables, to keep them from rubbing against the fuselage frame.

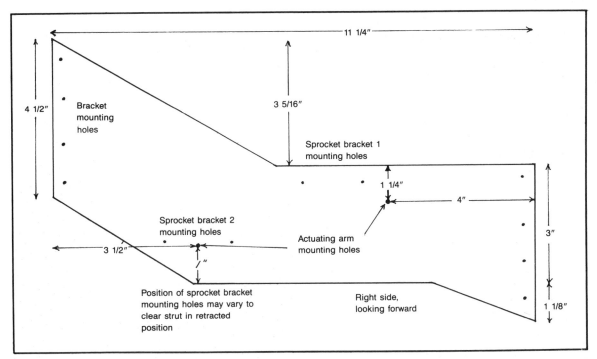

Fig. 17-19. Gear door close mounting board.

rods that attach to the doors themselves. The orientation of these arms is a little different than that shown in the plans. The long outer arm will go through the truss assembly rather than over it, and the short inner arm will also reach to the middle of the truss assembly instead of stopping just short of it.

These changes will also necessitate small modifications in the lengths and/or angles of the lower gear door arms. At this point, only work on what is required to finish off each end of the rod. This would consist of the mounting bolt hole and the eye bolt. Drill the holes in the gear door bulkhead to attach these arms as shown in Fig. 17-19, and temporarily pin just the shorter arm in place. Then retract the gear and position this assembly between the tire and the torque tube. The object of this check is to determine how much clearance is available between the rear of the torque tube and the forward face of the gear door bulkhead, and between the rear of the bulkhead and the tire.

Depending on how far back in the well the tire lies, this may be a very close fit. If this is the case, allow at least 1/8 to 3/16 inch between the tire and the bulkhead. There must be enough room left between the torque tube and the front of the bulkhead to allow the arm going to

the outboard door to clear the torque tube bushing as it operates. If these parameters can be met, mark the position of the bulkhead on the truss plates. Should things be too tight to give the tire some clearance and still allow the arm to miss the bushing, the tubular arm on that side must be replaced by one made from flat 1/8-inch aluminum.

Whatever type arm is eventually decided upon, mark the plate on the outer truss where a slot must be cut for it to pass through. When cutting this slot, do not get too close to the hole in which the bushing is mounted. As a minimum, there should be 1/4 inch of metal between these two openings. The slot in the truss plate should extend between the inside edges of the top and bottom truss members. When finishing this off, make sure the edges of the slot are filed smooth to allow the arm to operate freely.

Pin both arms to the gear door bulkhead and position it between the trusses at the marks previously made. The important thing to look for here is the proper clearance from the tire, and enough room between the arms and the torque tube for the former to work properly. If everything is okay, mark the final position of the bulkhead on the truss plates.

The next job is to make brackets to attach the bulkhead assembly to the trusses. These are bent from .064 aluminum, and 1/8-inch rivets are used to join them to the gear door bulkhead. All brackets should be long enough to reach from the top to the bottom of the particular truss plate to which it will be bolted.

Before drilling the holes for the rivets, make sure that the brackets are positioned to take up any excess room between the end of the bulkhead and the truss plate. Back out the long bolts through the truss assemblies at the rear corners of the plates to allow the gear door bulkhead with its brackets to be clamped in position. Once more make sure that you have all the required clearances mentioned above, and that the assembly is lined up vertically.

Using a long-shank drill, make as many of the holes as possible by drilling through the existing bolt holes. For those that cannot be done by this method, carefully mark where the hole should go on the bracket, then drill a 1/8-inch hole. Then, with a small round file, enlarge this hole in the proper direction so that it coincides with the bolt hole in the truss plate.

Gear Door Control Mechanism

The gear door bulkhead can then be removed for the addition of the remaining components. The first of these

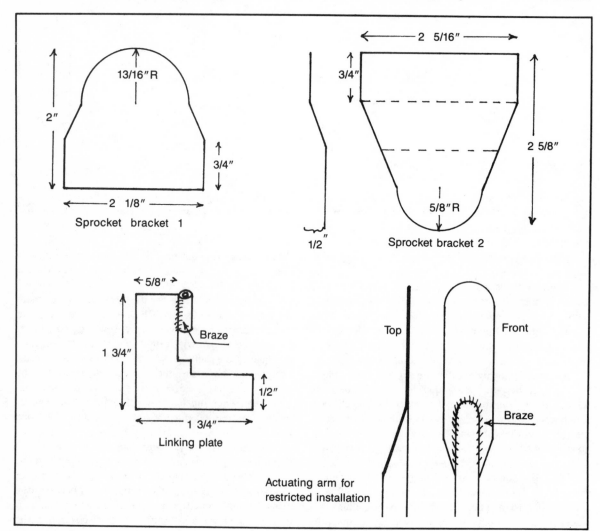

Fig. 17-20. Gear door control mechanism.

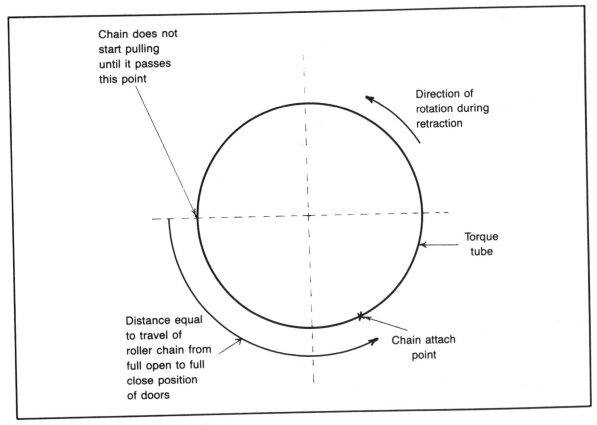

Fig. 17-21. Door close chain attach point.

is the adjustment screw attached to a short piece of #2 roller chain. The adjustment screw goes through the short tube brazed to the linking plate, shown in Fig. 17-20. This linking plate is attached to both of the door retract arms so that they act in unison and in the same direction. It also serves as an anchor point for the roller chain that transmits the actuating force to the door retract arms.

This chain goes over an 11-tooth sprocket attached to the upper sprocket mounting plate, and has a transition block pinned to the other end. This block is merely a short rectangular piece of steel that changes the direction of flex in the chain by 90 degrees. It is inserted in place of one of the links in the chain at a point where it will not engage the sprocket when the gear doors are full open. Position the upper sprocket mounting plate on the bulkhead so that the pull exerted by the chain acts straight up. The other end of the chain is pinned to a small rectangular plate with a hole in the middle for bolting it to the torque tube. The exact spot for attaching this plate to the torque tube is determined as follows:

First, measure how much chain travel is required to move the door retract arms from their full down position to full up. Then retract the gear and also tape or block the two arms attached to the gear door bulkhead in the up position. Set the locknuts on the adjustment screw at about midrange, so that small changes in either direction can be made later on. Stretch the chain up over the sprocket and down behind the torque tube to a point on its lower surface. This point is located by measuring off the chain travel distance, from the aft edge of the torque tube down around the bottom (Fig. 17-21). An alternate way of determining where this hole should go, is to place it as called for in the plans for mounting the door retract cam. In this case, it is 7/16 inch from the vertical axis of the torque tube, measuring aft and up from the bottom.

The open side of the gear door mechanism is a little easier to install. Attach the lower sprocket mounting plate to the bulkhead so that once again the chain acts in a straight down direction. This bottom piece of chain should be long enough to go over the 9-tooth sprocket and extend beyond it for a distance equal to the amount of chain travel measured previously, plus a half inch or so. Be sure that the mechanism is in the "door open" position when making this check.

A short piece of wire is attached to the end of this chain, which leads to a spring mounted at a convenient place on the truss assembly. This spring keeps tension on the entire system toward the "door open" position. Therefore, as the torque tube rotates when the gear is extended, the upper chain is slackened, allowing the spring to pull the mechanism in the opposite direction and open the doors.

The size of this spring depends in a large measure on just how much space is available in the builder's particular installation. By the time the door close bulkhead and the actuating arms are installed, things are getting pretty tight in this area. Before making a decision on where to put this spring, be sure to take a look at things with the gear in the up position. The scissors and the door actuating arms limit your available choices even more.

Depending on where it is mounted, a spring with an overall length of about two inches will fit inside the truss assembly and not interfere with the door actuators. The

use of a mounting bracket for the upper microswitch, such as that shown in Fig. 19-3, may preclude installing the spring inside the truss assembly. In this case, another small bracket may be used to anchor the spring, as shown in Fig. 17-22.

The strength of this spring is pretty much of a judgment call right now, and may not be finally determined until after the flight test phase. It must be strong enough to hold the doors open under air loads and the effect of propwash, yet not so strong that it will require a lot of extra force to retract the gear. A suggestion here is to try the same kind of spring that was recommended for the tailwheel retract cables (Ajax Wire Specialty Co. number 10). These are relatively small, and should not present an installation problem.

Once a clear path is found from the lower sprocket to the spot where the spring will go, so that the line of pull is straight, the attach point will most likely not be right on one of the truss members. This will require making a bracket that will hold the spring in the right position, and also be secured to the truss assembly by one of the existing bolts. If perchance you had to make a new set of the brackets used to hold the trusses to the main

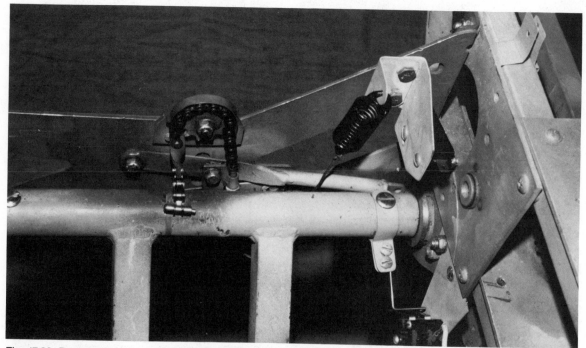

Fig. 17-22. Door open spring mounted on a bracket utilizing the same bolts used to attach a microswitch bracket to the door close bulkhead. The position of the bracket for the spring may vary according to the available clearances in each installation.

Fig. 17-23. Gear door close mechanism installed behind the torque tube. Note transition piece in the chain.

wing fittings, the old pieces provide ample prebent stock from which to cut the spring bracket.

Something to be aware of once this spring installation is complete is possible problems with the lower sprocket bracket. This latter piece is bent forward, out of line with its mounting points, and if the spring you select is rather sturdy, it may cause some bending in the bracket during the door cycle. Should it bend too much, the sprocket moves far enough to introduce the possibility that the chain will not feed onto it cleanly, and a jam may result. Therefore, if this occurs, about the only remedy is to replace the bracket with one made of thicker metal, or add a reinforcing plate to the existing one.

Crank the gear through a couple of cycles after everything is installed to see if it works as advertised. Some fine-tuning may be necessary by moving the locknuts on the adjustment screw, and there will undoubtedly have to be more adjustments made once the doors have been installed. For this reason, it is strongly recommended that the lower door arms be constructed with a threaded section and locknuts, so that these

changes can be accomplished as needed. If it is determined that large alterations must be made in the length of the chain, this can be done by removing or adding a link. See Figs. 17-23 through 17-25 for the complete gear door close mechanism as installed.

After the entire gear door-close mechanism has been bolted in place, a check should be made to ensure that the gear can be retracted with no interference from the newly installed components. As mentioned earlier, the big thing to check for here is adequate clearance between the retracted tire and the gear door-close bulkhead. If this looks close, some thought should be given to modifying the gear mounting brackets as described in the section on retraction problems.

Much like the tailwheel retract system, all the foregoing seems like an inordinate amount of trouble to get the doors to operate in proper harmony with the gear. If you elected to go the route of a manual tailwheel retract, it may be worth considering a manual door close system as well. It also shouldn't be too difficult to combine these two mechanisms to work from the same actuating lever. The

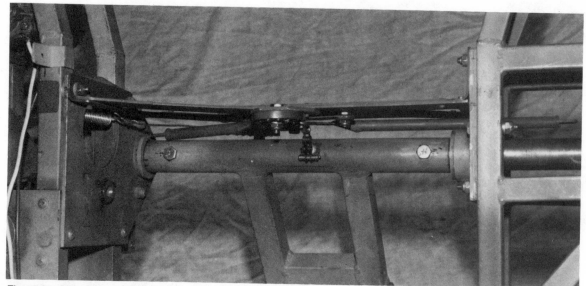

Fig. 17-24. Gear door close mechanism from above, showing modifications necessary to inner ends of door actuating arms, in order to maintain proper clearance between the tire and the bulkhead.

Fig. 17-25. Gear door close mechanism from the rear showing mounting brackets and sprocket bracket.

inclusion of these alternate systems for the tailwheel and the doors will probably result in fewer tedious adjustments and a more positive operation; however, there is still much to be said for hitting one switch and having everything work at the same time.

Although the installation of the actual doors is still quite a way downstream, you should be giving some thought to this area in the meantime. The bottom surface of the wing is curved where the doors will be attached, and the doors themselves may be curved in two directions in order to fit the wing and around the retracted gear. This will preclude fastening a piano hinge directly to the door and the wing.

One possible solution to this would be to bolt a plate at right angles to the hinge side of the door. The bottom edge of this plate would be curved to fit the contour of the door, and would be attached to it by tabs or angle brackets. The same type of plate would be made for the wing. Then the piano hinge could be attached to the two plates. However, a word of warning is appropriate here: Position the hinge line as close to the undersurface of the wing as possible to minimize the gap that will be required between the door and the wing. This gap is necessary because the hinge line is not on the surface, and the door and the wing surface will overlap in the "door open" position.

Another approach to this problem may be to use off-set hinges, similar to the design found on car doors. This method offers an advantage over the one previously discussed in that no gap is necessary between the door and the wing skin. The hinges that fit on the wing in this setup are longer than those on the doors, and this feature will allow the door edge to fold up inside the wing as the door opens. Using this type of hinge system permits a better-fitting and better-looking gear door installation.

Once you complete this phase of the project, you can look forward to pretty much of a downhill slide all the way. The gear and retract system are the major headache on the Corsair, and if everything works okay at this point, the rest is a piece of cake.

Although the work yet to come does have its exasperating moments, the biggest traumas are behind you. In fact, the next topic that will be discussed may even be somewhat enjoyable, since it allows for some creativity on your part. The following chapter will cover the design and construction of the cockpit interior.

Chapter 18

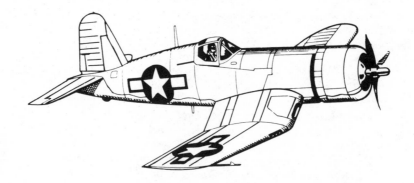

Cockpit Interior

Up to this point in the project you have been pretty much restricted by the plans, and a myriad of *dos* and *don'ts* dictated by good construction practices. Designing the layout of the cockpit interior is one of the few spots where you can just about have your druthers.

There are some practical considerations to take into account, which once again brings to the fore the old adage: "Don't start vast undertakings with half-vast planning." Before deciding on the location of any of the items in the cockpit not fixed by the plans, do yourself a favor and give each one fair amount of think time. Sit in the cockpit and physically determine where things should be so that they are most comfortable for you. It will quickly become obvious that, in the WAR Corsair, there is precious little elbow room—and even less for your legs and feet. During these trial fits, tape a cardboard replica of the instrument panel in place, and if it is available, drop the fuel tank into position. With these temporarily installed, and using something to simulate the cushions, climb back in and see how much of the usable space has disappeared.

As you are deciding on what switch panels to put where, you will most likely find that the narrowness of the fuselage precludes large, sharp projections from the cockpit walls. This is particularly true in the area around the main spar through which your legs will go when get-

ting in and out of the bird, and where your knees will rest during flight. Another factor to consider when placing switch panels is the possibility of their interfering with a rapid egress from the airplane in case of an emergency. When thinking about using the cockpit walls above your knees, be sure to determine just how much of this area will be obscured from your vision by the bottom of the instrument panel.

After all the exceptions and caveats have been considered, the most practical location for switch panels, the throttle quadrant, and circuit breaker panels is somewhere between your hips and your knees, preferably favoring the latter. Things that are used more frequently—such as battery, generator, and fuel switches—should be located in easier-to-reach positions than those used less often, such as circuit breakers. Also remember that the mechanisms used to connect the throttle quadrant to the engine must be placed along the left cockpit wall, so don't plan on installing anything along their route.

Rudder Cable Covers

Looking at the covers for the rudder cables first, you will note that the plans call for plastic tubes supported by Adel clamps for this job. These will work okay, but this

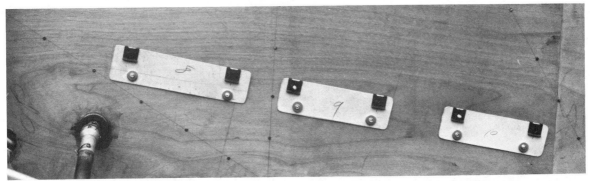

Fig. 18-1. Mounting plates with Tinnerman nuts for cockpit side panels, pop riveted to the fuselage skin.

is all they can be used for. Something to think about that is a little more functional (and a lot more aesthetic) is a set of cable covers bent out of sheet metal in the form of cockpit subpanels. These covers can then be used to mount circuit breakers, fuse holders, phone jacks, or other items that are not needed frequently. Since building these subpanels is another example of numerous trial fits being the name of the game, construct a posterboard mockup of the panel for each side. These are made by cutting out a pattern for each surface of the panel and taping them together with masking tape. Don't forget to include a piece on either side at least a half inch wide to be used for a mounting flange. The masking tape seams of these patterns allow them to be folded easily for the trial fits, which in turn gives you a realistic idea of how the finished product will look.

Before cutting any metal, tape these mockups in place and work the rudder pedals back and forth to see if the cables are rubbing. If everything is free and clear, unfold the pattern, lay it on a sheet of .032 aluminum, and draw the outline of the part to be made. Mark all bending lines on the appropriate side of the piece, and bend to shape using a bending brake.

Position the finished panels in place and once again check that they do not interfere with the rudder cables. Tape them to the floor and walls, and drill mounting holes through the metal flange and the cockpit wall. Undoubtedly you will want to make these covers removable, but attaching nuts to the outside of the cockpit wall with epoxy is not too satisfactory a solution. The plywood skin in this area still flexes enough to prevent a good permanent bond from being made here. One answer to this problem is to use mounting tabs, attached to the outside of the cockpit wall, to carry the nuts for the panel mounting screws. These mounting tabs are cut from .032 aluminum, and should be made long enough to cover two or three moun-

ting holes in the cockpit panel. The width of the tabs should allow for a minimum of 1/4 inch to hold the nuts for the panel mounting screws and should extend at least an additional 1/2 inch beyond the bent edge of the mounting flange. This latter amount will allow the pop rivets used for securing the tabs to the wall to be out of sight beneath the subpanel when viewed from inside the cockpit. Drill the panel mounting holes in these tabs using the holes already drilled in the panel flange as a guide. Slip Tinnerman nuts over the holes just drilled, and fasten the cable covers in place using sheet metal screws with the Tinnerman nuts (Figs. 18-1, 18-2).

The holes for attaching the mounting tabs to the outside of the cockpit wall are done next. While drilling the tabs and the plywood, be careful not to hit the cable cover with the drill. The tabs are then pop-riveted in place.

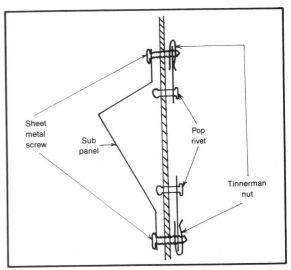

Fig. 18-2. Side panel mounting tabs, end view.

Fig. 18-3. Cockpit interior, right side, showing the panel for vent controls, tail wheel unlock, battery and generator switches, circuit breaker panel, and gear crank in stowed position.

A similar procedure is used to secure the cable cover to the floor. Small mounting tabs about an inch or so long are used to carry the Tinnerman nuts. Panel mounting holes are drilled into the *top* of the double floor, again using the holes in the panel flange as guides. The mounting tabs are then placed over the hole, and their outlines are drawn on the floor. This area is recessed slightly so that the mounting tabs are flush with the surface of the floor. The high-speed hand drill with a flat-ended burr makes this job fairly easy. The tabs are then pop-riveted to the cockpit floor. The plywood flooring is strong enough to hold the pop rivets in this blind installation, even without a washer on the bottom side. The sides of the forward ends of these cable covers will have to be trimmed to allow the slanted floor to be lifted while they are in place.

Switch Panels

There are numerous other switches, vent controls, tail wheel unlock, etc., that must be mounted in the more convenient positions in the cockpit. Since these are more accessible, they will also be the ones that catch on your clothes and bark your knuckles when you are reaching for something else. With this in mind, the best course of action is to mount these panels on the plywood part of the cockpit wall inbetween the fuselage frame members (Figs. 18-3, 18-4). Naturally, the top of the panel will have to be wide enough to accommodate the body of the switches and the wiring involved, and/or the mounting nuts for the push-pull knobs.

With these widths pretty much a given, it would be advisable to consider making panels with the the top surface slanted downward about 30 degrees. This type of design is no harder to make than a rectangular one, and offers three definite advantages. First, it reduces by a lit-

tle the distance that the panel projects beyond the fuselage framing. Second, it presents the switches and controls at a better angle, which allows for more finger room, especially when you are wearing gloves. Third, it angles the Bowden cables attached to push-pull knobs outward, so that holes do not have to be drilled in the structural parts of the fuselage frame.

This principle of not drilling holes in the basic aircraft framework, other than those called for in the plans, should be kept in mind throughout the project. It is very tempting to mount an Adel clamp to a frame member rather than going to the extra work of installing a mounting block or pad. Despite the additional work and time involved, the preferred course of action is to keep from weakening the frame whenever an alternate method is available or possible. The larger holes required for the handles of push-pull or Bowden cables should be avoided in particular,

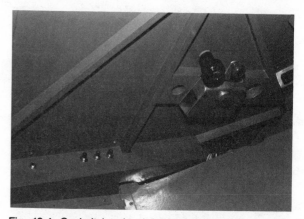

Fig. 18-4. Cockpit interior, left side, showing the throttle quadrant, external fuel tank switch, and circuit breaker panel with microphone jack.

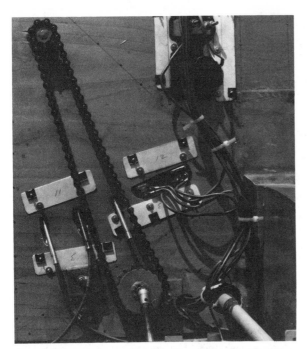

Fig. 18-5. Arrangement of the Bowden cable behind the lower gear retract sprocket, on the outside of the right cockpit wall.

and a slightly modified type of installation, such as that described above, should be tried.

These controls pass through the cockpit wall at such a shallow angle that they are easily positioned along the outside of the plywood to wherever they are needed. This reduces congestion inside the cockpit considerably. If the slanted top control panel is used, there is one area that requires a little caution and planning. Any push-pull controls installed on the right-hand cockpit wall should be positioned so as not to interfere with the retract chain and sprocket. There is enough room for these controls to pass behind the chain assembly if they are secured with an Adel clamp just above the lower longeron (Fig. 18-5). These clamps are only required at each end of the Bowden cable assembly; however, in order to achieve flush mounting along a desired path, some intermediate clamps will be needed. The mounting bolts for all Adel clamps should have a one-inch square backing pad if located near a structure member, and a two-inch square pad if in a relatively unsupported area.

Something else that should be kept in mind when making the patterns for the switch panels is some sort of closure or cover for the ends. If left open, they seem to have an unusually strong magnetic attraction for falling nuts, bolts, and washers. Since there will be exposed

switch terminals beneath these panels, anything falling inside could cause a short.

Instrument Panel Design

The design of the instrument panel is an area that depends almost entirely on the desires of the builder. It can be as fancy or as sparse as you choose, within certain limitations. Common sense and safety dictate that something above the minimum required instruments (compass, airspeed, altimeter, oil temperature and pressure, and tachometer) be included. Among these would be cylinder head temperature, fuel gauge, and ammeter (Fig. 18-6). You will probably have a couple of favorite instruments you would like to work in, such as a directional gyro, clock, artificial horizon, G-meter, exhaust gas temperature, turn and bank, etc.

The only problem with the extra gauges is the limited space on the instrument panel. Obviously, the critical flight and engine instruments should be given priority as far as room on the panel is concerned. These would be the instruments included in the primary flight group mentioned above. Gauges of secondary importance should be fitted into the remaining space on the panel, and any others relegated to subpanels. Some additional things to be considered in planning your panel are the ignition switch, primer, carburetor heat, and gear warning lights.

Plan the location of everything that goes on the panel very carefully so as to optimize all the available space. Sketch out a few different arrangements, then try a variety of combinations to see how everything fits. There are a couple of things that ought to be remembered while working toward the best configuration. The compass

Fig. 18-6. Instrument panel. Lights on the lower right show the gear in unsafe and down positions, and the light on the upper left illuminates when the trim tab is neutral.

should be centered on the panel, and is usually located at the top, or mounted above the panel. The latter arrangement, however, puts it right in your line of vision, which may or may not present a problem in flight.

Since most fighter pilots fly left-handed traffic patterns utilizing a 360-degree overhead approach, it almost becomes second nature to look out the left windscreen when landing, even on straight-in approaches. With this in mind, it might be advisable to locate the airspeed indicator on the top left of the panel. In this spot, it will be right in your field of view as you look at ground references during landing.

Starting the engine can be made a little easier and more comfortable if the ignition switch is on the right side of the panel and the primer is on the left, near the throttle.

Cutting Panel Holes

After the final arrangement is decided on, draw an accurate, full-size layout of the panel. Make this drawing light and erasable at first because, undoubtedly, some changes will have to be made. Place all the instruments face-down on the drawing in their proper locations, and check for adequate clearance between the cases. Some instrument housings are larger than the faces, which could cause problems behind the panel in a tight configuration.

When the drawing is finalized, transfer the measurements for the center of each cutout to the instrument panel blank, and lightly centerpunch. Clamp the panel blank down securely, using pads to protect the surface, and cut the holes for the instruments using a flycutter. A drill press is just about essential for this operation in order to keep the flycutter perpendicular to the surface being cut. As more holes are made in the panel, it becomes a little flimsy, and must be handled and clamped carefully to prevent inadvertently bending or creasing it. Any holes that are too small for the flycutter can be made with a regular drill, then enlarged to size with a round file.

The next job is one of those maddening tasks that seem to require a thousand tiny corrections to get things just right—and "just right" is the *only* way acceptable here, because any mistake on the instrument panel will be much too conspicuous to ignore. Therefore, the holes for the instrument mounting screws must be plotted and drilled *very* carefully. Mark the location of these holes by using the instrument, if possible. If this can't be done, there are patterns for most standard size instruments in the Aircraft Spruce and Specialty catalog. Once the holes have been made, check to see how they line up with the mounting tabs on the instrument. Also make sure that the face of

the gauge is properly oriented in the vertical. A dial that is rotated slightly in its mounting will be very noticeable, and detract from the overall appearance of the panel.

If the holes must be made bigger to accommodate the mounting pattern, consider making small enlargements in a few holes, rather than a large increase in one. What you want to avoid is expanding any hole to the extent that it projects beyond the head of the bolt used to secure the instrument.

Instrument Subpanels

Even after the gauges are installed, you will find that the panel still has some flex to it. A little more support can be gained by running a metal brace from the top rear of the panel to the plywood skin between the cockpit and the fuel tank. This can be pop-riveted to the panel, but will require a stiffening block under the plywood for the attaching bolts.

An even more sturdy panel can be realized by adding another brace on the bottom edge. Rather than using strips of metal here, the most advisable approach would be to utilize a plate whose forward end would be bolted in the same area as the upper brace. The advantage of having a plate here is that it makes it easier to mount the navcom, if you plan to install one at a later date. Therefore, the plate should be wide enough to accommodate the mounting bolt pattern of the type of set you have in mind. Having this option available until you actually purchase your navcom will save a lot of extra work later on, when this area is a lot less accessible. A wide plate in this location will also provide better support for the primer, if it is located nearby.

Other desirable instruments that could not be included on the panel can be mounted on the cockpit wall, or on top of the main spar. This will require bending some sort of mounting panels from thin sheet metal. These would be made up and installed in exactly the same fashion as were the switch panels and rudder cable covers. For easier reading of the instruments in flight, it would be advisable to angle these subpanels about 30 degrees out from the wall. This turns the instrument toward you somewhat, while still not having it project too far out into the cockpit (Figures 18-7, 18-8). The plywood skin behind these gauges will probably have to be cut out to accommodate the case of the instrument, but this also allows the wiring or tubing coming from the case to be routed outside the cockpit skin.

Before painting the completed instrument panel, it is a good idea to go over it carefully with fine sandpaper to

Fig. 18-7. Angled instrument subpanel for extra gauges.

remove any scratches on the side that will be visible.

Gyro Instruments and Filter

The limited space behind the panel just about precludes installing gyro instruments such as an artificial horizon or a directional gyro. There is simply not enough room for the bulky cases on most of these instruments, particularly the latter. However, the vacuum-driven artificial horizon used in a Cessna or a Piper can be utilized. The face is of standard size, but the case is quite long, and comes very close to the back of the fuel tank. The vacuum lines will fit between the tank and the case if 90-degree elbows are used to attach them to the instrument (Fig. 18-9).

The simplest and cheapest vacuum source for this installation is a venturi tube. Naturally, this is not a very aesthetic device to hang on the outside of any airplane, particularly a fighter. However, a four-inch venturi can be

mounted inside the cowling on the engine mount, where the airflow is sufficient to operate the system. Even though the air inlet port on the instrument is equipped with a screen, an air filter is highly recommended. This is easily made from a baking soda can with a hole cut in the bottom for a firewall-type fitting. Inside the can, a piece of fine mesh screen, cut to the inside diameter of the can, is placed over the fitting. The rest of the can is stuffed with glass wool; the plastic snap-on top is drilled with as many small holes as possible, and then put back on the open end. This filter can be mounted under the plywood skin between the cockpit and the fuel tank cutout. In this position, it is out of the way, yet can be reached for changing the glass wool.

Cushions

Cushions are another item in the cockpit that fall within your druthers. They definitely add a touch of class to any homebuilt, and since they are such a highly visible part of the cockpit, some care and planning should be devoted to their constructiong and installation. From the practical point of view, they should be made of material that looks good, is sturdy enough to be stepped on, and is easily cleaned. Also, they should be removable with little

Fig. 18-9. Vacuum line running from the artificial horizon down through the fuselage skin to the baking soda can filter, mounted with an aluminum strap as described in the text.

Fig. 18-8. Cockpit subpanels for clock, fuel shutoff/cold air vent, and gear switch.

111

or no effort, but still secured to the point where they don't slide around the cockpit.

When designing cushions for your bird, there are a couple of things to keep in mind because of the small cockpits common to most homebuilts, particularly the WAR Corsair. Thick cushions will move you closer to the top of the canopy and to the instrument panel. Wearing a back parachute will compound this problem to the point where the back cushion may have to be removed if a chute is worn. A combination seat and back parachute might preclude installing a cushion on the horizontal floor. After sitting in the cockpit for only a short time and working the rudder pedals, you will most likely decide that some form of cushioning over the front spar is a must.

Let's assume that you are of average size, and have figured that everything will fit with both a seat and a back cushion. The slanted floor and the rear floor can be covered with one cushion that has a cross seam over the hinge so that it will bend to match the floor line. Make all measurements with care, and ensure that the cushion extends the full width of the cockpit and up over the front spar. Although it requires a little extra trimming to make it fit around the fuselage frame, it's a good idea to have the seat cushion wide enough to reach the plywood walls of the cockpit. Having the edges fit up against the walls and the rudder cable covers helps prevent small objects from dropping out of sight, and possibly interfering with the control mechanism. This is particularly true where the forward sides of the slanted floor have to be cut away appreciably so that this section will clear the cable covers when it is lifted. The proximity of these open areas to the control system, and possibly the electrical buses, makes some method of covering them doubly important.

The seat cushions are held in place by a pair of Velcro strips glued to the horizontal cockpit floor. The forward ends that go over the front spar must also be held down tight against the spar with Velcro. This is easily done by having tabs sewn to the front of the cushion that hang down just ahead of the spar. These tabs can then be attached to the forward face of the spar with Velcro strips. When positioning these strips on the spar, make sure that they are down far enough to keep the cushion snug against the spar. As mentioned earlier, if these ends stick up, they will invariably catch on your heels as you work your way out of the cockpit. In an emergency, this could present a real hazard. If the interior of the cockpit has been painted before the velcro strips are glued in place, it is advisable to lightly sand the areas where they will be attached so that the epoxy will grip the surface better.

The cushion for the seat back is simply a rectangle

that extends from the top to the bottom of this panel, but not the entire width. With an eye toward giving you a little more elbow room in an already crowded cockpit, it is recommended that this cushion be only as wide as the narrow portion of the seat back. This size will still provide the necessary comfort, but will also allow easy access to the seat belt mountings, and permit you to use the top of the rear spar for hand supports in getting out of the cockpit. Again, Velcro strips are used here to hold the cushion in place.

The padded headrest on the Corsair is more for show than for function. Headroom in this cockpit (and in most other homebuilts) is restricted enough without being further reduced by a headrest large enough to use. But since it definitely adds to the realism of this bird, a small headrest should be included. The material used to make this item is mounted on a 3/4 to 1 inch thick wooden disk, after it has been sewn into a cylindrical shape and stuffed with foam rubber. See Fig. 18-10 for a typical installation.

Another addition to the cockpit that not only dresses it up, but is also practical, is a boot around the bottom of the stick. This can be made from the same material used for the cushions, and attached to the underside of the cutout in the slanted floor and the rear face of the for-

Fig. 18-10. Seat back cushion and headrest.

ward spar. Once again, Velcro strips can be used to hold the boot closed and to attach it all around. Since this piece of material will be a little tricky to fit and mount properly, it is highly recommended that an exact pattern be made beforehand so that the finished product will fit correctly. An extra like this is well worth the effort when considering the potential problems and aggravation of dropping things under the seat while in flight.

Since good-looking cushions add quite a bit to the overall appearance of your bird, some thought should be given to having them done professionally. Unless you or your better half are handy with upholstery, and have the heavy duty sewing machine required, a lot of work could be expended on cushions and floor mats that just don't hack it, appearance-wise. Rather than have a local upholsterer take a shot at it, a recommendation here would be to drop a line to Airtex Products in Fallsington, Pennsylvania. These people do excellent work on custom aircraft interiors, and have the lightweight-yet-durable fabrics and materials needed for aircraft use. They are also quite accustomed to working with the oddball patterns needed for homebuilts. Cushions, headrests, and carpets for the forward floor can be readily made up from your patterns, and their costs are quite reasonable.

One of the drawbacks of building an airplane of this size is the lack of any space to carry even the smallest piece of baggage. There is, however, a little bit of room available to carry a few items in the area behind the headrest. Since the space here is so restricted, and also because of the adverse effect on the CG, it should not be planned to carry anything heavy in this location. About all that should be considered would be a couple of maps, an emergency shaving kit, and a spare set of skivvies.

It would not be a good idea to build a plywood box behind the headrest to hold these items since this would block a major access to the inferior of the fuselage. Your best bet would be to utilize a small nylon bag that could be suspended by cords between the canopy guide rails, or attached by snaps to convenient spots on the framework. This will suffice to carry the few things that will fit here, and being easily removable, will also allow you to work in this area.

After the instruments and switch panels are installed in the cockpit, it's time to start work on the wiring for your bird so that a few of these components can be hooked together. The following chapter will go over some of the things to keep in mind concerning the electrical system and the various items that are included within it.

Chapter 19

Electrical System

The design of the aircraft's electrical system should be based on three things: *safety, simplicity* and *saving weight*. Paramount among these, of course, is safety, and the ability of the system to do what you want it to do. An electrical failure—or worse, an electrical *fire*—in flight is no fun; therefore, don't skimp on the wire size and protective devices.

Another thing to consider is to locate the key components where they will be accessible after the aircraft frame is covered. Undoubtedly, there will be some whose position is influenced by other factors of even greater importance. If this occurs, and easy accessibility becomes a problem, the only solution may be to construct an access panel in the aircraft skin to get at this unit. Some of these will be required anyway, but just from the added work and appearances standpoint, it is best to keep them to a minimum.

Even the simplest of electrical systems involves quite a few wires, and this number increases markedly as you start adding other "nice to have" items. Electrical instruments, fuel pumps, lights, and trim systems all increase the complexity of the system. However, this should not be a reason for doing without these conveniences. The primary thing to keep in mind when adding these extra components, is to plan the wiring layout to avoid large jumbles of wires. A disorganized approach to this system makes it hard to install, even harder to work on later, and also prone to short circuits. Although it may seem a little wasteful as far as the amount of wire used, and possibly a bit over-structured, a formalized routing of wires and wire bundles pays great dividends later on. Use square corners and an orderly arrangement when routing wires from terminal blocks, switches, and instruments into larger wire bundles.

Circuit Coding

Something that really helps in the installation of the wiring system—and results in even greater convenience when working on it after it is in place—is the use of color-coded wires for each subsystem. This, however, requires quite a variety of colors if each system is to be individually identified. These may be available if aircraft wire is ordered from one of the many supply houses, but the only drawback here is the high cost of this grade of wire.

Automotive wire of the appropriate gauge is acceptable for use in homebuilts, is more easily obtainable, and costs considerably less. The only limitation is the lack of more than about six colors.

A possible solution here would be to group similar aircraft systems and use a different color for each group. In lieu of a color for each subsystem or group, the hot and the ground sides of the electrical system should be separately coded. This only requires two colors, but even this basic distinction helps considerably during installation.

Since even automotive wire is not free, and the amount needed for almost any system is appreciable, another factor is added to the process of deciding where to locate electrical components. This deals with positioning these units so as to minimize the amount of wire needed to connect them into the system. If function and accessibility considerations do not materially affect the placement of a certain unit, then put it where the least amount of wire will be used. As an example, if you mount the switch controlling the pump for the external fuel tank on the left side of the cockpit, position the pump itself somewhere in the left wing or belly area of the aircraft. This same rationale also applies to circuit breakers and fuses incorporated in each subsystem.

Realizing that there is no standard electrical system for homebuilts, the one described below should be considered a typical system that can be modified to any extent required. It includes the basics and some, but not all, of the extras. The main purpose of the schematic shown in Fig. 19-1 is to propose a simple, easy-to-work-on installation that has the capacity for expansion.

In order to reduce the possibility of shorts caused by foreign objects and/or loose wires, consider the use of a system with separated hot and ground bus bars. These should be positioned relatively close to each other in an area that is convenient for installation and maintenance. Probably one of the most accessible spots after the aircraft is completed is in the truss area, adjacent to the wheel wells. However, this requires quite a bit of extra wire, and the bus bar assemblies would have to be weatherproofed to protect them from splashing. Putting the buses under the slanted floor almost guarantees a backache every time you work on the system, but is more protected and minimizes the use of wire. A note of caution here: Even if the bus bars are placed in this location, they should be isolated from each other and protected by a thin sheet metal cover.

Along with the backache, there is one more drawback that should be considered before placing the bus bars here. If you opt for an electrical retract system for the gear, it will probably have to include some sort of a declutch mechanism. Also, if the gearbox has to be modified as described in Chapter 17, things start to get quite crowded under the slanted floor. This is not to say that it is impossible to locate all these items here, but these are potential problems that may come up after the bus bars are in place, and thus should be considered at this time. A prudent choice would be to plan for the worst, and position the bus bars in a spot that gives you the most options. This would probably mean locating them as far outboard and to the rear as possible, if you choose to install them under the floor.

Terminal Blocks

Terminal blocks, obtainable as just about any electronics store, are used for the hot and ground buses. Because of the number of wires running to each, it is suggested that the hot bus be mounted on one side of the cockpit subfloor, and the ground bus on the other (Fig. 19-2). Such an arrangement allows for a neat and orderly routing of all wires, and maximum accessibility.

Since terminal blocks only connect opposing wire mounting stations to each other, all the stations on one side of the block must have a common connection to activate the entire block. This will require using either a jumper plate or jumper wires to connect all terminals on one side of the block. Although the plate is more work, it makes for a neater job than using individual wires between each mounting post.

The opposite side of the terminal block is where the leads for each subsystem are attached, but if you have a few more subsystems than terminals, it is certainly permissible to attach them to the jumper plate side of the block. If this is done, just be sure that the mounting screws are long enough to accommodate the jumper plate/wire, the mounting lug, and the lock washer.

Regardless of the type of bus bar system decided on, each terminal should be numbered and earmarked for a particular subsystem in the electrical network. If separate hot and ground buses are used, the numbering system should be the same on each. When considering what terminals to assign to each subsystem, keep in mind the location of the component involved and the available access holes to route the wire to it. Once the terminal assignment is finalized, it is a good idea to tape a list of what systems are serviced by each mounting post near the buses concerned. This will provide a handy reference for easy maintenance later on.

Wire Sizes

Wire size, or gauge, is another area that must be given particular attention. Safety of flight and common sense dictate that this is no place to cut corners, since an airborne electrical fire or a system malfunction could spoil

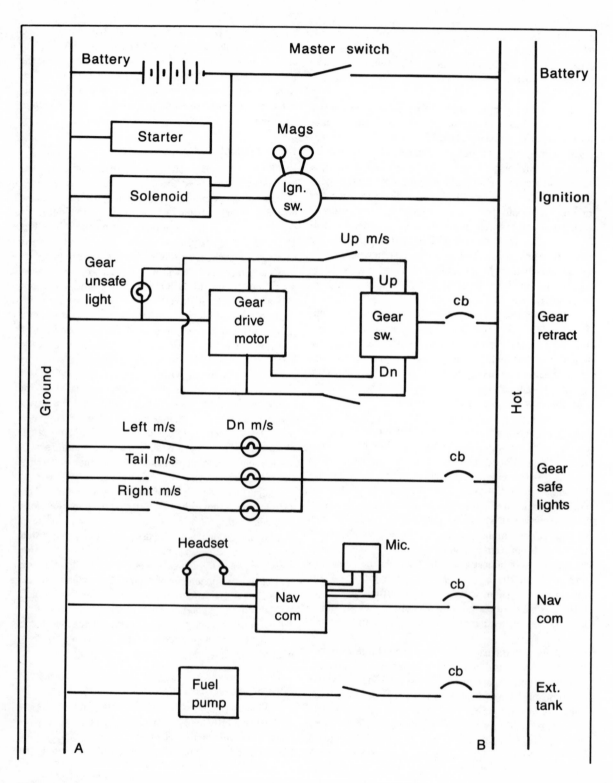

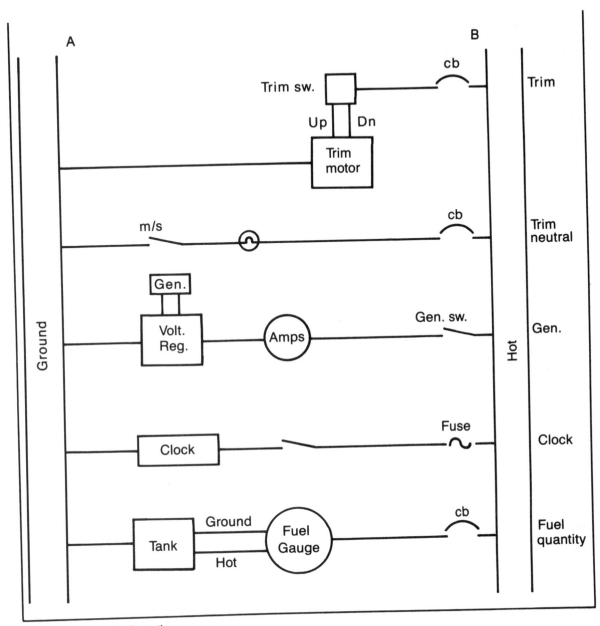

Fig. 19-1. Electrical schematic.

your whole day. Also, rewiring the bird later on to correct a deficiency would be a horrendous task, so *now* is the time to install wire that will handle all eventualities.

Use 10 gauge wire for connecting circuits where higher amperage is expected, such as the battery, battery switch, generator switch, ammeter and the starter circuit. Ten gauge wire is relatively heavy stuff, so keep any lines using it as short as practical. All other circuits in the airplane will use 14 gauge wire.

Given the shortage of space in the cockpit, and for appearance's sake, it is best to route wires on the outside of the fuselage frame around this section. Elsewhere in the bird they should be routed inside the frame for ease of replacement, if necessary. Another thing to remember

Fig. 19-2. Electrical system bus bars—hot on the right and ground on the left.

when planning the wiring routes, is to keep the number of holes that must be cut in the plywood skin to a minimum. Any holes that have to be made should have their edges padded with a rubber grommet before the foam is installed. Whenever possible, run the wires in a bundle, and tie them together every few feet or so to keep things manageable and secure. Cable ties are very handy for this job, but don't cinch them down all the way until you are sure that no more wires will be added to that bundle. *Padded* Adel clamps are used to hold these bundles in place, and to facilitate routing them around other components.

Circuit Breakers/Fuses

Another safety factor that is a must in the electrical system is the protection of each subsystem by a fuse or a circuit breaker. Fuses are cheaper, but are somewhat cumbersome to check and replace in flight—*if* you have a spare available. Circuit breakers, on the other hand, are quite expensive, but they can be reset if the problem was caused by a transient voltage. A repetitive malfunction of this type could eat up a lot of spare fuses in a short time.

As mentioned in the last chapter, a good place to install fuses or circuit breakers is in the small consoles formed by the rudder cable covers. Space is at a premium under these covers, and ensuring that there is proper clearance between the rudder cables and the fuses/breakers, with their associated wiring, is of primary importance.

Something else to consider here is the ability to remove the cable covers once these electrical items have been installed. This can be accomplished by using a little extra wire to connect each fuse or circuit breaker to its component. This extra wire is then bundled and folded

against itself, and secured with heavy rubber bands. This allows it to be neatly contained beneath the cable cover without interfering with control movement.

Fuses or circuit breakers should be positioned in each subsystem between the hot bus and the component being operated by that circuit. The amperage requirements for these devices are determined by the expected load for that subsystem. As a general rule, the following values can be used for circuit breakers/fuses in the systems indicated: gear retract motor—15 amps; radio—15 amps; fuel pump—10 amps; warning lights—5 amps; fuel quantity gauge—5 amps. Considering the expense of circuit breakers, some thought should be given to protecting strictly nonessential circuits, such as an electric clock, with an automobile-type fuse mounted nearby.

After the location of all the electrically given components has been pretty well determined, the wire used to connect them can be prepared for installation. Sections can be cut to the proper length, the connections soldered on, and a label attached to each end to indicate where it is hooked into the system. Figure the lengths of each piece on the generous side so that some slack is available to work around components that will be installed later on.

Battery Box Location

At this point, the lengths of the wires needed to connect the battery to the hot and ground buses can only be estimated. This is because the final location of this item cannot be determined until you are just about ready for the precover inspection. Since the battery is quite a heavy item, its position will have a definite impact on the CG of the airplane. In this light, the ideal location of the battery would be as close to the CG of the bird as possible. This will minimize its effect on the weight and balance calculations, and will also reduce the amount of counterbalance needed in the nose or the tail to achieve the proper CG.

The recommended procedure is to perform a preliminary weighing of the aircraft when all the construction is finished and the frame is ready to be foamed. The requisite calculations for this weight and balance check will indicate whether the battery should be installed fore or aft of the CG to get the latter within the specified limits.

The battery will most probably end up being mounted on the front of the firewall, or just behind the seat back. If it turns out to be the latter, an access panel must be cut in the skin to allow the battery to be removed and serviced. Plan on making this access panel large enough to permit the complete battery box to be removed. This box allows for the attachment of whatever mounting brackets are necessary to secure the battery to the framework. If it is to be mounted behind the seat, some form of stiffener and support will have to be glued to the frame and the plywood skin. The bottom skin has larger lightening holes in this area than do the skins for each side. This pretty well dictates that the battery box will be accessed through a panel in the bottom of the aircraft in order to minimize the amount of plywood that must be removed for this installation. A panel located here will also be less conspicuous, resulting in a better overall appearance.

Whatever spot is chosen for the battery box, remember to make the leads connecting it to the buses long enough to allow the box to clear the fuselage before it is disconnected. Also, the battery box must be vented if you use a lead-acid battery; however, this is not necessary if you install the gel type.

Microswitches

If the landing gear will be operated electrically, and/or cockpit lights will be used to indicate a down-and-safe condition, some form of microswitch will have to be utilized. These items are not carried by all of the larger aircraft supply houses, so a thorough search through a number of catalogs may be required to locate a vendor. If they are not listed as microswitches, look under leaf or roller-actuated switches.

Some break in this aspect may be realized by checking washing machine repair stores. The microswitches that are used in these appliances are quite serviceable for use in homebuilts, and are somewhat less expensive than those specifically designated for aircraft. If you have no luck with the repair stores, try a home appliance parts store. Should you get a blank stare when microswitches are mentioned, try asking for Cherry switches. These perform the same function as microswitches, but are made by another manufacturer. They are also a good bit larger than a microswitch, but not to the point that installation becomes a problem.

These switches can be mounted just about anywhere there is room after the other major components are in place. There are, however, a couple of things that should be remembered when planning this installation. The switches themselves should be mounted on something solid, rather than on a flange of sheet metal that could be bent out of adjustment. Securing these switches to a plate that can be bolted to the truss assembly will provide the necessary rigidity. However, if your particular installation just does not lend itself to mounting the switches on the truss (or something else just as solid), pick out the next

strongest component. If this turns out to be the case, the mounting plate or bracket for the switch should be of a fairly sturdy material that will not bend easily.

At least one of the switch mounting holes in the plate should be a slot that will permit fine adjustments of the action. The switch should also be activated by a spring tab or arm, rather than a part of the structure such as a bolt or a knuckle arm. Microswitches can be mounted in pairs so that the same action performs two functions, such as gear drive motor cutoff and gear down indication. The opposite actions called for in such an installation—that is, turning a light on and a motor off—are realized by reversing the connections on one of the microswitches.

The available spots for mounting a microswitch for the tailwheel are somewhat limited, and the spaces that can be used are very cramped. If it boils down to the fact that the switch must be attached to the plywood skin, pick an area near a structure member where the flex will be the least. Also, use a mounting plate that is a little oversize in order to give the entire installation the desired rigidity. See Figs. 19-3 and 19-4 for a typical installation of microswitches on the Corsair.

Toggle Switches

Toggle switches will most likely be used for two or three of the circuits in any installation. However, because

Fig. 19-3. Microswitch installation on the right main gear. One of the lower switches controls the safe indication on the instrument panel, and the other shuts off the gear drive motor when the gear is down. The large upper switch (known as a Cherry switch) shuts off the gear drive motor when the gear is retracted.

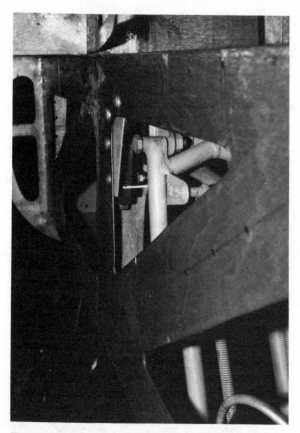

Fig. 19-4. Microswitch on tailwheel that controls the safe indication in the cockpit. The music wire "whisker" that actuates the switch is bolted to the tab on the tailwheel assembly that supports the retract spring.

of the crowded conditions in the cockpit, some thought should be given to preventing the inadvertent operation of these switches. Winter flying gear coupled with the usual squirming around the cockpit that is necessary on every flight could produce some nasty surprises if a switch is unknowingly turned off or on. The solution to this is to install switch covers, or to use switches that lock in position. Covers are okay for switches that must stay in one position, such as those used to control the generator or fuel pumps. The selection of whether the switch is on or off with the cover down depends on how this circuit is used

in normal flight conditions. Thus, a generator switch should be "on" with the cover down, while a fuel transfer pump would be "off." The positioning tab in the mounting hole of the switch cover may have to be filed off to turn the switch around so that it is in the "on" position with the cover down.

Some circuits in the bird should have switches that can be locked in both positions. Examples of these would be the battery switch and the gear up and down switch. Covers could be fabricated to protect these switches in either position, but an easier solution is to use locking toggle switches. These items are quite costly compared to a regular switch and cover, but they provide an excellent safeguard against the accidental movement of a switch to an unwanted position.

Along with their cost, another problem with locking toggle switches is that they are not listed in the catalogs of the major parts supply houses. A convenient way to find out where these items are available is to check at your local library for reference works entitled *The Thomas Register of American Manufacturers* and *Thomas Register Catalog File.* These volumes list all the manufacturing firms in the country and a rundown of the products they make. A short note to the company will usually produce the necessary information on prices and the exact type of locking action available for the different switches.

Like the cockpit interior, the design of the electrical system reflects the needs and wants of the builder, and the varieties are just about endless. The schematic included in the plans offers one solution to the problem, and the system depicted in Fig. 19-1 provides another. Before settling on any particular layout, the entire system should be drawn out on paper to make sure that it will work. This drawing, coupled with your decisions on where the various electrical components will be located, will help in minimizing the amount of wire used, and in positioning the circuit breakers/fuses.

A convenient follow-on to the installation of the electrical system is the fuel tank and all its associated plumbing. The tank and fuel gauge both have electrical connections, so these should be in place in order to estimate the lengths of wire needed for the required hookups. Some of the problems and caveats associated with the fuel system will be discussed next.

Chapter 20

Fuel System

The aircraft fuel system is a relatively straightforward installation; however, it is not without its share of difficulties. Foremost among these is the almost universal problem experienced by builders who purchased their fuel tanks from WAR. Leaks—especially in the seam areas—are a chronic problem with their fiberglass tanks. Therefore, whether you build your own tank from the plans or buy one from WAR, the first order of business is to test it *thoroughly.*

Support the tank adequately on the table, fill it with *gasoline,* and let it sit for a while to see if any seepage develops. If it does, mark the spot, drain the tank, and rinse it completely with water. If the tank was made by WAR, it is best to contact them as to the required procedure for fixing it. The materials used in some of their tanks is not compatible with the usual sloshing compounds. Therefore, tanks in this category must be returned to WAR for repair or replacement. Patching is another solution, but here again you must know the materials used to make the tank to be sure that the patch will adhere properly.

Fuel Tank Tiedowns

Another problem associated with WAR-built tanks is

the proper placement of the tiedown points for holding the tank in place. These fiberglass straps on the sides and bottom of the tank may not line up exactly with the vertical members of the fuselage frame used to anchor the turnbuckles. If this is the case, appropriate additions of 3/4-inch spruce of the proper thickness must be glued to the sides of the frame pieces. After these have been drilled, the plans call for using 3/16-inch bolts to secure the bottom end of the tiedowns.

Try to visualize the difficulties of removing the tank after the bird has been foamed and glassed. Sit in the cockpit and see how hard it is to reach these bolts with both hands to use a socket wrench and an open end wrench. The strain and contortions necessary for this job can be reduced considerably by replacing these bolts with clevis pins of the same diameter. The turnbuckle end and washer are held in place by a spring clip, rather than the cotter pin normally used with these fasteners. An added feature that makes this setup even more handy is a short length of wire soldered to the spring clip, with the other end wrapped around the clevis pin just beneath the head. This keeps the spring clip readily available while working in the blind to remove or replace the tank (Fig. 20-1).

There is something else that is not called for in the

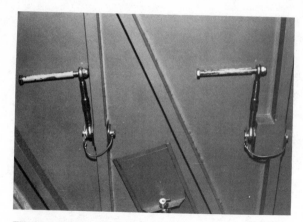

Fig. 20-1. Fuel tank tiedowns utilizing clevis pins and spring clips rather than bolts for mounting to the frame.

plans, but is definitely recommended for this installation. In order to prevent chafing between the tank and the framework, a piece of 1/4-inch thick felt, about 1 1/2 inches wide, is glued on the top fuselage skin around the fuel tank cutout (Fig. 20-2). Use five-minute epoxy to attach these strips, since rubber cement is absorbed too quickly by the felt to make a good bond.

Bending and Flaring Fuel Lines

Fuel lines, which are made from 3/8-inch aluminum tubing, must be flared at both ends to connect them to standard aircraft fittings. There are nuts and sleeves available that flare the end of the tube as the nut is being tightened on the fitting. Naturally, these are the easiest way to go if they can be obtained. If they cannot be found, locate a flaring tool and a tubing cutter to do the job yourself. Although a fine-toothed hacksaw can be used to cut the tubing, the cutter gives a much neater and cleaner edge, and in the long run is a little faster.

If you have never used a flaring tool before, it's a good idea to make a few practice flares before working on the lines that will be installed on the bird. There is a certain knack required to make the flare just the right length and not crimp the tubing in the flaring tool. Should the tubing be a little loose in the tool when the latter is tightened down, it may be necessary to wrap a short piece of masking tape around the tube to keep it secure while the end is being flared. If the tubing is a tad oversize for the tool, it will require some judicious tightening to grasp the tubing firmly without crimping it. An important thing to remember when flaring the tubing that will be part of the fuel system is to put all sleeves and nuts on the line *before*

the second end is flared. Forgetting this results in a lot of heartburn—and wasted tubing.

Another item that makes life easier while making the fuel and brake lines is a set of tubing benders. The coiled spring type are relatively inexpensive and work very well. Some form of bending device or technique is just about indispensable to make the various lines needed for your bird without kinking them. There are many times when the sequence of bending and flaring operations must be preplanned to avoid painting yourself into a corner. If a tube must be bent within an inch or so of an end that also must be flared, do the flaring *before* the bending if at all possible. If the order is reversed, there may not be enough straight tubing left on the end to install the sleeve and nut and still have the length necessary to fit through the flaring tool. Do not count on being able to slip nuts and sleeves around a bend. The sleeves fit the tubing fairly close, and will hang up on all but the slightest of bends.

Fuel System Design

Since the fuel system in most homebuilts is gravity-fed, the design of the plumbing should enhance this method of delivering fuel to the engine. Therefore, make sure that the fuel lines leading from the tank to the gascolator slope downhill all the way. The gascolator should be the lowest point in the system, and the line going from it to the carburetor must be flexible. Naturally, a firewall fitting is used at the point where the fuel line goes through the firewall, and a fuel shutoff valve must be installed somewhere in this line.

This valve must be operable from the cockpit, so the most convenient place to locate it is on the cockpit wall close to the tank. In this position it will require a sturdy

Fig. 20-2. Felt strip padding glued around the opening for the fuel tank to prevent chafing.

Fig. 20-3. Fuel shutoff valve with universal shaft to handle on instrument subpanel.

plywood backing pad for the mounting bolts, and some sort of an extension attached to the valve stem so that it can be operated handily from the pilot's seat. Depending on where and how this extension is mounted in the cockpit proper, you may have to use universal joints on one or both ends. These will allow the control handle to be located out of alignment with the valve, which may facilitate your particular cockpit layout. Quarter-inch steel tubing or rod can be used for the extension, and small universals are available to fit this size, which are held in place by roll pins. As was the case with the roll pins used in the retract mechanism, these too should be safety-wired in place as an added precaution (Fig. 20-3).

Depending on where you plan to locate the carburetor, the arrangement of the fuel line from the shutoff valve to the firewall may have to be altered. If the carburetor ends up more toward the center of the firewall than toward the bottom, this line may have to be angled directly from the shutoff valve to the firewall. This will allow some flexibility in placing the gascolator so that the downhill path can be maintained. If it looks like this is the way things are going to turn out, something else to think about is locating the oil access door in the cowling so that the fuel drain line on the gascolator can also be reached.

There is another important consideration to keep in mind when designing the fuel system: If maintenance ever has to be performed in the forward cockpit area or behind the instrument panel, the only way to get at things in these locations is through the fuel tank cutout. Since this is an eventuality that must be planned on, make life easier for yourself by ensuring that the job of removing the tank will be as painless as possible.

The fuel tank tiedown attachments mentioned earlier

are one way to achieve this. However, even with the tiedowns disconnected, the tank is still held in place by the main fuel line, and the external tank line, if you choose to include this latter installation. One such solution is to run all the fuel lines down the inside of the cockpit wall, and have disconnect fittings in the area of the main spar. But this is unsightly and will interfere with the throttle and mixture actuating cables. Try to visualize the problem of working on these fittings while sitting in the cockpit and doing the entire job by feel.

Therefore, the name of the game is to make the fuel tank detach points as accessible as can be without unnecessarily cluttering up the limited space in that area of the cockpit. A solution that is probably the most workable is to have a flex line coming from the top rear of the tank, down through the fuselage skin to a 90-degree fitting behind and beneath the instrument panel. If the navcom precludes working in the middle of this area, the flex line can be routed to one side of this unit so that the disconnect can be accessed easily. It would also be wise to use a piece of flex hose for the main fuel line going from the bottom of the tank to the shutoff valve.

External Tank

The relatively small amount of fuel carried in the main tank will most likely prompt many builders to consider an external tank system for added range and/or endurance. A working fuel tank and its mounting gear are not too difficult to make, and the design shown in Fig. 20-4 allows the tank to be removed when it is not needed.

The flat plate on the front of the aircraft mounting hardware is drilled to correspond to the bolt pattern for fastening the control stick mount to the main spar. It will also be necessary to cut a notch in the forward cockpit floor and fuselage skin just forward of the spar to allow this component to be slipped up into place. One thing to be cautious of when installing this post is to ensure that it is perpendicular to the frame after it has been tightened down.

When the front mount is in place, temporarily pin the tank mounting framework to it. The tank hardware should also have both pieces of the rear mounting assembly pinned together. Then, making sure that the metal strip connecting the two mounting posts is aligned with the centerline of the fuselage, mark the bottom of the skin where the holes must be drilled for the rear tank mount. This location will vary with the size of the external tank you plan to build, but if the dimensions shown in Fig. 20-4 are used, the attach point will fall just behind the crossmember beneath the hinge for the slanted floor.

Since the marked spot where the holes are to be drilled will be removed in the procedure described below, now is the time to make sure that it can be relocated after the mounting blocks are in place. This is accomplished by drawing a cross on the fuselage skin, with arms four or five inches long that intersect at the drilling point. Then, when the mounting blocks are permanently installed, lay a straightedge along the remaining line segments and redraw the cross, and once more the intersection will properly locate the bolt holes. Draw a two-inch square around the intended bolt holes and cut the plywood skin along these lines to gain access to the space between the cockpit floor and the fuselage skin.

Using the plywood squares just removed from the skin as patterns, cut the rear tank mounting support blocks from 3/4-inch scrap. These blocks will most likely have to be dimpled to allow for the pop rivets securing the piano hinge to the seat in order to get a perfect fit.

The wood sealer on the underside of the seat will have to be sanded off, and the easiest way to get at this restricted area is to use the high-speed hand drill with a tapered grinding stone. Epoxy the blocks into place, and after the glue has cured, re-mark the location of the mounting holes as described above, and drill them accordingly.

Once the blocks are in position, draw a rectangle at least one inch beyond the edges of the hole cut in the skin for the external tank rear mounts. sand off the wood sealer in this area along with any excess glue, and smooth down the edges around the holes for the blocks. Then cut a plywood patch the size of the rectangle just drawn, and

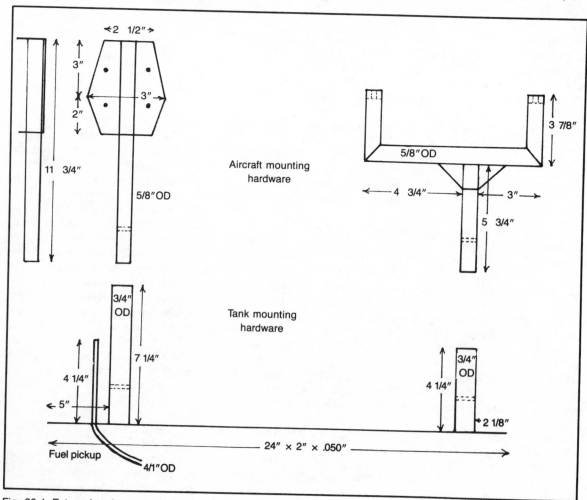

Fig. 20-4. External tank mounting.

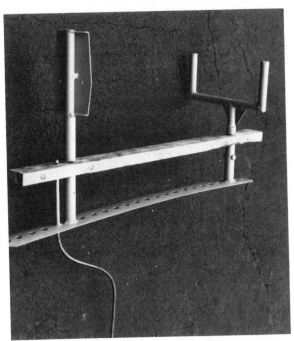

Fig. 20-5. External tank mounting framework in a wooden jig, including the metal strap that is fiberglassed inside the tank, and fuel pickup line.

epoxy in place to strengthen the entire section.

The rear tank hardware is then attached with 1/4-inch bolts going through the seat and the mounting blocks. Be sure to use an AN970-4 washer on the top surface of the seat to distribute the load.

When the external tank is mounted, make sure that its longitudinal axis is parallel to the thrust line of the aircraft. Any adjustments that have to be made can be accomplished by shortening either the fore or aft mounting tube, and/or moving the bolt holes in one of the tubes that join the aircraft to the tank hardware.

The entire tank assembly is attached to the aircraft mounting hardware by a pair of bolts and a fuel line connection (Fig. 20-5). The tank is made of fiberglass that is formed into two halves and epoxied together at the seam (Fig. 20-6). The mold for making the tank halves is shaped from styrofoam and then covered with two layers of fiberglass. When the epoxy for these layers has cured, the foam is trimmed around the edge and then glued to a sheet of plywood or paneling for use as a mold. The cured fiberglass is sanded smooth, and the mold is then painted with hot paraffin before laying up the fiberglass for the tank itself. Be sure to extend the paraffin about two or three inches beyond the edge of the mold on the plywood

so that a flange about an inch and a-half wide can be made around each half. This flange will provide the seam by which the halves are joined together. After the tank is completed, allow it to cure for two or three weeks before using a sloshing compound on the inside.

The major problem with an external tank is designing a reliable system to get the fuel out of it and up to the engine or main tank. Ram air pressurizing systems have not proven too effective. However, a small, electrically-driven air pump can be used to force the fuel up to where you want it. Of course, this method would require a completely airtight system to function properly.

A little simpler approach to this problem is to use an electric fuel pump to draw the fuel from the tank and deliver it to the main fuel system. Using this technique will require that the tank be vented to ensure proper fuel flow. A type of pump that can be used for this installation is an AC, Bendix, or Prestolite low-pressure pump that is rated at 1 1/2 pounds output pressure.

Although this pump could be mounted just about anywhere, it should be placed in a position where you can get at it for any maintenance needed. A spot that is

Fig. 20-6. Mold for the external fuel tank mounted on a plywood board. This particular mold measures 4 feet, 8 1/2 inches long, and 9 11/16 inches in diameter at the widest point.

Fig. 20-7. External tank fuel pump mounted in the left inner truss assembly.

Regardless of the system used, the line drawing fuel from the external tank should have a filter screen attached to the end inside the tank. The fuel pickup line is forced up off the bottom of the tank while the latter is being treated with sloshing compound to keep this material off the screen. It also helps to blow through the line when the sloshing is completed to ensure that the screen has not been clogged.

The fuel line from the output side of the pump can be routed directly to the main fuel tank (Fig. 20-8). This will require cutting a hole in either end of the tank near the top of the arch formed by the curved upper external section of the tank. If you have purchased a ready-made tank from WAR, this method could cause some problems in getting the washer and fittings in place inside the tank, and sealing them properly.

The front end of the tank is better for this hole because it is closest to the filler cap, through which any nuts and washers must be introduced on a length of wire. If the direct line method is used, as shown in Fig. 20-8, an access panel will be required between the instrument panel and the fuel tank so that the disconnect fittings can be reached for tank removal.

somewhat handy and will not require any access holes to be cut is inside the arms of the truss assembly (Fig. 20-7). In this location, the pump is mounted on an aluminum plate, which in turn is bolted to the truss members.

Fig. 20-8. Direct line from the external tank pump to the main fuel tank.

Fig. 20-9. External tank fuel line "T-ing" into the main fuel line coming down from the shutoff valve.

Fig. 20-10. Cold air duct leading from a simulated oil cooling radiator in the wing leading edge to a sliding gate valve inside the cockpit wall that is controlled by a Bowden cable.

A method that is less pregnant with problems is to have the output line from the pump "T" into the main fuel line at some convenient spot. If the main line is routed from the tank, through the shutoff valve, and then outside of the fuselage skin and down the side, an ideal location for the T would be where the line turns toward the firewall (Fig. 20-9). After these are in, the cold air duct shown in Fig. 20-10 can be clamped in position.

The fuel line from the pump that joins the main system should have a check valve installed to prevent draining fuel back down to the pump. This check valve should incorporate a light spring to ensure the ball is seated regardless of the attitude of the airplane. To determine if a check valve has a spring-loaded or free-floating ball, shake it. If the ball rattles around inside, a spring will have to be added. The pressure developed by the pump is sufficient to force fuel back up the main line to replenish

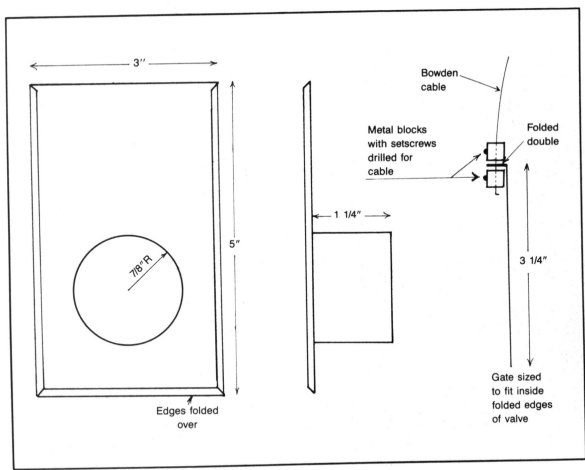

Fig. 20-11. Sliding gate air vent.

Fig. 20-12. Cold air vent on the right forward cockpit wall. Note that the Bowden cable wire is bent over after exiting from the retainer block with the setscrew.

the tank as required. If the fuel line goes directly to the top of the main tank, no check valve is required. This is because the fuel level will nearly always be below this port, particularly if it is in the front of the tank. Thus, fuel drainage back to the pump does not become a problem.

With either type of system, it's a good idea to check the feeding of the external tank as soon as possible after takeoff. When the fuel gauge shows a small decrease, hit the switch controlling the pump for a few moments. If the gauge does not show the tank filling back up, something is wrong with the system and the fuel in the external tank cannot be counted on.

Since the cold air vents for the cockpit were mentioned just above, perhaps some additional information on this system is appropriate at this time. The type of air duct installation shown in Fig. 20-10 varies somewhat from that depicted in the plans. The latter design was most likely

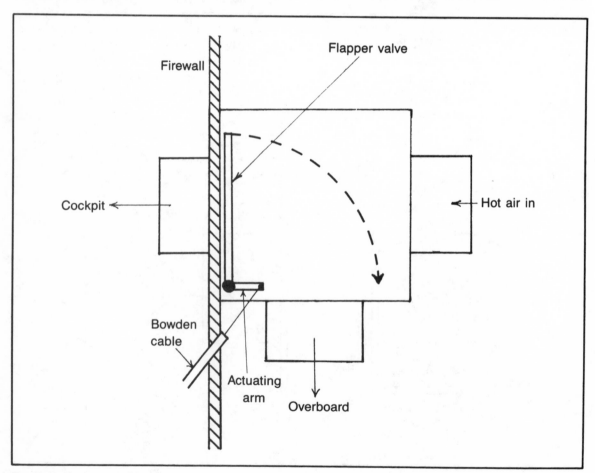

Fig. 20-13. Heater control box.

intended for people who fly in warm climates all the time, since the duct is always open and does not include a device to control the airflow. A more realistic approach—particularly for those who fly year-round in the north—is to incorporate a shutoff valve controlled by a push-pull cable. The details of a relatively simple sliding gate valve are shown in Fig. 20-11.

The valve assembly is mounted inside the cockpit, with a collar extending through the plywood wall to which the flexible ducting is attached. Because the portion of the valve on the inside is quite thin, it will not project beyond the side frame members to interfere with movement within the cockpit. There is no absolute requirement to attach this valve assembly to the fuselage skin. It can be held in place quite adequately by pressure from the flexible duct on the outside and the Bowden cable wire connected to the gate.

Using the flexible duct in this manner requires that the hole through the skin be just big enough to fit the collar exactly. Then, while pushing on the valve assembly from the inside, snug up the flexible duct on the collar as far as it will go and then clamp it in place. The gate valve in the open position is shown in Fig. 20-12.

The system for delivering hot air to the cockpit is a little more complicated. First of all, a heat muff must be installed on the exhaust stack that is close to the location where the hot air will enter the cockpit. The simplest solution here is to cut a hole through the firewall—preferably in the area of the rudder pedals—in a spot that is not congested with other components. At this point, the cockpit hot air control box will be mounted. The box incorporates two exits for the hot air—one through the firewall into the cockpit, and the other into the cowling area to be dumped overboard. The heater box contains a flapper valve that closes either one of these openings while allowing hot air to flow through the other. This valve is actuated by a push-pull knob in the cockpit. The system provides a steady flow of hot air to the heater box, which is vented overboard until cockpit heat is selected. Then temperature is controlled by regulating the position of the flapper valve. A representative schematic of this heater box is shown in Fig. 20-13.

The last major area of basic construction is the engine mount and its brackets, and the next chapter will detail the techniques and procedures needed to make and install these items. Also included will be a discussion on tearing down an engine before it is overhauled, or converted for aircraft use.

Chapter 21

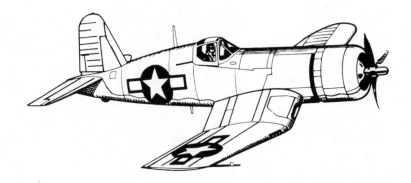

Engine Mount

The construction of the engine mount brackets involves a little more than cutting out the pieces as shown on the plans and welding them together. These brackets must fit the frame as closely as possible on all three sides at each corner in order to provide a very solid mounting base for the engine.

There is a good possibility that by the time construction has proceeded to this point, there may be a few variances from the ideal in the shape and alignment of the pieces forming the front corners. Rather than assume that these corners are perfect according to the plans, it is better to make new patterns for the individual bracket pieces so that these items will be custom-tailored for *your* bird. Even this does not guarantee an exact fit, since some irregularities may creep in during welding. However, the following procedure will get you a lot closer than taking a chance that the ones from the plans will fit.

Engine Mount Bracket Patterns

The first step is to measure on the plans how far the pieces extend from the corner in the horizontal, vertical, and rearward directions. Mark these distances on the fuselage frame at each corner and draw lines connecting the three marks.

If you start at the top left corner, lay a sheet of cardboard or posterboard on the skin so that one edge lies along the line running from the top front cross piece to the top left longeron. Tape or clamp the cardboard in position. Then, while holding it tight against the edges of the frame, draw lines on the bottom of the cardboard along the top left longeron and the top front cross piece to the corner. This will result in a triangle whose shorter sides represent the exact outline of the frame. Repeat this procedure for the front and side pieces, and be sure to label all patterns. This same technique is used to make patterns for the bracket pieces at the other corners.

After the metal parts are cut, just tack-weld them together at this time. Since good fit and alignment are critical with these brackets, once again make sure that they are securely clamped to a heavier piece of metal during any welding operations.

The smaller pieces forming the U-shaped attach points for the engine mount are also welded on at this time. Trial-mount each bracket to see what corrections must be made to ensure a snug fit along all three axes. If there are gaps of much more than 1/16 inch between the bracket and the frame, the tack-weld between the affected pieces should be cut and the seam line adjusted. This is done by heating the edges until they are malleable, then pinching them down by the amount necessary to move the seam snug up against the fuselage frame. This tight fit is particularly important in the area close to the weld lines, because this is where the mounting bolts will go, and a solid junction is required.

Bracket Shims and Mounting Holes

Spaces of 1/16 of an inch or less between the bracket and the frame are probably too small to be effectively corrected by the method described above. However, they should not be ignored, and the best course of action to follow is to use shims. These are made from thin pieces of aircraft plywood, initially cut to the same size triangle as the affected side of the bracket. Before the shim can be sanded to its final shape, the bracket must be temporarily pinned in place.

The important thing to remember when drilling the mounting holes in the bracket and fuselage frame is to ensure that the holes are centered in the frame pieces. With the brackets in place over the plywood skin and the firewall, it is a little tough to eyeball the centerline of these pieces. An easy way of solving this is to transfer the outline of the frame pieces from the skin to the outside of the bracket faces. Remove the bracket from the fuselage and, using careful measurements, draw the outline of the frame pieces on the skin. Don't forget to allow for the thickness of the plywood skin when drawing these lines, and be sure to extend them about four to six inches beyond the actual area covered by the brackets. Replace the brackets on the frame, lay a straightedge along the lines and over the bracket faces, and draw continuations of the lines on the brackets. The location of each hole can then be centered between these lines and drilled accordingly.

With bolts holding the bracket in place, slide the shim under the face with the gap as far as it will go. These trial fits will indicate where and by how much the shim must be tapered to fill the space under the bracket completely. Should the bracket fit fairly well near the corner, and the gap only exists toward the outside edges, the shim will have to be trimmed accordingly. This often results in the inner corner of the shim being rounded off considerably, and tapered down on the belt sander until it is almost paper-thin. When trimming has progressed to the point where the shim can be pushed under the bracket until their outside edges coincide, the shim is ready to be epoxied in place.

When the mounting holes for the lower brackets are drilled in the fuselage frame, you will find that four of them emerge between the cockpit floor and the bottom skin of the airplane. Access holes must be made that are long enough to allow an AN970-4 washer to be put on the end of the bolt, and wide enough to permit an open-end wrench to fit over the nut.

These access holes can be cut in either the floor or the bottom skin, but the former is probably the best way to go. If for some reason the engine mount brackets ever have to be removed, you can get at the bolts through the fuel tank cutout rather than cutting away a lot of foam and fiberglass from the belly of the aircraft. The washers mentioned above are quite a bit wider than the 3/4-inch frame members they will be resting on; consequently, their edges will have to be ground down before installation.

Bracket and Engine Mount Alignment

It is recommended that the final bolting of the brackets to the frame be delayed until the engine mount is finished. They should be temporarily bolted in place so that the exact dimensions between the four engine mount attach points can be used to line up the holes in the mount itself.

At this time the mount attach points on each bracket should have been line-bored to only 3/16 inch, as are the corresponding holes in the engine mount. With the brackets still only temporarily bolted in place, install one side of the engine mount and line-bore all the holes on that side to the correct size. This will allow that side of the mount to act as a hinge, so that the engine can be swung out to work on the accessory section.

After the final bolts are in place on this side, the mounting holes on the opposite side are line-bored to the correct diameter, and the final bolts are installed. When this has been done, the bolts holding the brackets can be tightened down for final installation. This sequence of operations minimizes the chance of small misalignment problems creeping in, which would preclude having a workable swing mount.

Before these procedures begin, the epoxy filler beneath the mounting brackets must be applied. Since the drilling and alignment procedures do take some time, do not use a five-minute epoxy for this job. The epoxy here is being used as a filler and there is no joint involved; therefore, one that takes overnight to cure will not pressure you to do a rush job with the drilling.

In order to keep the epoxy that is put on the vertical sections from running during the curing period, it should be thickened up considerably before application. This is done by adding microballoons or some other filler to the epoxy mix until it has the consistency of soft butter. Another alternative is to use an automobile body filler called "Bondo." When purchasing this item, be sure to get the lightweight variety that uses microspheres as a filler.

After marking centerlines on each, clamp the metal firewall to the plywood firewall and line up the centerlines as closely as possible. Mark the back of the metal where the U-shaped mounting bracket hits, and then cut small rectangular holes for the bracket in just *one* corner. If the firewall is galvanized sheet, these holes may be cut by using an old wood chisel, and having a flat wooden block directly under the area to be cut.

It also helps considerably if similar blocks are placed at a couple of other spots under the firewall for added support. Reposition the metal firewall over the plywood one, with the brackets sticking through the one set of holes. Try lining up the centerlines again, and if necessary, enlarge the holes to make this alignment possible. Then

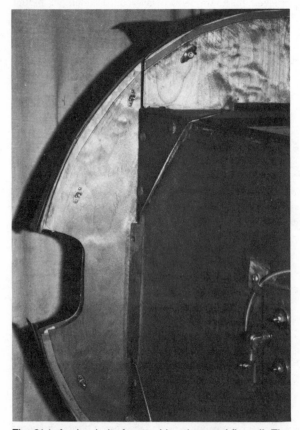

Fig. 21-1. Anchor bolts for attaching the metal firewall. The larger anchor bolt at the top is used to secure the cowl mounting bracket.

mark and cut the other holes in succession, using the same procedure. The final attachment of the metal firewall is accomplished by using anchor bolts on the rear side of the plywood, as shown in Fig. 21-1.

One last thought before leaving the discussion about the firewall: When the bird is finished, there will be quite a few wires, cables, and connections of one type or another running through the firewall into the engine area. *Do not* drill the holes in the firewall for these components until you are *absolutely* sure that their routing has been finalized. This is particularly true of the fuel lines, whose path can only be determined after the engine is mounted. Indeed, the engine will be the deciding factor in most of these cases; therefore, it is probably a good idea to hold off on as many as possible until it has been installed. When you are positive where all these holes will be made, drill them slightly oversized so that a rubber grommet can be inserted to prevent chafing. Another recommended procedure is to group as many items as possible for each hole—especially wires—but do not alter the paths of push-pull cables just to achieve this.

When all of the cables, lines, and wires going through each hole have been settled on and are in place along with the rubber grommets, there is one final step to be taken at each of these openings in the firewall. With a plastic sealer designed for use with wires going through walls in construction projects, completely fill in any openings remaining in the center of the grommet. This product can be obtained at an electrical supply store, and should be used on both sides of the firewall.

The engine mount itself is built according to the plans, but it is advisable to wait until you have obtained your engine before starting to work on this item (Figs. 21-2, 21-3). Having the exact dimensions of the mounting bolt pattern helps to avoid alignment problems in this critical area. If you are using a Lycoming or a Continental engine, there is a good possibility that a small adjustment will have to be made in the design of the engine mount. This will involve moving the centerline of the engine up about one inch so that the carburetor will fit inside the Corsair cowling. Getting all of these engines in the space available is a tight squeeze at best, and may even require making the cowling just a little bit bigger.

In this same vein, the cramped quarters inside the cowling bring to the fore another problem that must be given some thought. This concerns the placement of the carburetor air scoop, and how it can be squeezed into an already tight spot. Corsair builders who are trying to replicate the F4U-4 model have a break in this respect, because this series incorporated a chin scoop on the cowl-

Fig. 21-2. Engine mount temporarily pinned in place.

ing, which will facilitate locating the duct to the carburetor.

There is a rule of thumb that should be observed when planning the installation of the carburetor air scoop. The diameter of the passage should be at least twice the diameter of the venturi in the carburetor. If the design of your engine utilizes an updraft carburetor, a duct such as that just described is required. However, if you use a downdraft model, this type of installation is not necessary.

Another thing to consider here is the inclusion of a method of supplying hot air to the carburetor, regardless of whether it is an up- or downdraft type.

There is one additional item associated with the carburetor that must wait until the engine is installed before it can be done properly. This has to do with determining the exact length of the cables running back to the throttle and mixture controls. The path of these cables should be as free of slack and unnecessary bends as possible; however, this does not mean that they must run in a straight line from the quadrant to the carburetor. The thing to avoid here is trying to make an overly long cable fit by the use of S-curves or a loop.

Run-Out Engines

The engine for any homebuilt is undoubtedly the most expensive item in the entire project. The cost of a new engine is so prohibitive that it is not even considered by most builders; therefore, some alternative approach to the powerplant problem must be found.

The most practical solution used by just about all homebuilders is to locate a run-out engine in the size and horsepower range that is compatible with their pride and joy. A run-out engine is one whose time between overhauls has expired, or is just about to do so. Since these are operable powerplants, they are not exactly being given away; however, their price is considerably lower than the

tab for a new engine.

Naturally, these prices will vary according to what must be done to put it back in running condition. An engine whose crankshaft is probably bent could most likely be picked up for a lot less than one that merely needs rings and bearings. Despite the high cost of major engine components, you will doubtless come out ahead financially by refurbishing a run-out or damaged engine, as compared to buying a new one.

Along with cost, there are a couple of other factors that bolster the rationale for buying a run-out engine. First of all, you know it works, and all of the major service problems and adjustments have already been remedied. Secondly, a complete maintenance history on the engine should be available to give you some guidelines on what to expect in the future.

There is another source of engines that should not be overlooked in your search for an acceptable powerplant. These are engines used to run ground power carts for the military and/or the airlines. An example is the Lycoming 290G. This is a regular aircraft engine that has been adapted for use in a power cart, but does not require too many changes to return it to aircraft configuration. In the power cart, this engine is connected to a heavy flywheel and cooling fan, and to the electrical generator. This extra weight necessitates the crankcase having a beefed-up flange around the front end to strengthen this area. Another difference is that this engine uses only one magneto to power one set of spark plugs. Since this is mainly a stock aircraft engine, there are provisions for these additional items; however, they are plugged or covered by a plate on the power cart version. Engines such as these can most likely be obtained for a lower cost than a comparable run-out aircraft engine. But these added savings may be a lit-

Fig. 21-3. Hinged engine mount swung open to permit access to the rear of the engine.

tle deceiving, because converting this engine to aircraft configuration will require a little more work, and the purchase of the additional accessories. The best tack to follow in locating whatever type engine you are seeking is to go through all the trade publications thoroughly and regularly, particularly *Trade-A-Plane*. Also put out the word on the type of engine you are looking for to the members of your EAA Chapter.

Engine Disassembly

Once the powerplant is on hand, whether it be a run-out aircraft engine or a run-out power cart engine that must be converted, it will require disassembly and overhaul. This book will not discuss the latter, because the techniques and procedures involved constitute a book in themselves, and are different for every engine. In addition, the tools and equipment required to overhaul an engine are usually not available to the average homebuilder, especially the first-timer. Some of the sources of reference manuals for engine overhaul and conversion are listed in Appendix C. These manuals are designed for use by experienced mechanics, and are not intended as basic instruction books for someone who is not well-versed in this area. They may, however, give you an idea of the scope of the job and the difficulties involved, particularly with a conversion.

Assuming that an A & P mechanic will do the overhaul and conversion work required, there are some things that you can do to lessen the total cost for this job. An engine must be torn down completely before a mechanic can inspect it to determine what repairs and replacements are necessary. Simply dropping your engine off at his shop and letting him take it from there is, of course, the easiest way to go, but your A & P may not be inclined to do the routine work required to get the engine ready for the more specialized part of the task. If he does do this basic work, his bill will then reflect the time spent on taking the engine apart and cleaning it, along with the work on the actual overhaul.

Since a mechanic's time is both limited and expensive, a considerable saving can be realized by disassembling the engine yourself. This does not require any special expertise in this area or reference manuals, because common sense and care are the only guidelines needed. Nor are special tools involved, because about 95 percent of the engine can be taken apart with the normal tools found in any home workshop.

Then name of the game in tearing down an engine is to attack it progressively from the outside in, and, if something is bolted together, unbolt it. A few open-end wrenches and sockets of the more popular sizes are the main tools used in the disassembly.

These will work well for everything until you come to the cylinder bolts. Because of the limited space around the base of the cylinders, it will require some judicious maneuvering of the wrench to get a purchase on the bolt head. Again, because of the restricted working space, you will have to be content with moving the bolt by only a small amount before the wrench has to be repositioned. Things will go along slowly but surely until you come to one cylinder bolt that defies all attempts to get a wrench on it. This is why the manufacturers of both Lycoming and Continental engines designed a special cylinder head wrench just for this bolt—and why it is so expensive. If the engine is to be taken apart by anything short of dynamite, your only recourse here is to buy one or borrow one. Since this item will be used only once in a blue moon by the average homebuilder, ask around among the A & P mechanics in your EAA Chapter to see if they know anybody who would lend you one for about ten minutes.

Removal of the valves may require some special tool or technique, so this is better left to the one doing the overhaul. In this same vein, it would undoubtedly be advisable to check with the overhaul mechanic to see how far he wants the engine torn down before he starts to work on it. Also be sure to let him know the level of your experience and equipment for this job, and ask if he has any suggestions on how to approach it. A few words of advice here could save a lot of time and busted knuckles.

After you are about five minutes into the disassembly of the engine, you will discover that this is a very, *very* dirty job. Have lots of rags available, along with a couple of coffee cans filled with kerosene. These are used to soak the parts for a day or so after being removed from the engine. A stiff brush is used to clean all crevices, and the parts are wiped dry, wrapped in newspaper, and labeled.

A small dishpan is very handy for cleaning parts such as cylinders or crankcase halves. Before scrubbing down any unit, be sure to scrap off all gasket material with a knife. It's a good idea to clean and save everything, and let the overhauler decide on whether it's usable or not. Even rings and bearings, which are replaced as a matter of course, should be sent to the mechanic, since these may provide clues to other wear problems in the engine.

The next section will deal with a few areas that should be taken care of before starting to foam and fiberglass the airplane. While these topics present no special problems, they are covered at this time to make sure they are addressed before foaming so that they will not surface later as major difficulties.

Chapter 22

Miscellaneous

The purpose of this chapter is to tie up a few loose ends as far as certain areas of construction are concerned. These are the items that deserve some comment, but are not extensive enough to require full chapters of their own.

Trim System

The first topic of discussion is really an option with the builder as to whether it will be put in the airplane or not. This is an elevator trim tab that is controllable from the cockpit. An electrically driven system is a lot easier to use here than the wire cables attached to a trim wheel on the left console, as was done in the full-size Corsairs. This installation is much simpler, and acts like the beep-trim system used in modern fighters.

Starting at the cockpit end, the first thing you'll need is a miniature three-position toggle switch. This switch should be spring-loaded to the center position, which is "off," and provide a momentary "on" in the other two positions. The reason this switch is miniaturized is to allow it to be mounted on the top rear of the stick grip, where it can be operated by thumb pressure. This is the most practical and realistic setup; however, a regular size switch of the same type could also be used on a cockpit side panel.

After the switch is installed on the stick grip, use a continuity checker of some sort to test the circuit for proper operation in all positions. Make this test on the leads coming from the bottom of the control stick. This will make sure none of the wire attachment lugs on the switch got squeezed together when it was being pushed into the mounting hole.

The wires from the switch should be secured to the subfloor of the cockpit by a padded Adel clamp, and it is recommended that knife connectors be used on each for quick disassembly. Don't forget to cover these knife connectors with spaghetti tubing to prevent short circuits. Route wires from this connection to the trim drive motor, making sure that they are bundled and secured along the way.

The drive motor for the trim system is the device used on cars to raise and lower the antenna. These are obtainable at reasonable prices from just about any large auto parts dealer. The antenna and its housing are discarded, and the drive mechanism is modified as follows: Remove the outer cover and cut off a little over half of the Teflon rod that is coiled inside. An adapter is then made to connect the Teflon rod to the Bowden cable. This could take the form of a short cylinder with holes of the correct diameters drilled in each end (Fig. 22-1). Since this will be moving in both directions, a set screw or pin should

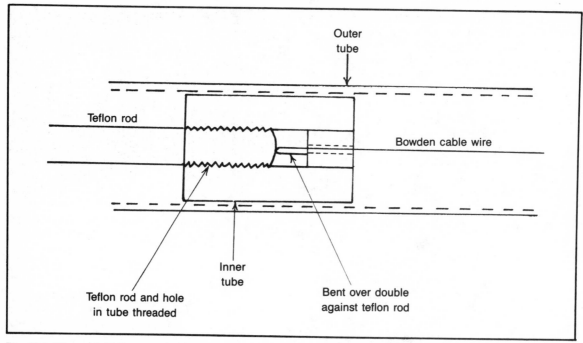

Fig. 22-1. Trim cable/Teflon rod connection.

be used to secure the rod and cable. Additional rigidity for this installation may be realized by allowing it to slide back and forth inside a larger tube that is fastened to the mounting board for the trim drive.

This drive unit can be placed just about anywhere, but probably the best location, considering CG and ease of maintenance, is behind the headrest. A piece of 1/8-inch plywood large enough to hold the drive is epoxied to the top fuselage frame skin just aft of the headrest (Fig. 22-2). The side chosen for this mounting board is the one opposite from the side where the trim tab will be located.

If you plan to include a system that gives a cockpit indication of a certain position of the trim tab, the mechanism to accomplish this can also be mounted on the same piece of wood. This would be useful to show a neutral or a takeoff position of the tab.

The fore-and-aft motion of the drive unit is transmitted to the trim tab by means of a Bowden cable. Secure the forward part of this cable to the frame with an Adel clamp placed as close as possible to the front end of the cable housing. This clamp—and any others used to route the Bowden cable—should have at least one-inch-square mounting pads epoxied to the fuselage skin. Run the cable inside the frame to a point about halfway to the forward stabilizer spar, and then outside the frame for the remain-

ing distance. The cable should pass just under the junction of the front stabilizer spar and the fuselage frame, run along the top corner of the frame between the stab spars, and straight through the tail web. Make the hole in the tail web a little oversize, and do not clamp the Bowden cable after it passes the front stab spar. This is to allow the cable to move slightly as the elevator spar rotates through its range of travel. To hold the cable par-

Fig. 22-2. Trim drive motor installed on its mounting board beneath the canopy guide rails.

allel to the spar, Adel clamps are used under both nuts on the elevator control horn mounting bolts.

If the enlarged hole through the tail web does not give the Bowden cable enough freedom of movement, or if this method of installation necessitates too sharp a turn for the cable, a slightly modified route must be used. Try running the cable through the lightening hole in the tail web. This should ease the problem of the sharp turn, and also give the cable considerably more room to move with the elevator. When installed in this manner, the cable can be attached to the mounting bolts by one elongated clamp so as to minimize drastic changes of direction at this point (Fig. 22-3). The rear end of the Bowden cable must also be supported by an Adel clamp very close to the end of the cable housing. It may be necessary to epoxy a mounting block to the aft spar face for this clamps so that it is held securely and lined up properly with the bellcrank.

At this point it is time to make a check to see if the antenna drive motor is powerful enough to push and pull the Bowden cable around the sharp bend at the elevator. Clamp the cable in place on the control horn mounting bolts and hook up a car battery to the motor. Actuate the switch in both directions and check for the desired movement.

If nothing happens, or if the action is erratic, the cable might be too heavy for the drive motor. This may be the case if 3/16-inch diameter Bowden cable was used;

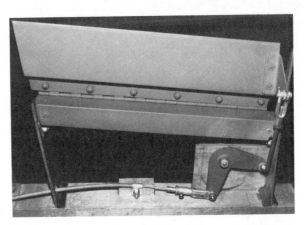

Fig. 22-4. Trim tab bellcrank mechanism mounted to the extra rib, as viewed from the underside of the elevator.

therefore, a smaller size should be tried to see if it corrects the problem.

If this does not work, or a thinner cable cannot be located, a second alternative can be tried. This involves replacing the 90-degree turn in the cable behind the elevator spar with a bellcrank assembly like that used on the outer wing spar for the aileron control. The base of the bracket holding the bellcrank will have to be widened to accommodate the bolting pattern of the elevator control horn (Fig. 22-4).

Should the antenna drive motor still not have the power to move the control wire easily in both directions, it should be replaced with a larger unit, if one is available. As a last resort, you might try replacing the antenna drive motor with a linear actuator. This latter device is an electric motor with a threaded shaft running through the center, and is a lot more powerful than the antenna motor. The shaft moves in and out depending on the direction of rotation of the motor, and can be connected directly to the Bowden cable, or to a lever assembly if a force multiplier is needed. An electric motor with the appropriate gearing to convert rotary motion into linear could be used in place of the actuator.

If, in the course of trying the various options listed above, you decide that the second bellcrank system offers the best solution to your problem, there is another variant that will make this mechanism work even better. If you have already invested in an antenna drive motor that is not exactly the world's strongest, and have modified it for your bird only to find out that the Bowden cable still offers too much resistance, the following alternative may be the answer to your prayers. This procedure involves removing the outer coiled wire from the inner push-pull cable,

Fig. 22-3. Bowden cable for the trim tab attached to one of the bolts used to mount the elevator control horn.

137

by sliding it off the aft end of the trim drive assembly. Then install, along the same routing as the Bowden cable, a 1/4-inch OD *steel* tube. Feed the inner Bowden cable wire through the tube back to the trim bellcrank. Stop the tubing about 18 to 24 inches in front of the elevator spar, and use the regular Bowden cable outer housing for the remaining distance to the spar. Clamp the cable end to a small block epoxied to the rear face of the elevator spar. The cable must be secured to the elevator and free to flex back to the tubing, as the control surface moves from full up to full down. If the cable is not clamped to the elevator, any movement of the latter will cause the trim tab to move in the opposite direction, giving the same effect as a servo. This principle also applies if Bowden cable is used all the way from the actuator. The reason steel tubing is emphasized above is to maintain compatibility with the steel inner wire. If aluminum were used, wear points would develop that could eventually cause jamming of the mechanism.

The trim tab itself should be as near to scale as possible; for the Corsair, this results in a tab that is 3 inches wide and 12 inches long. This is bent from .032 sheet aluminum, and is bolted to its spar by a piano hinge running its entire length. The tab spar is bent from the same size stock into a U-shaped channel, with the arms of the U spread slightly to conform to the double taper of the elevator ribs. Be sure to include mounting tabs on both ends of this spar when making the pattern.

On the real bird, the tab extends to the inner edge of the elevator. Therefore, cut the existing inside rib on the elevator to allow the trim tab to line up flush with the remaining portion of the rib once it is installed. Another rib will have to be made and epoxied in place to support the opposite end of the trim spar. Since the trailing edge of the elevator tapers toward the tip, draw the outline on the plans so that the exact length of this extra rib can be determined. This part is cut from 1/8-inch plywood, and a 1/16-inch duplicate of the root rib is epoxied to the existing rib to give it some added strength (Fig. 22-5).

The bellcrank mechanism is mounted on a 1/4-inch piece of plywood epoxied to the extra rib and the elevator spar. The bellcrank should have a short sleeve brazed to the pivot corner that has an inside diameter of 3/16 of an inch. This sleeve will provide a more positive movement of the mechanism by keeping the bellcrank from wobbling. The arm going back to the control horn should have a threaded portion to allow for small adjustments in alignment. Large changes in the amount of travel of the tab for a given application of trim (e.g., a one-second "beep") can be made by moving the attach points for the control

arm on either the trim tab horn or on the bellcrank. It may be necessary to move the holes on both these parts to achieve the desired sensitivity. The actual effectiveness of this trim tab will only be known after the plane has been test-flown. Therefore, at this stage, set up the tab so that it moves plus or minus 30 degrees before it hits a stop.

If the antenna drive motor is used for the trim installation, there is a procedure that should be followed when making the final attachment of the Bowden cable to the trim bellcrank: Connect power to the drive motor and run it to the full-out position—that is, with the wire in the Bowden cable extended as far as it will go. Then put the trim tab in the full-up position, and cut the Bowden cable accordingly to hold the tab at this extreme. This technique will ensure that you have full travel available on the tab

Fig. 22-5. Alternate method for trim tab actuation, utilizing a second bellcrank mounted to the elevator control horn attach bolts. Note that the end of the Bowden cable must be secured to the elevator spar.

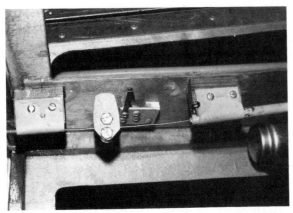

Fig. 22-6. Spring switch to indicate the neutral position of the trim tab. The contacts are closed by the cam on the trim actuating wire passing beneath them.

in both directions. if the two-bellcrank system described earlier is used for the trim, this method will apply to the bellcrank mounted on the elevator control horn bolts. In this instance, the two bellcranks should be connected to each other, and the tab held in the up position as before.

If you opt to include a cockpit indicator of the neutral trim position, the easiest method is to install a cam on the Bowden cable wire that trips a spring-type switch. A handy place for this cam is just aft of where the wire exits from the antenna drive motor housing. If this is to be added, the sheath portion of the Bowden cable must be moved back from the drive motor by a few inches, and then secured to the frame. Make sure this distance between the housing and the sheath is long enough to accommodate the full travel of the wire in both directions, with the cam attached. This installation is shown in Fig. 22-6. When the elevators are being foamed and fiberglassed, don't forget to include an inspection plate over the bellcrank mechanism.

Cowling

The building of the cowling for the Corsair can be approached in two ways. The first is the method described in the construction manual for making a fiberglass cowling with a styrofoam core. This, however, involves quite a bit of work to make both the mold and the glass/foam sandwich for the cowling itself.

A simpler way to go, which results in a stronger unit, is to roll the flat portion of the cowling from sheet metal and attach it to a fiberglass nose ring. The aft edge of the latter is recessed slightly with a rasp so that the metal portion of the cowling will fit flush. These two pieces are bolted together with countersunk 10-32 machine screws and anchor nuts.

When positioning the rolled sheet metal, it is advisable to locate the split where the two edges come together at the midpoint on one side. Then the nose ring is cut on an extension of this split line. A similar cut is made on the opposite side of the cowling and continued through the sheet metal portion to its aft edge. Dividing the cowling into two halves like this makes it easier to handle during installation and for maintenance. The two halves are held together by 10-32 machine screws and anchor nuts through an overlapping joint.

The plans call for using small angle brackets around the circumference of the firewall to mount the cowling. A more sturdy installation can be had by supporting the weight of the cowling by a pair of large brackets that are bolted to the upper part of the firewall (Fig. 22-7). These brackets extend forward to the air baffle behind the engine. Three small peripheral brackets can still be used on each side, but they are more for maintaining rigidity than for carrying the load. These are attached by 10-32 bolts through the fiberglass wrapped around the firewall edge to anchor bolts on the back side.

Whether you make the fiberglass or the metal cowl, don't forget to provide an access door to check the oil. A recommended feature that lends itself to the metal cowling is a set of cowl flaps on the bottom rear edge. These are a pair of ground-adjustable doors used to control the exit of cooling air in order to regulate engine temperature. The construction and installation of these flaps is relatively straightforward, as shown in Fig. 22-8.

Of course, for the perfectionist, there is the possibility of putting in a system to allow the pilot to adjust these

Fig. 22-7. Cowl mounting brackets. The exact position of these brackets will be determined by the location of the engine accessories.

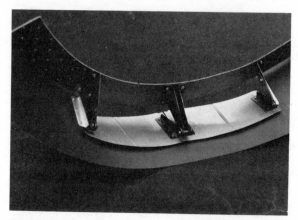

Fig. 22-8. A mockup of the bottom inside of the cowling, to show how the mounting brackets/hinges are attached to the firewall and cooling flaps.

cowl flaps in flight. It would not be too difficult to design a mechanism to connect the two center brackets so that the doors could be operated in unison by means of a Bowden cable. Such a system would allow the pilot to fine-tune engine temperatures for optimum performance. Since there will be an air load on these flaps, a locking T-handle control would probably be more advisable than the standard push-pull control, which would have a tendency to creep closed. The decision to install such a system should be made before the cockpit interior is finalized, since a place will have to be found to mount the control handle.

Setting Wheel Toe-In

Something that is not talked about in either the plans or the construction manual is the toe-in adjustment for the wheels. This is a fairly critical procedure, because if any toe-out is present, the aircraft will be very difficult to control while taxiing and during the takeoff and landing roll.

The amount of toe-in is a function of the length of the airplane. It is set by aligning the fore-aft centerline of each tire with a point that is located at a distance of ten times the aircraft length, on the extended centerline of the bird. Since the WAR Corsair is 15.9 feet long, the aiming point would be 159 feet away.

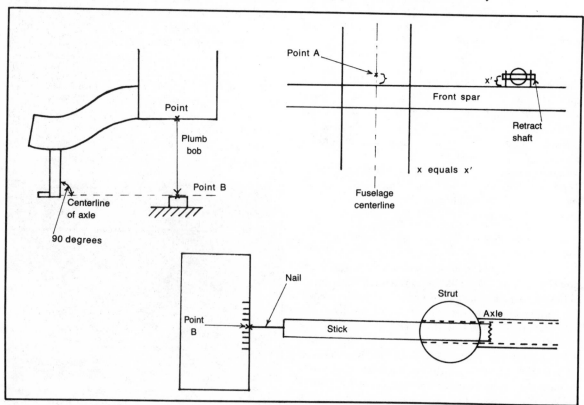

Fig. 22-9. Toe-in setup.

It is easier to solve this problem by trigonometry than by actually sighting over the tire to this point. Measure the distance between the centers of the tires and then halve this amount. This figure (about 3.07 feet), along with the 159 feet from above, give you two sides of a right triangle. Dividing the 3.07 feet by the 159 feet results in a number that is the tangent of the angle you are seeking. The angle is found by looking through a table of trigonometric functions until this value of the tangent is located, or is very closely approximated. The desired angle is then read from the table (about 1 degree).

The toe-in angle found by these calculations is fairly small, and as such is difficult, if not impossible, to set by the eyeball method. A more precise way of doing things involves measuring the distance from the front spar face to the inboard center of the wheel axle. Then wedge a *straight* piece of wood inside the axle from the inboard side. This should be just long enough to reach about half an inch short of the aircraft centerline. The remaining half inch or so is taken up by a nail driven in the end of the stick, after which the head is clipped off and the end ground to a point. Make sure that this stick is pushed inside the axle all the way, so that it forms a true extension of the axle centerline toward the middle of the airplane.

Draw a line across the bottom fuselage skin that is directly beneath the front face of the spar. Draw another line perpendicular to the first, along the centerline of the airplane, and measure off on it the same distance that was found between the axle and the spar. Drop a plumb line from this spot down to the end of the stick extending from the axle. Twist the wheel so that the end of the nail touches the string, which now makes the axle parallel to the spar face.

The problem now becomes one of how much more to twist the wheel to achieve the proper toe-in. Block up a board beneath the airplane with one edge directly below the centerline of the bird and just touching the point of the nail in the end of the stick. A plumb line dropped from the front of the fuselage will help in lining up this board. Mark the spot where the end of the nail touches.

The next step is to calculate the distance *rearward* from this spot that the nail must move to set the toe-in. This is done once more by using the tangent of the angle. The value of the tangent was determined in the original problem, and the only measurement needed is that from the end of the nail to the center of the great strut. Multiply this amount, converted to inches, by the value of the tangent and you have the distance the nail must move *aft* of the first mark to set the toe-in (.67 inches). (The numbers used in both these examples are representative

figures *only;* you should make actual measurements from your aircraft and set of plans.) All of the procedures described here must be accomplished with the aircraft resting on the gear with the engine installed, and the tail propped up so that the fuselage is level. The reason for making these adjustments after the engine is mounted is to approximate the actual weight distribution of the finished airplane as closely as possible. It would help even more to have someone sit in the cockpit during this procedure (Fig. 22-9).

Seat Belt and Harness

Anchoring the shoulder harness and seat belt to the fittings made from the plans can present some problems with the standard hardware used with commercial belts. The normal attachment buckles for the harness are of a size that will interfere with the rudder cable and pulleys in the Corsair installation.

A much easier approach to securing the shoulder

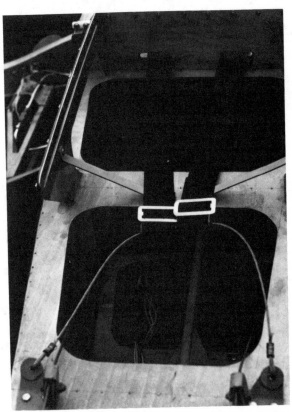

Fig. 22-10. Shoulder harness bridle with belts attached to a steel tube between retaining washers.

141

harness is to make a bridle from a short section of rudder cable. Before mounting this permanently on the airplane, slide a small piece of steel tubing on the cable. The length of this tube is about a half inch greater than twice the width of one shoulder harness belt. Make up two washers about an inch in diameter from scrap aluminum, with a center hole equal to the outside diameter of the tube. Slip these on the tube, and then flare both ends to keep them from falling off. The ends of the cable can now be swagged to the fittings, using a thimble to prevent kinking and chafing. Each harness belt is then looped around the tube and cinched down with an adjustment buckle (Fig. 22-10).

Installing the seat belts presents a similar problem, since the attachment fitting it set at an angle that does not lend itself to commercial mounting buckles. A small bridle arrangement like that used for the harness, or a mounting buckle cut from sheet metal with a safetied hook, can be used here. Whatever the arrangement, the line of pull should be direct from the belt to the fitting, with no angled pieces in between.

This just about wraps up all the major construction areas on the aircraft before it is foamed and fiberglassed. Needless to say, before this phase of the project starts, there are a lot of odds and ends that must be taken care of first. Finalizing the instrument connections; hooking up the throttle, mixture, and primer to the engine; and making the final adjustments on the control system to make sure the surfaces line up and operate properly, are just a few.

Once all these are finished, it's time to press on to the next topic—some of the dos and don'ts about foaming and fiberglassing, which will be covered in the next chapter.

Chapter 23

Foaming and Fiberglassing

This phase of the project marks a real milestone, from which you just start to perceive the light at the end of the tunnel. A lot of hard work lies ahead, but the frustrating, never-ending, ever-changing problems of construction are all behind you. This part of the building process undoubtedly provides the most aesthetically pleasing aspects of the entire project. The bare skeleton that has been sitting on your work table for so very long finally starts taking shape.

However, before gluing very much foam in place, take a little time out to go over each section of the plans very carefully. The object of this review is to make absolutely sure that *all* parts of *every* system that will be on the inside of the airplane have been installed. It would really water your eyes later on to discover that holes must be cut in the foam to add a forgotten component.

If you are building a replica such as the Corsair, a final decision will have to be made prior to any foaming as to what particular model of the aircraft you want to duplicate. As the original airplane went through the various stages of its development, quite a few of its features were changed along the way. Check as many reference works as you can to find pictures that show each item in question from a couple of different angles. Two excellent sources of the kind of photos and drawings you need for the Corsair are

the publications *F4U Corsair in Action* and *F4U Corsair in Color* ($4.95 and $5.95 respectively, from Squadron/Signal Publications; address in the Appendix). Sketches illustrating the prominent design changes are included in these books, and similar references are also published for other military aircraft. Of course, if a full-size version of your bird is available in your area, make arrangements to look it over at close range, and don't forget your camera and sketch pad. Bringing along a tape measure to get exact dimensions is also recommended. The things to be concerned about here are the obvious, major differences between the various models. Examples of these on the Corsair would be the canopy framing, carburetor air scoop, and the arrangement of the exhaust stacks.

Access Panels

Another topic that must be addressed at this time is the provisions for access panels. Look the bird over and decide on the best way to get at the various control mechanisms, and plan the cutouts in the foam accordingly. The size of these openings should be large enough to allow all parts of the item to be reached by your hand *and whatever tools are required.*

At the very minimum, access panels should be planned

to allow work to be done on, or the removal of, the following items: Control stick connections beneath the cockpit subfloor, rudder and elevator control horns, battery, aileron bellcranks, trim bellcrank, chain and sprocket mechanism in the retract system, and the elevator idler arm. Depending on the type of fuel tank mounting used, it may be necessary to have small access holes to the tank tiedowns so that it can be removed for maintenance or other work in that area. The need for an access panel to get at the rear of the instruments hinges on whether you plan to glass in the space between the tank and the gauges down to the fuselage frame. If this is done, a panel or two will have to be cut behind the instruments to allow access to the connections and wiring inside.

While deciding on the location of the various panels, some thought should be given to the possibility of servicing two components through a single opening. The judicious placement of one slightly larger access panel can sometimes save the extra work of building two smaller ones. Possible combinations to consider here are: Battery and elevator transfer crank, gear drive motor, stick mount and declutch bellcrank, chain and sprocket mechanism and push-pull control anchor points.

Since even at best these panels detract somewhat from the external appearance of the airplane, they should be located on the less conspicuous bottom surfaces whenever possible. Another advantage is realized by doing this: Panels located thus will minimize the seepage of rainwater into the interior of the airplane, where it could collect in inaccessible areas and cause structural deterioration.

Access panels are made after the airplane has been fiberglassed. Decide where the openings will go, and using a felt-tip pen, draw their outlines on the foam after it has been sanded to shape. It would also be a good idea to sketch these in on the plans for a permanent reference. After the fiberglass has cured, the outlines are visible and the openings are cut with a high-speed hand drill, using the miniature circular saw attachment. If the edge is cut carefully, this piece can be used for the access panel cover. However, if the edges turn out a little rough, it can serve as the pattern for the sheet metal cover.

When the edges of the hole have been smoothed, fasten strips of sheet metal around the underside of the opening with either rivets or epoxy. If the latter is used, be sure to sand the surface of the fiberglass so that the epoxy will adhere properly. The strips of metal should also have a lot of holes drilled in the half that will be epoxied. The reason for this is the same as for the three-sided channel used to attach the windshield bow to the fuselage frame: These holes make for a much stronger bond be-

tween the metal and the fiberglass. The strips will act as backing plates for the cover; therefore, they should be drilled for Dzus fasteners or anchor nuts before installation. In order to ensure perfect alignment, temporarily fasten the backing plates in position, and drill the cover and plates in one operation.

Before any foam is attached to the frame, there are a couple of things that need to be done. The first of these is to bevel the spars slightly so that the airfoil shape will be maintained. This can be done with a wood rasp or a razor blade block plane. Care must be taken here, since not much material is removed in the beveling operation, particularly near the tips of the spars. A good indication of how much should be taken off, and where, can be gained by checking the sheet of the plans that shows the patterns for the wing and tail ribs. Measure off the amount of the bevel of each rib and mark it on the appropriate spar face. Then connect these marks with a line that will serve as a guide once you start shaving down the spar. Use careful measurements and markings here, since the depth of the bevel at each rib and mark it on the appropriate spar face. spar and the position on that spar. Try to avoid overcuts here to preclude having to "fill in" later on. A slight excess can be sanded down after the foam is in place, when the entire surface can be eyeballed better. Don't forget to bevel the spars in the fin, rudder, stab, and elevator, and remember that the bevel is on the front of the forward spars in the wing and stabilizer.

The other remaining item to be accomplished before foaming is installing the navcom antennas and ground plane, if this type of equipment is planned for the bird. Because this is such a high-cost item, you may want to hold off on the decision to put in a navcom until your checkbook has had a chance to regroup. However, the parts needed for the antenna system are very inexpensive, and should be installed now, even though a navcom isn't in the cards for a while. Because of the susceptibility of the aluminum foil ground plane to tearing once it is epoxied in place, it is recommended that this be installed just before the foam for that section. Since connections have a way of working loose, and electrical components can burn out, it might be a good idea to locate these parts of the antenna system where they can be reached through an access panel, or the opening for the tailwheel.

It is highly recommended that you obtain a couple of new tools before starting to work on the foam. The first of these is a Stanley Surform Plane, with some additional blades of varying roughness. The other is a butcher knife for cutting the foam. This material dulls a knife quickly, so a lot of time and aggravation can be saved by having a knife sharpener handy.

Some homemade tools will also be required, such as the large and small sanding blocks for the final contouring. Another item that will be very useful is a supply of large rubber band clamps. These are made from sections cut from old inner tubes, and short pieces of dowel, exactly the same as the smaller ones used to hold gussets when building the fuselage frame. Tie enough of these sections together so that the clamp will encircle the structure being foamed. The pressure exerted by these clamps does not have to be very great, since their primary purpose is to hold the foam in place while the epoxy dries. Weights, such as bricks, shot bags, or scrap metal, can be used on flat surfaces. This sure beats having to sit there holding the foam while the "five-minute" epoxy sets up to the point where it will keep the foam block in position. For those areas where the rubber band clamps cannot be used, try masking tape.

Another thing that can be picked up while shopping for the above items is a package of dust masks. These are essential once you start sanding the foam, when you'll be living in a cloud of dust.

Foaming Procedures

The procedures and steps for applying foam to the Corsair are outlined very well in the construction manual. The method of building up the round shape of the fuselage using the contour pieces as guides in fairly straightforward, and does not need elaboration here. The same can be said for the wing and tail surfaces.

The major thing to keep in mind during this portion of the project is to work carefully and achieve a good fit between adjacent foam blocks. This will minimize any seam lines, which will require filling after the foam is sanded to shape.

If a space between two pieces of foam is unavoidable, it can be filled with two-component polyurethane foam. When the resin and catalyst are mixed, they expand to 40 times their liquid volume. The resulting foam can be allowed to work its way to the surface of a joint, since it will not present a dissimilar surface for sanding, as does epoxy. Gaps of up to 1/4 inch can be filled by this method, and blocks of polyurethane foam can also be joined by this substance. Using it as a glue, it works just like Aerolite, where the resin is brushed on one surface and the catalyst on the other. The pieces are then brought together, slid back and forth to mix the components, and then weighted or clamped into position. The materials used for this "instant foam" are fairly toxic items, and the manufacturers' recommendations as to use and protection

required should be followed closely.

When foaming the leading edge of the control surfaces, the overall appearance of the bird can be enhanced by enclosing the hinge bolt openings. This is done by foaming completely around the hinge, then marking the foam on one side where the opening will be to allow access to the hinge bolt. After glassing, these areas are cut out just like a miniature access panel. Wooden blocks, with anchor nuts installed, are then epoxied in the opening and a thin sheet metal cover is screwed to the anchor nuts.

As the sanding progresses, be sure to make frequent use of a long straightedge on all flat surfaces. This, in combination with the large sanding block, should preclude any "hills and valleys" in the finished surface. Such irregularities would be particularly noticeable along the leading edges of the wings and tail.

Scraps of foam are great for the final sanding of any foamed area. The scrap wears down as fast as the surface being worked on, and not very much material is removed with each pass. Because of this, it's a good method to use for final contouring, since it results in a very smooth finish.

The warning in the construction manual about keeping the epoxy used to join foam blocks from squeezing to the surface of the joint is *well* worth heading. The many problems this can cause during sanding can be avoided by a little care in applying the epoxy when the blocks are installed.

Once the shaping and sanding starts, the shop area becomes a mess with all the dust and small pieces of foam. A lot of points can be made with the better half by the regular use of the shop vacuum during this phase.

There are many varieties of foam on the market to choose from, and the selection depends on your druthers. However, be sure to pick a type of foam that is compatible with the epoxy you plan to use. And, Murphy's Law being what it is, another criterion might be to limit your choice to those that are fuel resistant.

Fiberglassing

If you have never worked with fiberglass before, a little time should be taken at this point to get properly briefed on the subject before proceeding. Burt Rutan is the acknowledged expert on fiberglass used for aircraft construction; therefore, no attempt will be made here to reinvent the wheel. It is highly recommended that you obtain a copy of his book *Moldless Composite Homebuilt Sandwich Aircraft Construction.* Although this work is mainly directed at people building the VariEze and Long-EZ, the description of the fiberglassing process is clear, well-written, illustrated, and definitely worth your time.

After digesting this information—and any additional you can dig up on fiberglassing—it is also strongly suggested that you visit someone who is in the glassing stage of his project. Watching the entire procedure, and seeing firsthand how the glass looks when it is too wet or too dry, will save you a lot of heartburn later on. Bring along a notebook and a list of any questions you may have about the process, and take lots of notes on any hints that may be offered.

When ordering Burt Rutan's book you will probably notice that there is a practice kit available that includes the book. For those new to fiberglassing, this is probably the best way to go, since a little trial-and-error work is just about mandatory before starting to glass the airplane.

Glancing through the price lists for aircraft epoxies is enough to cause cardiac arrest, particularly when you figure it will take about 10 gallons for the Corsair. The bottom line for these materials quickly brings home the fact that this is precious stuff, and not to be wasted. Therefore, the time to learn all about it is on the practice items, not the bird. This will also give you a chance to try one type of epoxy before deciding on which one will actually be used on the airplane. If you are sure of the kind of epoxy you will be using, and can scrounge some cloth and foam, all you will need is the book to build the practice parts. Make sure that you understand each step of the process before making any layups on the bird itself, because this is where you start using relatively large amounts of epoxy and fiberglass.

Epoxy Measuring Devices

You will find in any written material on epoxies that accurate measuring of the components is an absolute *must*. There are various methods and devices recommended to accomplish this, and all will work if care and precision are used for making each batch.

But glassing large surfaces of the airplane is definitely not a one-man job, and the skill and interest of your helpers becomes a definite consideration. Given the accuracy called for in measuring the ingredients, and the careful application of the mix to the glass, where do you put yourself when the pace gets fast and furious? Having someone who is not familiar with fiberglassing mix the epoxy, could result in less-than-exact proportions, or a batch that exotherms and is ruined. In either case the result is the same-wasted epoxy, and with the cost of these materials, it doesn't take too many of these mishaps to really water your eyes.

A possible solution here is equally eye-watering in cost, but it assures consistent accuracy and avoids the frustration of ruined batches at critical times during the glassing procedure. This is an epoxy measuring machine that works much like a restaurant cream dispenser. It simplifies and expedites the measuring and mixing process to the point where all hands can be used for applying epoxy and squeegeeing. The consistency between batches of epoxy obtainable by using a mixing machine has additional advantages after the bird is fiberglassed. Any filling-in that must be done by using a microspheres/epoxy mix (micro) will have to be sanded after curing. If the proportions of the epoxy used on the glass vary from those used for the micro, two different hardnesses will result. This will cause problems when attempting to sand both areas into one smooth surface.

There is another epoxy measuring device that is only slightly less accurate than the mixing machine described above. This is called "The Poor Man's Epoxy Pump," and is available from Scientec Services, whose address is listed in the Appendix. The most attractive feature of this product is the price, which is about one-tenth that of the mixing machine. The system consists of two plastic bottles with calibrated syringes sticking through the caps, and its advertised accuracy is well within the mixing error tolerance of Safe-T-Poxy. The only drawback in using the Poor Man's Epoxy Pump is the slightly longer time it takes to fill the syringes and empty them into the cup, as compared to the instant response of the mixing machine. Given the price differential of these two items, the extra time spent filling the syringes amounts to just a minor inconvenience. And, when considering the time spent in preparing an epoxy mix by weighing the components on a scale, the choice as to which measuring system to use becomes obvious.

Safety Precautions with Epoxies

The selection of epoxies is another area left to the discretion of the builder. If, from among the varieties that are compatible with your foam, you choose one that has a tendency to exotherm, the following suggestion may save you from a few spoiled batches: Instead of using a relatively deep and narrow container to mix the epoxy, such as a coffee or soup can, use one that is wide and shallow. The aluminum foil pie pans sold in supermarkets are ideal for this purpose. The larger surface area allows for faster heat dissipation, which results in less chance that the heat buildup during mixing will become uncontrolled.

Regardless of the type of epoxy you settle on, there

is one thing common to them all, to one degree or another, that deserves to be mentioned here: *Believe what you hear about the harmful side effects of epoxies.* They are dangerous substances, and the manufacturer's recommendations as to the protection for the skin, lungs, and eyes should be followed *religiously*. A dramatic example of the toxicity of epoxies happened to an individual who only had a brief exposure to the fumes of an epoxy-based paint. The vapors from this paint so inflamed the tissues in the lungs and around the heart that a coronary was induced. *There is no remedy for this type of coronary if a sufficient amount of the toxin has been ingested.*

Some of the commonsense precautions that should be followed during the fiberglassing phase of the project are listed below: Keep your shop clean and make sure it has adequate ventilation. An electric fan in the back of the garage would at least keep a little air moving on calm days. Wear protective clothing at all times. This not only includes rubber gloves or a recommended hand cream, but also long-sleeve shirts and trousers to protect the skin from drips and spatters. Keep plenty of clean rags handy to wipe off any accidental spills. Some form of breathing mask or respirator should be used to preclude your breathing the fumes. These devices are also necessary if you are dry sanding fiberglass, since the sanding dust is just as dangerous as the fumes, and its effects are cumulative with repeated exposures.

Something else is the safety line that should not be overlooked is allowing unprotected people in the shop during fiberglassing operations. The activity is usually hectic during these times, and you don't need any bystanders in the way who could be injured by the fumes, dust, or epoxy. The same goes for pets.

Some of the hazards associated with epoxy may be decreased by using Safe-T-Poxy, which is advertised as being less toxic than other brands. Although Safe-T-Poxy is only available with a one-speed hardener, its advantages far outweigh the small increase in cost over the other epoxy systems. It is also less prone to exotherm than other mixes, unless you really screw up in measuring the hardener. Another plus is that it can be used indoors without smelling up the entire house.

Some additional recommended reading on epoxies and other composite construction materials and their properties is found in the Aircraft Spruce and Specialty catalog.

As work on fiberglassing the aircraft gets under way, you may find it helpful to use reference marks, made with a felt tip pen on the glass and foam, to help align the cloth properly as it is being positioned before the epoxy is applied. Another place these reference marks can be used

is at the lap joints. Because of the overlaps necessary to achieve structural integrity between sections of cloth, the eventual thickness of the glass will be doubled at these joints. This may cause a bulge in the skin that would detract from the bird's appearance once it is painted. A solution that could be tried here is to mark the seam line carefully on the foam, and then sand a *very slight* depression in the foam where the overlap will lay. This is by far a lot easier than sanding down the cured glass, which would also effectively weaken the joint.

Temperature also plays a very important part in fiberglassing. Follow the manufacturer's recommendation as to application temperatures. This pretty well restricts this job to the summertime if your garage or shop is not heated. Since this temperature is so important, it may be necessary to rent a torpedo heater for the glassing sessions, rather than waiting for just the right day.

On days when you're working near the minimum temperatures and you find that the epoxy mix is stiffening up and getting hard to work, some localized heating may be advisable. Make a few passes over the area with a hair dryer set on low, and the epoxy will soften right up to a workable consistency. Another trick is to put the containers with the epoxy components in a pan of hot water on top of a kerosene heater for a few moments. *However, before trying this, make sure that the epoxy you are using does not have flammable fumes.* Some mixes are almost as volatile as gasoline in this respect.

Some builders find that the squeegees cut from coffee can tops are too flexible. They feel that more control is available by using squeegees purchased from an auto body supply store. These are thick at the top and taper to a sharp edge at the bottom. Store-bought squeegees come in different widths, and the larger ones may lend themselves better to working on large flat areas such as the wings.

The most natural way to use a squeegee is to pull it across the surface with the blade slanted toward the direction of motion. Try it this way and see how it works, but it may be worth your time to experiment with a slightly different method. Tilt the squeegee away from the direction of motion, and *push* it across the glass surface. This technique will pick up more epoxy than the other, and would be particularly useful in areas where you used a heavy hand in applying the epoxy.

The ideal situation in any glassing operation is to finish the entire surface you are working on. However, there are bound to be times when, for any one of a million reasons, you must stop working when you reach the edge of the cloth being epoxied. If this happens, do yourself a favor and cover the edge of the cloth with a strip of "peel ply." This will eliminate the need for lot of hard work in sanding down the cured glass edge before the next section of cloth is applied. It is a good practice to use peel ply on any lap joint that will be cured before the next layer of cloth is put on—and leave the peel ply in place until the last minute before the new cloth is laid on. Since fairly large amounts of this fabric tape are used on even a small airplane, it may be more economical to buy sheet Dacron and cut the strips as you need them.

Sometimes a problem may develop in glassing where the cloth will not lay flat as it goes around a sharp corner, such as a trailing edge. To prevent the cloth from lifting and forming a bubble along the edge, clamp it down with strips of wood over a sheet of Saran Wrap or Mylar. The latter can be obtained from art supply stores. Both of these materials keep the strips from adhering to the epoxy, and enables them to release cleanly after the curing process is finished.

There is one portion of the glassing instructions given in the construction manual where you may want to deviate just a little. When finishing off the canopy and windshield trim frame, the manual calls for wrapping the fiberglass around the plex and the tubular metal frame. This, however, results in a very rigid bond between two materials with dissimilar expansion and contraction properties in heat and cold. Therefore, extremes in temperature could result in a cracked canopy or windshield because of unrelieved internal stress. With this in mind, you may want to apply the cloth only to the outside of the canopy and windshield to make the trim frame. In this way the plex is free to "float" on the frame during temperature changes.

Another suggestion, which is more of a variation than a deviation, is the use of two different speed hardeners for successive layers of cloth if you are using a product other that Safe-T-Poxy. Using a faster-curing epoxy for the first layer of cloth may preclude it from creeping while you are squeegeeing the second layer, which utilizes a hardener giving a slower cure.

Final Painting

After all the glassing, sanding, and surface preparations are done, the bird is ready for its final color scheme. Once again, there is a wide choice of products and manufacturers available. The main thing to be wary of here is to be sure to choose a primer that is compatible with the final finish product. Select the latter first and then follow the manufacturer's recommendations as to the primer.

The final paint job is another area where it might be wiser to farm it out if you have no experience in spray painting the type of finish you choose. The entire appearance of your airplane is wrapped up in this last operation, and anything less than a professional handling of the task could ruin a great deal of hard work on your part. Check with some of your local body shops to see if they could do the job, and what it will cost. Since they do this type of work for a living and have a touch with the spray gun, the quality of the finish will probably be very high.

Another area to look into—where the quality might not be as great, but the price will be considerably better—is a vocational school that offers an auto body course. If you happen to catch a class near the end of the program, there is a very good probability that the quality of work will be excellent. Talk the project over with the instructor before committing yourself. Normally, these schools do not charge for labor, since students will be doing the work under the supervision of a qualified instructor. Expect to pay for all materials used, plus a nominal shop charge.

Professional and educational auto body shops have spray booths for this type of work that eliminate the chance of any blowing dust ruining the finish, along with heat lamps to expedite the drying process.

Should you decide to have a go at painting the bird yourself, an air compressor and a good-quality spray gun are essential. These can be obtained from an equipment rental shop, but make sure you get completely checked out on how to use the particular brand of spray gun they have available. Dust and moisture are the major bugaboos you will have to contend with during this phase of the operation. Keep the shop squeeky clean while painting is going on, and if the work is being done in your garage, it may have to be reserved for relatively calm days. Proper ventilation is once again of prime importance for health reasons; therefore, the doors will have to be open, which could present problems if you live in a dusty area and the wind is kicking up.

A safety note on any sanding that must be done, particularly between coats of paint: it's a good idea to connect the surface being worked on to a water pipe or other suitable ground. Sanding builds up large static charges that could cause some nasty surprises, especially in an area containing paints and solvents.

After any session of wet sanding, make absolutely sure that the airplane's surface is completely dry before any paint is applied. Rushing the next coat of paint before all the trapped moisture has evaporated could cause a lot or problems with the resulting finish.

For the same reason, painting sessions should only be held on dry days with as low a humidity as possible. It is definitely not recommended to do any painting while it's raining.

The compressor itself is another source of moisture that should be compensated for. The hose from the compressor acts as a condensation coil; therefore, a water/oil separator should be installed in this line as close to the spray gun as practical.

Obviously, all the tricks of the trade and techniques for foaming, glassing, and painting are not discussed here. The variety of materials available and the different properties of each make a comprehensive analysis of this phase of the project well beyond the scope of this book. The best course of action to follow is to talk it over with someone who has worked in this medium, and who can discuss it knowledgeably. Run through the advantages and disadvantages of various combinations of composite materials, and then decide on which will work best for you. Once this decision is made, look up people who have used these items, and find out as much as you can on what problems they encountered, and any pointers they may have to offer.

After all the dust has settled and all the fumes have blown away, your pride and joy is at last ready for rollout. This moment is the culmination of a lot of time, effort, and money that has been spent on this project over the years, and you should justifiably savor it. After the tumultuous acclaim of the gathered masses has subsided, the real proof of the pudding is yet to be measured: *Will this turkey actually get off the ground?*

The proper way to find out just how high and how well it will get off the ground is outlined in the following chapter on test flying. Now that all the hard work is done and it's time to start enjoying the bird, don't bring things to grief by taking a cavalier attitude toward finding out what makes your airplane tick—right down to the smallest detail.

Chapter 24

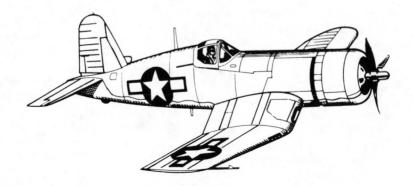

Test-Flying

Test-flying any aircraft—*particularly* one that has not been in the air and whose characteristics are unknown—should be approached with caution, discipline, and a definite game plan. Until you are completely familiar with how the aircraft handles throughout its flight envelope, each mission should be designed to learn something new about the bird.

The learning process should be a gradual, step-by-step sequence, beginning with the easy yet critical items, and then proceeding to the more difficult things and subsidiary information. *Don't* get ahead of yourself and try some fancy maneuvering or high-speed flight without knowing how the bird reacts under less demanding conditions. Trying something advanced before you are thoroughly grounded in the basics could result in serious problems cropping up suddenly for which you have no immediate answers. These same difficulties may still occur in a carefully planned and flown test regimen, but in this setting, you are a lot better prepared to cope with them.

Another word of caution: All of the test program items mentioned below should be flown while wearing a parachute. This is almost too much of a commonsense thing to mention, but when investigating the unknown, charity begins at home and practicality is the watchword.

Checklists

Although it sounds like an overly structured way of doing things, especially for the average lightplane pilot, checklists are just about essential to test-flying a new airplane. Unless you fly every couple of days or so, checklists should always be used to preclude missing some small but important step in any given procedure. Even after a checklist has been committed to memory, the written word should still be carried to counteract an occasional mental block.

Once the normal operating procedures become routine, the most important reason for carrying a checklist is for emergency procedures. If something goes wrong in the air, where the stress of the moment may preclude a logical sequence of thought, it sure is comforting to have the ungarbled word right at your fingertips.

Checklists should be made for *every* major phase of operation for your bird. As a minimum, this would include the following: Preflight, Prestart check, going from left to right in the cockpit, Start and Taxi procedures, Pretakeoff, Climb, Cruise and Descent, Pre-landing, and Shutdown and Postflight. (See the Appendix for suggested checklists.) Some of these may only contain a few items, but until they become second nature, make sure they are included. These lists should be drawn up before the first flight, when you have time to plan an orderly and logical sequence. Then, as your program for testing the bird progresses, they can be modified as the test data indicates.

The thrill of the first flight in an airplane you have built is something that every homebuilder eagerly looks forward to. However, this next suggestion should be given serious consideration by anyone who does not have a good amount of lightplane time under his belt: If all your flying experience has been in heavier, faster airplanes, or your overall time is relatively low, *it is highly recommended that you have an experienced lightplane pilot make the first flight.*

This may sound like heresy, particularly in view of all the time and money you have sunk into your project. It is natural to feel that the first flight is your just reward for hanging in there in spite of all the problems encountered during the building process. At this point you have an almost overwhelming urge to get it into the air and start enjoying the culmination of all your work.

This is *precisely* why someone whose heart is less involved than his head should be at the controls. Sitting in the run-up area at the end of the runway, the builder is probably the worst judge of the seriousness of small problems at this point. Pride is the biggest obstacle to this decision. Therefore, if you are light on flying time in small aircraft, take heed of the old saying: "Pride goeth before a fall." In this situation, the "fall" could really spoil your whole day.

Flight Testing Plan

The approach to testing a new airplane should be thought out in advance of the flight, and then executed in detail after you're airborne. To be sure that nothing will be overlooked, prepare a card for each test flight, outlining the sequence of events for that mission. Leave blanks at the end of each item so that data may be recorded as it happens, rather than relying on your memory after you have landed. It is a good idea to have two or three blanks to fill in for those items that are critical and should be known fairly accurately. Examples would be stall speeds, gliding distances, altitude lost in a high-speed dive. Don't crowd too many items into each flight, since you may want extra time to investigate some more thoroughly. Also, at this stage it is important to get an overall general impression on the feel and sounds of the aircraft while you're just boring holes in the sky.

Once you have a game plan on how you will proceed on each test flight, there are a few things that must be done before you ever think about getting the bird in the air. The first of these is to check the entire airplane over very thoroughly to make absolutely certain that every nut, bolt, cotter pin, and safety wire is in place and secure. The importance of this inspection can't be overemphasized, so take plenty of time to make sure that every detail is covered completely. It is highly recommended that even after taking such a good look at the bird, the entire procedure be reaccomplished so that nothing is missed. The consequences of a loose nut or a missing cotter pin could be disastrous once the bird is airborne.

Before starting this inspection, all access panels and the cowling should be removed so that everything can be seen, and a flashlight should be used to check out the interior of the airplane. There are an awful lot of things that can cause an engine to quit on a first flight, so the name of the game at this point is to eliminate all the obvious ones. Are all electrical connections secure with no wire scraps or stray nuts and bolts in the area that could cause a short? Is everything properly and solidly grounded? Have the plugs been cleaned lately? Is the gas tank full, and has the oil been checked for the correct level? These may seem like very apparent things that could cause problems, but in the hustle to get your aircraft in the blue, they could be very easily overlooked.

Noise-High Engine Check

There is another check for reliable engine operation that is a little more work, but should nonetheless be accomplished. This is a test to ensure that the fuel system will deliver the proper amount of fuel to the engine with the aircraft in an exaggerated nose-high attitude. Since most homebuilts utilize a gravity system, it is essential to see if it operates correctly under these conditions.

One way to make this check is to suspend the airplane from the ceiling and hold the tail down until the nose is 30 degrees above the level flight attitude. Another way is to block up the gear on a set of ramps such as those used for working under a car. In either case, the tail of the airplane should be securely anchored to hold the bird during the engine run-up. What you are trying to determine during these tests is: Can the fuel system deliver at least twice the fuel flow required by the engine at full power, in this attitude?

This is a fairly tough requirement, and if the engine coughs, runs rough, or gives any indication of fuel starvation, corrective measures should be taken. This may involve installing a larger finger screen, or possibly replacing all the plumbing with a bigger size. The fuel system should have at least a 5/16-inch clear bore throughout the lines from the tank to the carburetor.

While making these checks to ensure that the engine will run in a variety of aircraft attitudes, it is also advisable to look for fuel leaks, loose or unsafetied throttle connections, and an operable carburetor heat system. Be sure to check that the oil cap does not have a tendency to work loose due to engine vibration.

Even though it may sound a little foolish, there is one more important thing to do before taking the bird out to the airport. This is to make sure that the controls are hooked up correctly, and the surfaces move in the proper direction. This is especially true with controls systems that use cables, and given the number of times that everything has been taken apart and put back together again, there is a good chance for an error to creep in.

Taxi Checks

Once the airplane has been assembled at the field, there are some essential checks that must be made before leaping off into the wild blue. These are the low- and high-speed taxi tests—and, as with any other phase of the test program, they should be developed slowly and cautiously.

Tow the bird to a clear area on the ramp and see how it handles at slow and normal taxi speeds. How much power does it take to start it moving? How much to maintain a comfortable taxi speed? This is also the time to check on the effectiveness of the brakes, and to find out how much differential braking, rudder, and power are needed for turns. If the bird has conventional gear, it is particularly important to determine if it has any tendency to nose over with a hard application of the brakes.

While working at these slow speeds, you should also find out if the airplane will track in a straight line. Problems in this area could result from a dragging brake, or an improperly set toe-in or toe-out on one of the wheels.

If things are working okay at the slower speeds and the aircraft can be maneuvered safely, it's time to take it out on the runway for some high-speed runs. Here again, increase the speed gradually on successive runs, because problems that are not too apparent while taxiing around the ramp may become magnified at the higher speeds. Shimmy and wheel misalignment are examples of these.

If you are testing a taildragger, these runs are useful to determine at what speed the tail can be lifted off, and how well the bird handles when riding on the main gear alone. The effectiveness of the rudder to maintain directional control is something else to note during these runs.

Liftoffs

Successful testing of the low- and high-speed handling characteristics of the bird does not mean that you are ready to launch it on the first flight. Now that you know that you can control the airplane right up to takeoff speed, you are ready for some *small* liftoffs. The word *small* is emphasized here because you should only just break ground, and hold it about six inches above the runway. Fly along for a few seconds and then put it back on terra firma as smoothly as possible.

It goes without saying that this type of testing requires a runway long enough to get the bird stopped after setting it back on the ground. The necessary stopping distances for speeds in this range are determined during the runs just short of liftoff speed. It is highly recommended that, while making these runs, you select a runway marker or some other prominent checkpoint alongside the runway as the spot where the bird *must* be on the ground with the throttle in idle. Failure to observe this point as an *absolute* criterion will necessitate ground-looping the bird with probable structural and/or gear damage, or finding yourself in the overrun with a lot of serious dents in the airplane.

During all these taxi and high-speed checks, the brakes will undoubtedly get quite warm. This is turn will cause them to lose their effectiveness, so a little cushion should be worked into establishing your checkpoint to make allowances for brake fade.

The things you are looking for on these small liftoffs relate to the basic controllability of the airplane at this critical point in flight. How effective is the elevator in maintaining the attitude of the airplane? Do things get squirrely with a small movement of the stick, or is the response to pitch inputs sluggish? At what speed does the bird become unstuck from the ground? Are there any tendencies toward wing heaviness on one side or the other?

After it has been determined that the airplane has no oddball traits close to the ground, try increasing the altitude to a few feet above the runway. This is an area where some very unexpected control responses can occur; therefore, anticipate the unusual and be ready for it. As the airplane rises more than (roughly) one wing-chord length above the runway, it runs out of the ground effect region. This can produce changes in attitude and control effectiveness that you must be prepared to counteract.

All of the high-speed taxi checks, including those involving small liftoffs, should *never* be attempted if there is a crosswind present. In fact, even strong winds on the nose are sufficient reason to scrub these checks until a calmer day. The reason for this is that any gust could cause the bird to get airborne prematurely, or to pay off on a landing before you are ready.

There are two more very important areas to look at during these taxi runs and liftoffs. The first of these is engine cooling problems, which are indicated by high oil temperatures. Given the immutable character of Murphy's Law, if your engine is overheating on the ground, you can bet your bottom dollar that you will have cooling problems in flight. The time to find out these things is *now*, when an oil temperature or cylinder head temperature running in the red does not precipitate a major emergency. Problems like this emerging once you are committed to flight could result in a very sticky wicket indeed if another runway is not immediately available.

After you get a handle on the fundamental control characteristics of the bird during the small liftoff phase, another aspect of its flight envelope should be investigated. This concerns the all-important question of how the bird reacts to a sudden loss of power on takeoff. The necessary changes in pitch attitude, and the control inputs required to achieve this, should be determined for both a sudden and a gradual loss of power. These simulations of power failure should be tried in stages, progressing from the easy-to-handle to the more difficult situations.

The whole idea of all these checks is not to test your ability to endure tedious or nitpicking procedures. Rather, they are designed to systematically build confidence in your ability to control the aircraft completely, so that the early stages of test flying your airplane will produce no surprises. As a result of this program, you should be so familiar with the basic handling characteristics of your bird that the first flight around the traffic pattern may actually seem a bit anticlimactic.

Aircraft Sounds and Feel

Even after you've determined that your bird will take to the blue and get back down again, there are still quite a few things—both critical and noncritical—that must be learned about your airplane. Along with the items discussed below, there is another, more indefinite, characteristic of the aircraft that you should be learning about during the succeeding flights of your test program. This is the sound and the feel of the airplane in all flight conditions. Make mental notes of the sounds that change with varying speeds, attitudes, and G loadings, and those that don't. How do the controls respond under these different conditions, and how does the aircraft itself feel?

What level of vibration is present in each of these situations? Your ears and your tailbone are two very important "instruments" that should not be disregarded on any test flight. And inputs from these sources is not limited to low-level, barely discernible changes in the sounds and feel of the airplane. *Any* loud noise or sudden unusual vibration is cause for *immediate* investigation. "Immediate" in this sense is relative, and does not mean an emergency landing in the nearest field if the engine is still running and you have control of the aircraft. In this case it is much better to slow the airplane down and check the instruments and as much of the exterior of the bird as you can while heading for the nearest runway. Don't try to be a hero in a situation like this—or with any other emergency. Let the tower know you've got problems so they can clear out the traffic pattern and give you priority to land. They can also alert any crash equipment available in case you've got *big* problems.

Initial Test Items

One of the more important things that must be initially determined about your airplane is the final approach speed and landing speed. A fairly close approximation of the latter should be known as a result of the liftoff runs. A "hip pocket" final approach speed is found by using the speed where the airplane quits flying as a basis, and adding 8 to 10 knots. This latter figure can be used until more accurate data can be calculated after the stall series has been run.

The first flight up and away from the airport should be devoted exclusively to finding out information that will be essential for all succeeding flights. Don't try to crowd too many test items in on this ride, since thorough investigation of a few characteristics is more important that amassing a lot of data.

While staying within a conservative gliding distance to the field, get a little altitude and try a series of *gentle* climbs and dives, and turns in both directions. At this point do not worry about bank angles over 30 degrees, because all you're interested in now is how the aircraft handles in basic maneuvers. Monitor all instruments for both proper operation and staying within the prescribed limits.

Stall Series

After you are comfortable with how the bird flies within this restricted envelope, it's time to investigate the stall characteristics of the airplane. Get some altitude, point the bird toward the airport, and try some straight-ahead stalls in a clean configuration.

The first few of these should only be *approaches* to a stall, with the throttle midway between cruise and idle. Ease into it slowly, and note the early signs of the stall and at what speed they occur. Is there a tendency toward wing heaviness as the stall starts to nibble at the wingtips? Don't let the stall proceed too far before applying the power and starting a recovery. Jot down the information, and then try a couple more until you feel comfortable with how the bird handles at this stage.

If all goes well, climb back to altitude, pull the throttle to idle, and try a full stall. If at any time while the bird is progressing through the various stages of a stall things start to get a little squirrely, or the stall symptoms become too severe, get the power back on and affect a recovery immediately.

Some things to look for as the airplane progresses toward the stall are: Does wing heaviness continue to develop? Can it be corrected by aileron? If ailerons aren't too effective, will opposite rudder pick up the heavy wing? Does the nose start to wander other than that caused by torque? Do the stall warning signs develop smoothly from a nibble through a shudder to a shake? Are either of the latter two signs missing before the final payoff, or is their duration too short to be a reliable stall indicator? Is the final stall violent or mushy? Will normal recovery techniques break the stall, or must they be exaggerated?

After getting the hang of the way things go during a clean stall, the same characteristics must be investigated with the airplane in a landing configuration. Learning how and when the bird stalls with the gear and flaps down is probably the most important outcome of the first flight. This information is critical to establishing a safe approach speed, and knowing what to expect on landing when the bird is ready to quit flying.

The procedures and all of the questions pertaining to clean stalls are also applicable to stalls in the "down and dirty" configuration. However, one additional bit of information can be obtained from this series: since the gear will be cycled for these stalls, this is a good opportunity to record the time it takes to extend and retract the gear under actual airload conditions. The former time will come in handy when gliding distances and high key points for power-out landings are tried. After the stall speed in the landing configuration is known, add 10 knots to this figure to come up with the airspeed you should hold on final approach.

Stalls in Turns

Since just about all traffic patterns involve turns at relatively low speeds, the bird's stall characteristics while turning should also be examined. Get some altitude under the aircraft, put the gear and flaps down, and see how it reacts to problems that may crop up in the traffic pattern. These usually result from a failure to maintain the proper altitude before making the turns to base leg and to the final approach. The end result is a nose-high turn at a low airspeed with the gear and flaps down. With your attention concentrated on the landing, it is very possible for the bird to slip into a stall in a position where there is insufficient altitude to recover.

An aircraft in a turn stalls at a higher airspeed than one in a wings-level attitude. Therefore, it is very important to know the sounds and the feel of your bird as it approaches a stalled condition in a turn. Then, if your cross-check doesn't pick up the decreasing airspeed, you won't be caught by surprise.

Practice these nose-high turns while flying a simulated traffic pattern at altitude, and note what your minimum airspeeds should be in the turns to preclude a stall. If everything is coordinated in these turns, there will be some rudder in to keep the ball centered. Because of this, your recovery from a turning stall should also include neutralizing the rudder, as well as dumping the nose.

After the bird's initial full-fledged exposure to the wild blue, it should be given a *very* thorough postflight inspection. Look everything over quite carefully to see what shook loose, started to leak, or got out of adjustment.

After these basics are well in hand, it's time to investigate some of the follow-on items in the test regimen. A fairly important thing that should be determined early is the best glide speeds and distances with a simulated dead engine. This will require knowing the distance between two ground objects with a fair degree of accuracy. If these can't be measured from your local area charts, it may be necessary to clock off some distances along a road in your car. Paved runways of sufficient length can also be used for this check.

With the throttle in idle, try gliding between these two points at a few different speeds, and note the altitude lost on each run. Refine this down to the nearest 5 knots, but remember to take into consideration the fact that with an actual dead engine, your altitude loss will probably be a little greater than that with an idling engine. When you have determined the best glide speed for your bird in a clean configuration, do the same thing with the gear down.

Dead Engine Procedures

Once the best gear-down glide speed has been found, this will be used for another important test procedure.

Climb up to 3,000 or 4,000 feet AGL and point the bird toward a prominent road or section line so as to cross it at a 90 degree angle. Retard the throttle to idle, put the gear down, and set up your best glide speed. Note the altitude when the wingtip crosses the road or section line, and immediately start a 30 to 45-degree bank turn in either direction. Keep the turn going for a full 360 degrees, and note your altitude after completing 270 degrees of the turn, and again when the wingtip recrosses the road.

The altitude lost in this complete turn determines the high key point for a deadstick landing, after the fudge factor has been added for the difference between an idling and a dead engine. The altitude at the 270 degree point (low key) is your base leg altitude for an engine-out approach. The object of this exercise to establish a high key point is to firmly set the altitude you must have above the runway in order to effect a safe landing with a dead engine. Knowing how far your airplane will glide, gear up and gear down, could make the difference between putting your bird in the woods or on the concrete in the event of an engine failure.

An example of how to use all these figures is as follows: Let's assume that your bird loses 1,000 feet of altitude for every mile of horizontal distance while gliding with the gear up, and that figure jumps to 2,000 feet per mile with the gear down. Another assumption would be that the high key point has been determined to be 2,000 feet above the runway. To set the problem, say you are 6 miles from a runway at 8,000 feet and the engine quits. Can you make it? (Let's also assume that aside from an engine failure, this is your lucky day, and you are headed toward the field.)

The most preferred way to handle a deadstick landing is to make an approach from the high key point. The reason for this is that if you make high key at the proper altitude, you are assured of landing on the runway, unless you screw things up by some gross error of judgment in the pattern. Also, a straight-in engine-out approach is very difficult to judge correctly, and a gusty headwind or tailwind could play havoc with the best of estimates. Everything must go exactly right on a straight-in approach if you are to hit the first third of the runway, including your guesstimate of how far you are from the field.

Back to our problem: As soon as the engine stops, maintain altitude until the airspeed falls to the best gear-up glide speed, and then lower the nose to hold this speed. Turn the aircraft gently so as to line up with the runway most nearly aligned with your heading. As you traverse the 6 miles to the field, you will lose 6,000 feet of altitude. In a no-wind situation, this will put you over the runway at 2,000 feet, which is exactly the high key altitude you are shooting for.

At this point, drop the gear and start an immediate turn in the direction of traffic, utilizing at least 30 to 45 degrees of bank. Allow the airspeed to bleed off to the best gear-down glide speed, and hold it there. Play the turn to hit the low key at the right altitude, while planning your touchdown point for one third of the way down the runway. The reason for aiming at this spot is to provide a little cushion in case of some misjudgment in the pattern that causes you to end up short. Errors in the other direction, which result in your being long, can be compensated for by slipping, or by an intentional ground-loop at the far end of the runway. An important thing to remember in this type of emergency is that it is much better to go off the far end of the runway at a slower, more controlled speed, than it is to hit short at a higher speed in a near-full stall condition.

As can be seen from the above example, an aircraft must be relatively close to the field, and/or have a good deal of altitude to play with, in order to make a high key approach. Going back to our original problem, if the distance to the field was 7 miles, this type of approach could not have been made. The next most desirable choice is to try to hit your low key altitude on a heading that is 90 degrees from the runway, about a half mile from the threshold. This would amount to hitting a high base leg, and all that remains is to adjust the turn on final to compensate for the wind and glide on in.

Obviously, there are a lot of other variables that come into play on any engine-out approach. Winds, terrain obstacles, and cloud cover, along with your ability to estimate distances accurately and hold a glide speed right on the money, are all major factors in the process of getting your bird down in one piece. With this in mind, the name of the game on an engine-out approach is to be *conservative* in your estimates and *precise* in your techniques. If things turn to worms and it doesn't look like you're going to make the runway, use these same procedures to set up an approach to a field or a highway that you are sure of making.

It's a good idea to practice simulated engine-out approaches to your airport frequently, utilizing the high key method. This will help reinforce the mental picture of just how everything should look during the 360 degree turn from the high key to the runway.

Follow-On Test Items

Other things to investigate during these follow-on test

flights are the slip characteristics of the bird and the optimum climb speed. The latter will probably result in two figures, whose use will depend on the situation. If maximum altitude is the major factor, then holding about 10 knots over the stall speed will be the way to climb out; however, engine temperatures should be closely monitored until you level off. When distance is the criterion, a speed about 10 knots below cruise could be used. Naturally, as you get more time on the bird, these speeds will be refined to those that best suit the individual traits of your airplane.

The climbouts made during the initial phase of flight testing afford another opportunity to check for potential engine cooling problems, so keep an eye on the temperature gauges until you are sure everything is okay.

Finding out how your bird behaves in a slip should be approached more or less gingerly. Try a few gentle slips at altitude to see how it reacts, and if no unusual tendencies develop, try some with increased control inputs. The whole idea of attempting these with plenty of air below you is to provide ample room for a recovery in case the airplane shows some nasty characteristics during this maneuver. These traits should not be discovered the first time you slip the bird in a landing pattern. As with the stall series, it's advisable to try these slips in both the clean and dirty configurations.

During any of the flights in this phase of the program, the cruise speed of the aircraft should be determined. Set the throttle at the recommended cruise position (usually 75 percent), and when the airspeed settles down, make a note of this reading for reference later.

After all this preliminary, yet necessary, testing, there is probably one nagging question still in your mind: *"What will this baby do wide open?"* As with other parts of the test program, you are going into an unknown area, so ease into it gradually. Once more, get some altitude under you, and open the throttle until the speed stabilizes at 5 knots above cruise. If there are no problems at this setting, increase the airspeed by another 5 knots and let it sit there for a few moments. If everything is okay, increase the speed another 5 knots, and so on until you reach the maximum continuous power setting on the throttle. *Do not* use the full-open position of the throttle during this check, since operation at this setting is usually limited to five minutes.

As the speed builds through the various ranges, stay alert for any unusual sounds or vibrations, particularly the latter. If things start to shake a little, slow it down until the cause can be determined. Control surface flutter, a loose cowling or inspection plate, or improperly adjusted

gear doors may not become apparent until the higher speed ranges. Make sure that any problem cropping up here is thoroughly explored and corrected before hitting these speeds again. Disregarding these warning signs may result in the airplane shedding some of its parts at a very inopportune time.

In addition, if you plan to hang anything on the bird such as an auxiliary fuel tank, dummy rockets or bombs, etc., make the first cruise and maximum speed runs with these items removed. An even better idea is to hold off installing such extras until the airplane is thoroughly tested. There is no sense in adding things at this time that may be a source of problems in themselves, or may mask symptoms of other difficulties.

High-Speed Flight Checks

While you're operating the airplane at these higher speeds, the control responses for this region should be tested. Try gentle turns and dives at first to see how everything reacts and what control pressures are needed. The increased speeds will undoubtedly result in heavier controls, but if this does not occur, you may have a very dangerous situation on your hands.

Unconventional or not-previously-tested designs may be prone to control reversal, where pressures lighten with increased input, and the controls seem to want to keep on moving in the same direction. If this happens, slow down and get the airplane on the ground, and analyze the problem thoroughly before trying it again. An aircraft with this quirk could bring on an out-of-control situation that could ruin your whole day.

If the control response is okay, try some steep turns at the higher speeds, using 45 and then 60 degrees of bank. Should no irregularities develop during these turns, the next step is to check out the bird's high-speed stall characteristics. As soon as the bank angle for the turn has been established, haul back on the stick rather smartly until you experience the pre-stall warnings. It is not necessary to completely stall the bird out in the turn. All you are looking for is any unusual tendency toward pitch-up or rolling inverted. If the airplane feels like it wants to go in either of these directions, release the back pressure immediately and roll the wings level. It is sufficient to know the attitude and speed at which these traits exist, and what corrective action is effective.

Final Test Items

Now it's time for a little more enjoyable part of the program. When all the foregoing has been accomplished, you are fairly certain that the aircraft is controllable in just about any flight condition. Needed adjustments in fixed trim tabs will have been determined by this time, and the corrections made.

Since you are now familiar with the handling and the feel of the aircraft in a variety of basic flight situations, some mild acrobatics should be tried. Do some easy wingovers and chandelles at first, and see how the bird handles throughout these maneuvers. Then steepen them up gradually until you reach the classic execution of each. A series of lazy eights is next, which will also point out what it takes to fly your airplane in a smoothly coordinated manner with rapidly changing altitudes and speeds.

This stage of flight testing is also a good time to gather some preliminary data on fuel and oil consumption. These numbers will most likely be refined as you accumulate more hours on your airplane, but you should get a pretty good handle on these values early in the test program.

Another thing that ought to be determined during this phase is how the aircraft behaves in a light crosswind. Again, work into this gradually until you are confident that you can handle the bird in a 10 to 15 knot wind across the runway. Also look to establishing a personal crosswind component for flying, just below the point where things get a little hairy on the approach, touchdown, and rollout.

The above described procedures will wring your bird out pretty well as far as basic airworthiness and controllability are concerned. Once the information from these flights has been gathered and averaged out, it's time to see how the external tank will affect things. Even though this tank will normally be used only for cruising situations, it still should be tested for stability at high speeds.

Undoubtedly, the tank will create a new noise for you to get accustomed to, but here again, if vibrations out of the ordinary start to develop, slow down and investigate what's happening. Another set of fuel consumption figures will have to be determined for cruising with the tank installed.

Aerobatics

If you intend to horse your bird around and get into some unusual attitudes, you should extend your testing program to include these areas. The same ground rules apply here as they did in any other part of the test regimen: Approach each new event by degrees, and be absolutely sure that everything is under control before proceeding to the next step.

Something to be especially wary of is how the engine performs in these exaggerated attitudes. If it cuts out in high-angle climbs or less than one-G conditions, such maneuvers may have to be excluded from your aircraft's repertoire. Overhead aerobatics, including momentary inverted flight, are particular areas of concern here. Aileron rolls, slow rolls, and barrel rolls should be tried first to see how the bird responds to being on its back. Be sure to maintain positive Gs on the airplane throughout these maneuvers to keep the engine from quitting due to interrupted fuel flow caused by zero or negative-G conditions.

This caveat also applies to all overhead maneuvers. The rolls should be tried in the sequence listed above so as to gradually increase the time the bird will be inverted. If all of the other test items were passed successfully, there should be no surprises in the handling characteristics of the airplane during the roll series.

Prerequisites for Overhead Maneuvers

Overhead maneuvers—such as loops, Immelmanns, Cuban eights, and cloverleafs—present the greatest potential for problems due to the extremes in attitudes and airspeeds involved. Because of this, there are a few preliminary maneuvers that should be mastered before any of the above are attempted.

The first of these is the spin. Be very, *very* cautious about feeling out the spin characteristics of your airplane, since this gyration can develop into a hairy, if not catastrophic, situation quickly. Let it go for only one turn initially, and then break it to see how fast the aircraft responds. If all is well with no oddball tendencies, try two turns. A clean recovery here should be sufficient to prove that your bird can be brought out of a spin with no problems. If the spin wants to tighten up, or the recovery is unusually slow, give some second thoughts to trying overhead maneuvers.

The next thing to attempt is a split-S, in order to find out what it takes to bring the aircraft out of a vertical dive. In keeping with the incremental approach, it is probably advisable to roll into a couple of 45 and 60-degree dives before doing the first split-S. Try these first at idle and then at some mid-range power setting, so that you'll be familiar with the effect of power on recovery procedures. After these are under your belt, roll the bird into a split-S, remembering to keep positive Gs on it throughout the entry. Once more, the first few attempts should be at idle power, followed by a couple with the throttle half-open. Note the altitude lost in both varieties of the split-S for reference later.

Before actually trying any overhead maneuver, you should be prepared for the possibility that your bird won't make it over the top. This could result from inadequate power, too low an entry airspeed, or improper technique by the pilot. Regardless of the reason, the consequence is the same—you fall out of the maneuver before completing it. A stall in the vertical or nearly inverted position could produce some unpleasant complications that should be avoided at any time, but most certainly during a test program.

The way to stay out of trouble when it looks like the bird won't make it through an overhead maneuver is to use the vertical recovery. Before attempting a loop or any of its variations, you should be quite familiar with the correct procedures for executing a vertical recovery. However, like parachuting, this maneuver does not lend itself very well to practice or simulation. It would be very impractical—and even a little foolish—to set up actual conditions for practicing a vertical recovery. Adding rudder to an aircraft in a nose-high attitude at a low airspeed is providing all the ingredients for a spin—maybe an inverted one. Therefore, the whole idea in learning how to do vertical recoveries is to fly an *approach* to a stall, and then start the recovery.

The entire problem is precipitated by the aircraft being in a stalled condition, or losing airspeed at a rate that will soon produce a stall. Simulate this by pulling the bird into a straight-ahead 45-degree climb with the wings level. Maintain this attitude until the symptoms of a stall start to appear. When a good shudder has developed, add full power and release the excessive back pressure on the stick. Start a coordinated roll to the nearest horizon, and *ease* in some rudder in the same direction to help bring the nose down below the horizon. This will most likely produce a near-vertical bank by the time the nose is pointing downward. Don't worry about this excessive bank angle until the nose is well below the horizon and the airspeed is increasing. The important thing is to break the stall and regain flying speed, after which you can roll the wings level again. Since you are flying close to a stall throughout this maneuver, the key to a successful vertical recovery is *smooth, coordinated* control inputs that do nothing to aggravate the stalled condition.

If everything goes well with the vertical recoveries, and you feel comfortable that you could handle one should the need arise, it's time to press on with the overhead maneuvers. However, prior to starting this phase of the testing, there are a few criteria that *must* be observed when performing aerobatics. Sufficient entry speed is the first of these. This is a prime requisite for all aerobatic maneuvers, and not having it at the entry point will guar-

antee more practice at vertical recoveries. Nothing is learned from falling out of a loop when you're only partway through, except that you've reproven a basic aerodynamic law.

Although the exact entry speed for each maneuver varies with the different designs of aircraft, the rules of thumb given below are good starting points. After you've gotten some experience in your bird, they may be adjusted as necessary. The minimum entry speed for aileron rolls, slow rolls, barrel rolls, vertical recoveries, loops, and Cuban eights is 2 1/2 times your stall speed. Immelmanns and cloverleafs require 3 times the stall speed. If your airplane can reach 2 1/2 times its stall speed in a shallow dive at the maximum continuous power setting, it's okay to try the maneuvers listed above for that speed. Even if your bird can reach three times its stall speed, it's a good idea to see how things go in a couple of loops before trying an Immelmann or a cloverleaf. Check your airspeed at the top of a loop that you entered at three times the stall speed. Do you have enough push left to do a half roll? Are the controls still responsive, or are they fairly mushy? Think about these factors before actually completing either of these maneuvers.

The second essential item for aerobatics is somewhat obvious, but should *never* be skimped on, especially in an airplane you are just getting acquainted with. *Always* start any aerobatic maneuver at more than enough altitude to recover from a spin or a powered dive in case anything goes amiss. Remember, if things turn to worms in the middle of any aerobatic maneuver, the unusual attitude and the few moments it takes to sort things out while the airplane is deciding what to do all cost you altitude. Recoveries from high-speed dives and spins will not normally be of the controlled, textbook variety. Therefore, give yourself an insurance cushion of an extra few thousand feet before honking the bird around in overhead maneuvers.

The last prerequisite for trying these gyrations is another one that's fairly apparent. No one should ever attempt aerobatics without having first been cleared by a qualified instructor. If you plan to do aerobatics in your homebuilt, but haven't had any training in this area, get some dual time under your belt with someone authorized to teach this phase of flying. There is no substitute for the experience of having been there before, even in another type of bird. These maneuvers provide the perfect setting in which one can run out of airspeed, altitude, and ideas all at once. Don't let the lack of adequate preparation allow you to get caught in this predicament.

Other Test Items

The flight testing program outlined in this chapter will give your new pride and joy a pretty good shakedown; however, it's by no means all-inclusive. Depending on how you want to use your bird, there are a lot of other items that should be checked out and recorded so that unpleasant surprises are kept to a minimum. Such things as fine tuning the cruise control procedures to get maximum range from a load of fuel, the best power setting for maximum endurance, navcom reception at various ranges and angles from the field, etc., all should be investigated at some time before the test program is wrapped up.

The operation of any additional systems that you put in your airplane should be tested under normal and emergency conditions. If trim tabs that are controllable from the cockpit are installed, are they too sensitive, or ineffective to the point where they are not worth the weight penalty? Can the aircraft be handled safely in the event of a runaway trim in either the up or down position? Could the airplane be landed in this condition? Flaps, steerable tailwheels, auxiliary fuel pumps, or any other innovation that you came up with should all be subject to the acid test: *Does it work effectively in flight under normal, and, more particularly, emergency conditions?* If problems develop during the testing of these systems, and an easy fix cannot be found, the best course of action may be to remove the system entirely.

Every homebuilder will have to tailor his own test program according to the design of his airplane and how he intends to fly it. Regardless of how basic or how involved the testing procedures become, the overriding name of the game is safety. It's *your* tailbone that will be strapped to this machine, so approach every phase of the test program with careful preplanning, careful execution, and careful documentation of the results. Anything less marks you as a fledgling, and if problems develop later on that should have been investigated during the flight test phase, the sweaty palms on the stick will be yours.

One final note on testing: Remember that every homebuilt is unique, and even if it is a proven design and flies well, it is still a one-of-a-kind item. Because of this, you must *always* be ready for the unexpected—which means that, in reality, your bird is always in the test phase. Piper and Cessna have many designs with a lot of flying hours on them, and most of the bugs have been picked up long ago. Not so with your homebuilt, and, as a consequence, you will have to find all its bugs by yourself.

Therefore, the smart homebuilder never really considers his test program as completed.

Chapter 25

Conclusion

Before wrapping up this discussion on building and flying the WAR Corsair, it's probably a good idea to reiterate a few things that were mentioned at the outset. The techniques and procedures described throughout this book are most certainly not to be construed as the *only* solution to the particular problems under discussion. There are undoubtedly many ways of solving the numerous difficult areas of construction that crop up when building any airplane. The methods presented here offer but one answer; however, it is an answer that flies, both literally and figuratively. Building an airplane in your spare time takes long enough without wasting more time and money on blind alleys. Therefore, the primary rationale for this book is to save you both of the above by providing feasible solutions to the major problem areas in constructing an aircraft of this type. The name of the game is to get the bird finished and get it into the air.

Also, there is the distinct probability that not all builders will experience problems in the same areas of the project. What is duck soup for one may be a real backbreaker for another. However, the phases of construction discussed here will most likely present difficulties, or at least some anxious moments, for just about all average first-time homebuilders.

Another variable that makes or breaks problems is the availability of tools and equipment. Having access to a complete metal and woodworking shop will certainly ease the pain in many troublesome areas, but not everyone is fortunate enough to be in this boat. While there are a lot of items that must be done in a well-equipped shop, all the processes talked about in the foregoing chapters can be handles by the usual stock of do-it-yourselfer tools. Most people do acquire a few new tools during the course of a project such as this, and if it is something that is used often enough, it will be money well spent. Airplane building has enough aggravating experiences without creating more by having to stop work at a critical time for the lack of a more-or-less common tool.

Another factor to keep in mind is the time frame with which we are dealing. The WAR Corsair is a relatively new design, and the building problems described here are not too unusual at this stage in its development. As more and more Corsairs are built, there will doubtless be a variety of ways to tackle these difficulties. Innovative approaches to some of the major stumbling blocks of the Corsair are already being worked on, such as a completely hydraulic gear retraction system. As mentioned earlier, the best way to keep abreast of these new ideas is to read the newsletters from WAR or the Replica Fighters Association. However, just because somebody describes a new way of doing things, don't accept it as gospel until you discuss it thoroughly with an A & P mechanic.

Throughout this book there are numerous references to metals of a certain thickness, and hardware of a specific size. There are also many things that are mentioned as either advisable or recommended. These are suggestions only and are not to be considered as absolutes. However, they are presented here as the considered opinion of builders who have worked on the WAR Corsair. As such, they will hopefully save you the frustration of experimenting with methods and techniques that either do not work, or are the hardest way to go.

The two overriding factors that should govern every decision in a project such as this are *safety* and *simplicity*—in that order. Think about any suggested procedure in these terms while considering the work environment of your particular project. Attempting something that your shop cannot handle from either the size or equipment standpoint will do nothing but raise your blood pressure and lower your bank balance.

A lot of compromises must be made during this project between what you would like in your bird, and what will fit—or can be paid for. But, there should *never* be a compromise on the quality or the size of the *basic* construction materials. If it's a tossup as to the size or thickness of a certain part, it pays to favor the safe side. There may come a time, when you're flying the bird, that a little extra beef in a few areas will stand you in good stead. Naturally, you should avoid going to extremes in this regard. You could make the bird so strong and so safe that it will never get off the ground. The best course of action to follow when thinking about adding something not called for in the plans, is to ask the advice of an A & P mechanic. A few questions here could save a lot of heartburn later on, when you discover that the new item won't fit, or interferes with other components.

Anyone who sticks with an airplane project until it is completed deserves a lot of credit. It is not an easy undertaking, but with a little diligence coupled with thorough planning and careful construction methods, the impossible slowly takes shape before your eyes. During those times when progress seems maddeningly slow, don't give in to the temptation of taking a shortcut. Follow prescribed and recommended procedures so that when the bird is finished, there won't be any nagging doubts as to its complete airworthiness. It is really heartbreaking to ding a bird for any reason, but even more so if the problem was caused by the failure of a component that wasn't quite up to specifications.

The thrill of owning and flying a replica fighter you have built surely ranks among life's most rewarding experiences. It is a unique accomplishment in which you can be justifiably proud. Long after all the hard work is but a memory, and you've put the bird through its paces to the point where you know you've got a good one, is the the time when the harvest is the richest. Knowing that you've accomplished something that most men wouldn't even dare brings to the inner man a particularly rewarding sense of having done something special.

As you sit in the cockpit before cranking up for an early morning flight, and you look out at the bent wings of your Corsair with their meancing gun ports, it's very easy for the imagination to run rampant. The sun starbursts off the cowling and obscures your surroundings in the glare, and you can almost feel the flight deck heaving beneath your aircraft as the carrier plows through heavy swells, while the adrenaline pumps faster in anticipation as the bullhorn blares: "All fighters—start your engines!"

Go get 'em, tiger!

Appendix

Where To Find It

All of the items listed below can no doubt be found in one or more of the popular aircraft supply catalogs. However, the sources indicated may offer prices that are more reasonable for merchandise that is just as serviceable.

Aluminum sheet, .063, for nonstructural use—aluminum siding dealer.

Canopy—Gee Bee Canopies Inc., 18415 2nd Avenue South, Seattle, Washington 98148.

Chain for gear retract system—bicycle repair shop.

Cockpit vent ducting, 2″—auto supply store.

Cushions, seat belts and shoulder harness—Airtex Products, 259 Lower Morrisville Road, Fallsington, Pennsylvania, 19054, (215) 295-4115.

Electrical wire, grommets, plastic wire clamps—auto supply store.

Engine parts:
El Reno Aviation Inc., 1004 South Country Club Road, P.O. Box 760, El Reno, Oklahoma, 73036
Lou Leebe, Selma, California, 93662

Felt stripping—yellow pages under Felting and Felt Products.

Flexible fuel and brake lines—auto supply store or J.C. Whitney & Co., 1917-19 Archer Avenue, P.O. Box 8410, Chicago, Illinois, 60680, (312) 431-6102.

Locking toggle switches—H S Electronics, Inc., 1665 W 33rd Place, Hialeah, Florida, 33012, (305) 821-5802.

Microswitches—washing machine repair store and home appliance store.

Navcom kits—Radio Systems Technology, 13281 Grass Valley Avenue, Grass Valley, California, 95945

Plywood—Violette Plywood Co., Lunenburg, Massachusetts, 01462

Poor Man's Epoxy Pump—Scientec Services, P. O. Box 2872, Sarnia Ontario, Canada N7T-7M1.

Tailwheel—grocery cart

Terminal blocks, cable ties, connectors—electronic parts store.

Trim drive motor—auto parts store or J.C. Whitney & Co.

Tubing benders and flaring tools—J.C. Whitney & Co.

Used parts and engines:
R. Ellington, Ellington Airport, 30982 East Broadway, Walbridge, Ohio, 43465

Wheel bearings—yellow pages under Bearings-SKF 07100 Cone 7 TK may replace Timken bearings called for in plans.

Wheel hubs—Go-kart shop or speed shop.

Suitable Substitutions

Before substituting materials other than those called for in the plans, the manuals listed below should be consulted to determine appropriate sizes and allowable replacements.

Reprint of CAA Manual 18
Aircraft Hardware Standards Manual

Available from the Experimental Aircraft Association, Wittman Airfield, Oshkosh, Wisconsin, 54903-2591

Wood for Aircraft Substitutions for Sitka in High Strength Roles

U.S. Forest Products, Milwaukee, Wisconsin
Aircraft Construction, Repair & Inspection
TAB Book No. 2377.

FAA Advisory Circular #43.13
Available from Supt. of Documents, Washington, D.C.

Rodger Sell, Slatington Airport, Slatington, Pennsylvania, 18080

Bud Wagner, Oak Street, Old Bridge, New Jersey

Engine Manuals

The required manuals for aircraft engine overhaul or conversion may be obtained from the sources listed below.

Continental Motors
1801 Touhy Avenue
Elk Grove Village
Illinois 60007

ESSCO
Akron Municipal Airport
Akron, Ohio 44306

Lou Leebe
Selma, California 93662

Lycoming
AVCO Manufacturing Corporation
Williamsport, Pennsylvania

Maintenance/Overhaul Guide to Lycoming Aircraft Engines
(TAB Book No. 2277)

Organizations of Interest

Air Force Association
Suite 400
1750 Pennsylvania Avenue, N.W.
Washington, D.C. 20006

Confederate Air Force
P.O. Box CAF
Harlingen, Texas 78550

Experimental Aircraft Association
Whitman Airfield
Oshkosh, Wisconsin 54903-2591

EAA Antique/Classic Division
EAA International Aerobatic Club
EAA Ultralight Association
EAA Warbirds of America
Same address as above

Replica Fighter Association
2789 Mohawk
Rochester, Michigan 48064

Publications of Interest

Books

Every Pilot's Guide to Aviation Electronics by John M. Ferrara, El-Jac Publishing Co., Box 240, Yardley, Pennsylvania, 19067

Military Aircraft Replicas by Louis F. Langhurst, Lourene Ventures, Rt. 1, Box 315, Carriere, Mississippi, 39426

Moldless Composite Homebuilt Sandwich Aircraft Construction by Burt Rutan, Rutan Aircraft Factory, Mojave, California, 93501

The Sportplane Builder by Tony Bingelis, 8509 Greenflint Lane, Austin Texas, 78759

163

Catalogs

Aero Sales and Supply Co., Fleming Field, South St. Paul, Minnesota, 55075, 612-451-2040

Aircraft Spruce and Specialty Co., Box 424, Fullerton, California, 92632, 714-870-7551

BJG Aircraft Supply, 40 Countryside Drive, St. Peters, Missouri, 63376, 314-278-1622

J & M Aircraft Supply, Inc., 1037 Hawn Avenue, P. O. Box 7586, Shreveport, Louisiana, 71107, 318-222-5749

The Aeroplane Factory, 196 Palisade Avenue, Cliffside Park, New Jersey, 07010, 201-628-7011

Trade-A-Plane, Crossville, Tennessee, 38555

Wag Aero, Box 181, North Road, Lyons, Wisconsin, 53148, 414-763-9586

Wicks Aircraft Supply, 410 Pine Street, Highland, Illinois, 62249, 618-654-7447

Magazines/Newsletters

Kitplanes, P. O. Box 4030, San Clemente, California, 92672

Replica Fighter Association Newsletter, 2789 Mohawk, Rochester, Michigan, 48064

Sport Aviation, Experimental Aircraft Association, Whitman Airfield, Oshkosh, Wisconsin, 54903-2591

WAR Newsletter, War Aircraft Replicas, 348 South 8th Street, Santa Paula, California, 93060

Reference Manuals/Pamphlets

Aircraft Design Manual, Third Edition
Building the Custom Aircraft with Wood, Vol. 2
Sport Aircraft You Can Build
All available from the Experimental Aircraft Association, Whitman Airfield, Oshkosh, Wisconsin, 54903-2591

F4U Corsair in Color
F4U Corsair in Action, Squadron/Signal Publications, 1115 Crowley Drive, Carrollton, Texas 75011

Safety Guide for Private Aircraft Owners
Tips on Engine Operation in Small General Aviation Aircraft by J.A. Diblin
Both available from the U.S. Department of Transportation, Federal Aviation Division, Washington, D.C. 20590

Stits Poly-Fiber Covering & Painting Manual by Ray Stits, P. O. Box 3084, Riverside, California, 92519, 714-684-4280

Regulations/Circulars

Advisory Circular 20-27C dated 4/1/83
Amateur-Builder's Information and Guidelines, revised 3/84
Guide to FAA Publications
Pilot's Weight and Balance Handbook
All available from U.S. Department of Transportation, Federal Aviation Division, Washington, D.C. 20590

Suggested Checklist

This is a generalized checklist, and all items may not be applicable to every airplane. At first glance it may seem overly long; however, in keeping with the inevitability of Murphy's Law, and the fact that a homebuilt is just about always in the test phase, it is highly recommended. The overriding consideration is, of course, safety and its length may be made more palatable by keeping in mind whose tailbone the airplane will be strapped to.

Cockpit

☐ Ignition off.
☐ Control locks removed, if installed.

Walkaround

Nose Area

☐ Cowling—Secure.
☐ Oil—Visually check quantity, retighten cap, door secure.
☐ Battery—Check security and connections if installed here.
☐ Fuel drain—Open for water drainage and re-close.
☐ Prop—Nicks, dents, or cracks; mounting bolts secure.
☐ Engine—Leaking fluids; electrical and mechanical connections secure.

☐ Carburetor intake—Clear of foreign matter.
☐ Fuel—Visually check quantity, re-secure cap.

Right Gear Area

☐ Tire—Proper inflation, cuts, bruises.
☐ Brakes—Worn pucks, leaking lines.
☐ Strut—Proper extension, leakage if hydraulic, scoring.
☐ Scissors/retract arms—All connections secure and safetied.
☐ Microswitches—Operational, connections secure, free of obstructions.
☐ Doors and actuators—Properly secured.
☐ Door close mechanism—General condition and security, free of obstructions.
☐ Landing light—Condition and security, if installed.
☐ Tiedown—Removed.

Right Wing Area

☐ General condition, free of ice and snow.
☐ Pitot boom—Cover removed, ports clear.
☐ Aileron—Gust lock removed, if installed; freedom of movement, hinge pins secure.
☐ Light—General condition and security, if installed.
☐ Access panels—Secured.

Aft Fuselage, Right Side

☐ Battery—Check security and connections if installed here.
☐ General condition, access panels secured.

Tail Surfaces

☐ General condition, free of ice and snow, gust locks removed, if installed; security of hinge pins.
☐ Light—General condition and security, if installed.
☐ Access panels—Secured.
☐ Trim tab—General condition, actuating arm secured, access panel secure.
☐ Tailwheel—Condition of tire, unlocking cable secure, doors secure, tiedown removed.
☐ Microswitch—Operational, connections secure, free of obstructions.

Aft Fuselage, Left Side

☐ General condition, access panels secure.

Left Wing Area

☐ General condition, free of ice and snow.
☐ Aileron—Gust lock removed, if installed; freedom of movement, hinge pins secure.
☐ Light—General condition and security, if installed.
☐ Access panels—Secured.

Left Gear Area

☐ Tire—Proper inflation, cuts, bruises.
☐ Brakes—Worn pucks, leaking lines.
☐ Strut—Proper extension, leakage if hydraulic, scoring.
☐ Scissors/retract arms—All connections secure and safetied.
☐ Microswitches—Operational, connections secure, free of obstructions.
☐ Doors and actuators—Properly secured.
☐ Door close mechanism—General condition and security, free of obstructions.
☐ Landing Light—Condition and security, if installed.
☐ Tiedown removed.
☐ Fuel transfer pump—Condition, security, connections, leaks.

External Fuel Tank

☐ Visually check quantity, re-secure cap.
☐ Fuel transfer line connected, no leaks.
☐ Mounting bracket—General condition and security.

Pre-Start Check--Power Off

☐ Seat belt and shoulder harness buckled.

Left side:

☐ Emergency gear retract declutch—Engaged.
☐ Communications leads—Connected.
☐ Circuit breakers—In.
☐ Fuel transfer pump—Off, guard down.
☐ Throttle—Closed.
☐ Mixture—Full rich.
☐ Gear selector switch—Down position.
☐ Fuel shutoff—Open position.
☐ Cabin vent—As desired.

Instrument panel:

☐ G-meter—Zeroed, if installed.

- [ ] Primer—Locked.
- [ ] Carburetor heat—Cold.
- [ ] Altimeter—Set.
- [ ] Clock—Wound and set, if applicable.
- [ ] Ignition switch—Off.
- [ ] Navcom—Off, if installed.

Right side:
- [ ] Battery switch—Off.
- [ ] Generator switch—Off.
- [ ] Cabin vent—As desired.
- [ ] Tailwheel unlock—Locked position.
- [ ] Manual gear retract handle—Stowed.
- [ ] Circuit breakers—In.
- [ ] Light switches—Off, if installed.

General:
- [ ] Flight controls—Check for freedom of movement and proper operation.
- [ ] Stow all loose equipment.

Engine Start
- [ ] Battery—On, check for gear indicator lights illuminated.
- [ ] Carburetor heat—Cold.
- [ ] Throttle—Open to start position.
- [ ] Mixture—Full rich.
- [ ] Primer—As required.
- [ ] Clear nose area.
- [ ] Ignition switch to "Start" until engine catches.
- [ ] Throttle to idle rpm.
- [ ] Oil pressure—Check for an immediate indication and rising into green.
- [ ] Generator switch—On.
- [ ] Ammeter-check for charge indication.

Pre-Taxi Check
- [ ] Fuel quantity gauge—Indicating properly.
- [ ] Oil temperature, pressure, and cylinder head temperature—Approaching or in the green.
- [ ] Gyro instruments—Caged and released, set as required.
- [ ] Navcom—On and frequency set, if installed.
- [ ] Clock—On and set, if electric.
- [ ] Cabin vent—As desired.
- [ ] Trim—Set for takeoff.
- [ ] Tailwheel—Unlocked.
- [ ] Lights—As required, if installed.
- [ ] Clear area before taxiing.

Before Taking Runway
- [ ] Point aircraft into wind.
- [ ] Tailwheel—Locked.
- [ ] Carburetor heat—Check operation.
- [ ] Mixture—Recheck full rich.
- [ ] Oil and cylinder head temperatures—Within limits.
- [ ] Mag check—Set rpm, check for proper drop on right and left mags, return switch to "Both."
- [ ] Controls—Recheck for freedom of movement.
- [ ] Seat belt and harness—Tightened.
- [ ] Canopy—Closed and locked.

Pre-Takeoff
- [ ] Tailwheel—Locked.
- [ ] Check compass heading for runway alignment.
- [ ] Throttle—Takeoff rpm.
- [ ] Engine instruments—In the green.

Climbout
- [ ] Gear up when safely airborne.
- [ ] Climb rpm set.
- [ ] Carburetor heat—As required.
- [ ] Cabin vent—As desired.

Pre-Landing
- [ ] Gas—Check fuel quantity and external tank emptied.
- [ ] Gear—Down at proper speed, check for safe indication.
- [ ] Mixture—Full rich.
- [ ] Carburetor heat—As required.
- [ ] Tailwheel—Locked.
- [ ] Landing light—As required, if installed.

Shutdown
- [ ] Lights—Off, if installed.
- [ ] Navcom—Off, if installed.
- [ ] Clock—Off, if electric.
- [ ] Generator switch—Off.
- [ ] Throttle—Closed.
- [ ] Mixture—Idle cutoff.
- [ ] Ignition—Off.
- [ ] Battery—Off.

The Great Verities of Homebuilding

The following is a collection of some of the basic laws, precepts, axioms, postulates, theorems and rules that invariably have a profound influence on any homebuilt airplane project. They are all developed from the one great maxim that governs all human endeavor: *Murphy's Law.*

Undoubtedly you will discover a host of corollaries, principles, and observations that are peculiar to your own situation. This tongue-in-cheek offering is made, however, not to discourage but to forewarn.

When building an airplane, if anything can go wrong, no matter how remote the possibility, it will. This event will take place at the worst possible time.

Nothing in homebuilding is as easy as it looks in the plans.

Every phase of a project, no matter how simplistic it appears, will take longer than you think.

When major subassemblies are installed on the airframe, the probability of several things going wrong is a given. However, the one that will cause the *most* damage will be the one that will occur.

For every solution found in homebuilding, multiple new problems will be generated.

If any component on an airplane is damaged during construction, the extent of the damage will be in direct proportion to its value.

During all phases of putting an airplane together, whenever things are proceeding smoothly, something will go wrong.

Whenever things appear to be going well during a project, extreme caution is advised, since you have most certainly overlooked something.

While building an airplane, the probability of anything happening is in inverse ratio to its desirability.

During the construction process, and even more so during the test flying stage, sooner or later the worst possible set of circumstances is bound to occur.

Pressure proliferates problems.

When ordering supplies, the reliability of the expected delivery date is inversely proportional to the urgency of need.

All parts cut to length from plans or dimensions will be too small.

All promises of delivery of custom-made parts must be multiplied by a factor of at least three or four.

Interchangeable airplane parts won't.

When considering alterations to the plans, the more innocuous the modification appears, the more profound its impact will be, and the more the plans will have to be redrawn.

Any part dropped during assembly will fall so as to do the most damage, and the most delicate component will be the one most likely to drop.

Small tools—and in particular aircraft hardware—when dropped will immediately roll out of sight, and will most likely come to rest in the most inaccessible part of the work area.

The ease of recovering dropped parts varies inversely to their importance to the work at hand.

While working on an airplane, any tool put away because you are certain you have finished with it will be needed instantly.

If tools are kept in two work locations, the one absolutely essential to the completion of the job in one area will always be found in the other.

Experience in the art of homebuilding is gained in direct proportion to the amount of materials and equipment ruined.

When everything else fails, read the plans and/or the construction manual.

Selected Bibliography

Books

Aircraft Spruce and Specialty Company Supply Catalogue 782. Fullerton, California: Aircraft Spruce and Specialty Company, 1982.

Bingelis, Tony. *The Sportplane Builder*. Austin, Texas: By the Author, 1979.

Building the Custom Aircraft with Wood, Vol. 2. Hales Corners, Wisconsin: EAA Air Museum Foundation, Inc., 1970; reprinted., Hales Corners, Wisconsin: EAA Air Museum Foundation, 1976.

Constructing the WAR F4U Corsair. Santa Paula, California: WAR Aircraft Replicas, Inc., 1976.

Rutan, Burt. *Moldless Composite Sandwich Homebuilt Aircraft Construction*. Mojave, California: Rutan Aircraft Factory, 1978.

Sport Aircraft You Can Build. Hales Corners, Wisconsin: Experimental Aircraft Association, Inc., 1977.

Wiley, Jack. *The Fiberglass Repair and Construction Handbook*. Blue Ridge Summit, Pennsylvania: TAB BOOKS Inc, 1982.

Articles

Taylor, M.B. "Testing Your Homebuilt." *Sport Aviation*, January 1977, pp. 24-27.

Index

A

access panels, 143
Adel clamps, 118
aerobatics, 157
aileron and elevator controls, 65
aircraft hardware, 20
aircraft sounds and feel, 153

B

battery box location, 118
bevel gear installation, 83
Bowden cable, 137
bracket and engine mount alignment, 131
bracket shims and mounting holes, 131
bracket shims, mounting, 61

C

canopy and windshield, 68-75
canopy frame, fitting, 69
canopy lock, 72
canopy, cutting, 70
chain and sprocket assemblies, 85
checklists, 150
circuit breakers/fuses, 118
circuit coding, 114
cockpit interior, 106-113
compression bushings, 41
control stops, 37

control surface rib alignment, 32
control systems, 63-67
costs, 4
cowling, 139
critical measurements, 51
cushions, 111

D

dead engine procedures, 154
dihedral and incidence problems, correcting, 78
dihedral, setting, 77
doublers, 25

E

electric retract system, 90
electrical system, 114-120
engine check, noise-high, 151
engine disassembly, 134
engine mount bracket patterns, 130
engine mount, 130-134
engines, run-out, 133
epoxies, safety precautions with, 146
epoxy measuring devices, 146
Experimental Aircraft Association, 6
external tank, 123

F

fiberglassing, 145
flight checks, high-speed, 156

flight testing plan, 151
foaming and fiberglassing, 143
foaming procedures, 145
forward cockpit floor, 58
forward fin alignment, 34
fuel lines, bending and flaring, 122
fuel system design, 122
fuel system, 121-129
fuel tank tiedowns, 121
fuselage frame construction, 22-25
fuselage frame, completing, 24

G

gear door control mechanism, 100
gear door mechanism, 98
gear mounting brackets, 80
getting ready, 14-21
glues, 18
gluing procedures, 23
gussets, 25
gyro instruments and filter, 111

H

hinge alignment, 32

I

installation checks, 71
instrument panel design, 109
instrument subpanels, 110

L

landing gear and retract system, 80-105
liftoffs, 152

M

manuals, 12
metal components, 19
microswitches, 119
MIG welding, 48
mounting holes, 41

O

outer fittings, 42
outer spar installation, 76-79
outer spars, alternate method, 78

P

painting, 148
panel holes, cutting, 110
plans, 5, 9
plex to frame, mounting, 71
plywood skins for the frame, 26-28
polyurethane, 38
preliminary considerations, 7-13
prerequisites for overhead maneuvers, 157
project selection, 3

R

references, 12
retraction problems, 86
rubber cable covers, 106
rudder cable clearance, checking, 61

rudder cable holes, 66
rudder pedal assemblies, 60-62
Rutan, Burt, 145

S

sanding, 39
scarfing, 26
sealer for open grain wood, 39
seat back and floor installation, 58
seat back and floor, 57-59
seat belt and harness, 141
setting wheel toe-in, 140
skins, assembly and preparation of, 27
skins, attaching to frame, 28
slot patches, 46
space, 8
spar construction, 29-33
spar slots, 44
spar varnish, 38
spars and fuselage, joining, 44
spars, outer, 31
spars, skinning, 30
Sport Aircraft You Can Build, 6
Sport Aviation, 7
stab spars, 36
stall series, 153
stalls in turns, 154
stick grip, 63
switch panels, 108

T

tailfeathers, 34-37
tailwheel installation, 95
taxi checks, 152
terminal blocks, 117

test items, final, 156
test items, follow-on, 155
test items, initial, 153
test-flying, 150-159
The Thomas Register of American Manufacturers and Thomas Register Catalog File, 120
TIG welding, 48
time, 8
toggle switches, 119
tools, 15
tools, 16
torque tube installation, 54
Trade-A-Plane, 7
trim system, 135
trunnion mounting holes, 81
truss alignment, 50
truss assemblies, 47-56
truss mounting holes, drilling, 55
trusses, building, 47

U

underspar blocks, 46

V

ventilation, 39

W

War Aircraft Replicas, 2
WAR Corsair, 2
webs, 25
wheel assemblies, 88
wheel well clearance, 83
wing fittings, 40-43
wire sizes, 117
wood sealers, 38-39

Edited by Steven H. Mesner